# Virtual and Augmented Reality

AF675099

**Dr. Rajiv Chopra**
**Associate Professor**
Guru Tegh Bahadur Institute of Information Technology,
CSE Department, GGSIPU Delhi

*Assisted by*
**Mr. Damandeep Singh**
(Final Year CSE)

**KHANNA PUBLISHING HOUSE**
NEW DELHI (INDIA)

Dear Readers,

To prevent the piracy, this book is secured with HIGH SECURITY HOLOGRAM on the front title cover. In case you don't find the hologram on the front cover title, please write us to at *contact@khannabooks.com* or whatsapp us at +91-99109 09320 and avail special gift voucher for yourself.

Specimen of Hologram on front Cover title:

Moreover, there is a SPECIAL DISCOUNT COUPON for you with EVERY HOLOGRAM.

How to avail this SPECIAL DISCOUNT:
Step 1: Scratch the hologram
Step 2: Under the scratch area, your "coupon code" is available
Step 3: Logon to *www.khannabooks.com*
Step 4: Use your "coupon code" in the shopping cart and get your copy at a special discount
Step 5: Enjoy your reading!

Thanks,
Khanna Publishing House

**Price: ₹ 199.00**

# VIRTUAL AND AUGMENTED REALITY

**Dr. Rajiv Chopra**

**Copyright © Khanna Publishing House**

This book is sold subject to the condition that it shall not, by way of trade or otherwise, be lent, resold, hired out, or otherwise circulated without the publisher's prior consent in any form of binding or cover other than that in which it is published and without a similar condition including this condition being imposed on the subsequent purchaser and without limiting the rights under copyright reserved above, no part of this publication may be reproduced, stored in or introduced into retrieval system, or transmitted any form or by any means (electronic, mechanical, photocopying, recording or otherwise), without the prior written permission of both the copyright owner and the above mentioned publisher of this book.

**ISBN:** 978-93-90779-00-0

**Edition:** 2021

*Published by:*

**KHANNA PUBLISHING HOUSE**
4C/4344, Ansari Road, Darya Ganj, New Delhi-110 002
**Phone:** 011-23244447-48 **Mobile:** +91-9910909320
**E-mail:** contact@khannabooks.com

*Printed in India by:*
S.P.S. Printers & Binders, Delhi

# Preface

This book provides you the clarity on terms like VR, AR, UNITY 3D and the like in practice for everyday life at work and home. This includes the implications and changes this technology brings.

We remember the lines of Douglas Hofstadter, Pulitzer Prize Winning Author and Cognitive Scientist-

***"Sometimes it seems as though each new step towards AI, rather than producing something which everyone agrees is real intelligence, merely reveals what real intelligence is NOT."***

Another Russian Novelist and Philosopher said-

***"It takes something more than intelligence to act intelligently."***

This book guides you through the complex web of intricacies brought by combination of AR and VR. It discusses the stark aspects of such transformative technologies. It gives the bright and bleak sides in order to give holistic view of VR technologies. The need is to minimize the barriers and blend both VR--AR and AI together. Also it covers the latest **AICTE SYLLABUS of VR.** This book is suitable for B. Tech. (CSE), M. Tech. (CSE), MCA and other courses of all Indian Universities.

Let us go for a brief tour of this book.

Chapter-1 starts with VR and AR with their history, benefits and applications.

Chapter-2 provides context that is often overlooked today, describing how VR came about and why it had so many false dawns. It also explains why this generation of VR is different from those that came before. It explains the concept of Geometric Modeling in VR. It is short but pivotal to our exposition.

Chapter-3 shows how the virtual environment is created with techniques for handling different types of objects virtually. Virtual environments are central to VR. The tricks that are used to handle with collision detection of objects, object picking, head tracking, teleporting and feedbacks have been introduced.

Chapter-4 illustrates various hardware and software required to set up a virtual environment. Also it introduces the reader to VRML.

Chapter-5 portrays various applications of VR and AR. Also it delineates the use of an interactive platform-UNITY 3D. It shows how UNITY 3D can be used to achieve VR, AR and AI.

Several practical experiments in VR and a demo-project has also been added for the student's benefit.

The book is grounded in fact rather than opinion. It is a concise introduction to a complex subject. It is a mix of academic, general and specialist references to more in-depth coverage of the ideas covered. Audiences will be amply rewarded with a very satisfying understanding of VR concepts and its applications. It is a splendid book for all levels of the readers. The range of activity and the massive interconnected-ness of Internet has driven the growth of a king of VR where smarter algorithms are needed. Practical virtual and augmented realty still seems more than a decade away. Researchers have not even identified what the best practical implementation of VR and AR will be. There is a real need in the scientific literature on these topics and looming roadblocks. This book provides a doable roadmap with signposts that guide in building a VR environment.

I am sure that this book will prove as an important and a very useful addition to the literature in this space.

**Author**

# Acknowledgements

My book has been benefited from the insights and directions of several people. I use this opportunity to express my heartfelt thanks to all those who supported me during the writing of this book. I offer my deep gratitude to the divine essence within me for bestowing on me the strength to follow my heart.

I would like to thank my entire college staff of Guru Tegh Bahadur Institute of Technology (Aff. To GGSIPU, Delhi) along with my Director and my Chairman for showering blessings on me.

Special thanks to the MD and the entire team of Khanna Publishing House of Computer Books for getting such a fine book in a short time span. The ceaseless cooperation by the team is greatly acknowledged. I owe my deepest gratitude to my parents (Dr. J. R Chopra, Ms. Sushma Chopra, my spouse, Ms. Shakti Chopra and my kids (Arjeesh Chopra and Arshitha Chopra) for allowing me to write such a book.

Last but not the least, I would also like to shower my blessings on my final year student, Damandeep Singh, who wrote the newer concepts of the UNITY 3D platform for the completion of this book.

**Dr. Rajiv Chopra**

# Contents

# 1 Introduction to Virtual Reality

## 1.0 INTRODUCTION OF VIRTUAL REALITY (VR)

In this book, we have used two terms- Virtual Reality (VR) as well as Augmented Reality (AR). AR is cousin of VR. It is the amalgamation of Artificial Intelligence (AI) and VR (or AR) that can provide better business revenues (expected to be more than \$100 billion by 2021). In spite of these facts and the eye-popping numbers, the wave of AR and VR is still in its infancy. Time has arrived to brush these technologies before the mass consumers adopts hits. This book arms you with a broader Knowledge Base (KB) of VR and AR fields and their blend with AI. Many fortune 500 companies are currently waging war in this field of VR so that they are the winner. The fields of VR and AR are in a state of constant flux. Hence, one must have an open mind regarding AI + VR (or AR). **Please note that the AI's (VR + AR) have been called as the "fourth wave" of transformative technology.** The first three being the Personal Computer (PC), the Internet and the mobile computing (see figure 1.1). So, we can say that:

Personal Computer (PC) — first wave
↓
Internet — second wave
↓
Mobile Computing — third wave
↓
VR + AR — fourth wave

**Fig.1.1:** The 4 waves of Transformative Technology

The ideas of VR and AR themselves seems to be outlandish (a group). Scientific-fiction writer Arthur C. Clarke quoted that **"Any sufficiently advanced technology is indistinguishable from magic."** The promises of VR and AR that were a science fiction earlier has been brought to life now.

**Let us now compare VR and AR.**

Virtual Reality (VR) is an **"umbrella activity"** that covers the entire gamut of augmented reality, mixed reality and extended reality. VR means **an immersive computer-simulated reality that creates a physical environment that does not exist.** It creates a wholly new environment. On the other hand, Augmented Reality (AR) is **a method of augmenting real-world visual with computer generated input such as still graphics, audio or videos.**

AR is different from VR as AR **augments** (adds to) a real-world or existing scene instead of creating a new one from the very **beginning. This means that in AR, the computer-generated content is an overlay on the top of the real-world content.**

VR and AR do not communicate with each other. However, AR and mixed reality have been used recently. **For examples,**

1. A real environment (say, a football field) has been augmented with digital information (the yellow line) to enhance user's viewing experience in a way that feels neutral to the viewers.
2. One of the most popular game. 'Pokeman Go' is an example of AR only. It places a digital Pokeman character within your real-world environment.

## 1.0.0 Father of VR

A cinematographer named as **Morten Heilig is considered to be the father of VR** (1995). He imagined a multisensory theatre called **"The Cinema of the Future."** He created the **'sensorama'** i.e. an arcade -style mechanical cabinet build to simulate the senses, for which he then developed a number of short films. It included many features like:

- Stereoscopic 3D display.
- Stereo speakers.
- Feedbacks by vibrations in the user's chair.

Later, in 1990, Tom Caudell modified Boeing's large plywood boards with reusable boards. Tom Caudell et. al coined this as **Augmented Reality.** Gartner claims that VR is just leaving the **'Trough of Disillusionments'** and headed into the **'slope of Enlightenment'** by 2017. But there will be a mass adoption within 2 to 5 years. On the other hand, AR is listed as currently **wallowing** in the **'Trough of Disillusionment'.** It's mass adoption will be five to ten years out. AR as a **mass consumer** device is in its infancy. Developers need time to figure out:

- What **form factor** it should exist in?
- What problems it can solve?
- How best can it solve?

**This physical world is 3D.** But our decisions and actions (data) need to be mapped on 2D screens and pages. This bridge between real and digital worlds limit our ability to take the advantage of the volumes of information available to us. AR solves this problem by superimposing digital images directly on the real objects. This will untap the hidden human capabilities. According to an estimate, companies would be spending about $60 billion in 2020, on AR only. This will have impact on Universities as well as social enterprises. The impact of this would be:

- Transformation on how we learn.
- Transformation on how we make decisions.
- Transformation on how enterprise serve users.
- Transformation on how we train employees.
- Transformation on how we design and create products.
- Transformation on how to manage their value chains.

**AR** will amplify their power to create value. In nutshell, AR will become an interface between humans and machines. Thereby, bridging the gap between digital and physical worlds.

World company giants like GE, AMAZON, FACEBOOK, U.S. NAVY are already using AR to see its ramifications into quality and productivity for increasing **value creations.**

At the core, AR transforms deluge (flood) of data and analytics into images or animations that are overlaid on the real worlds. Today, most of the AR applications are delivered through mobile devices and will very soon shift to **smart glasses.**

AR applications put navigation, collision warning and other information directly in car driver's LOS (Line-of-Sight). AR creates a new info-delivery paradigm (model) that will have huge impact on how data is structured, managed and delivered on the Internet.

By **superimposing digital information directly real objects (or environment), AR allows us to process both physical and digital simultaneously.** This improves our ability to rapidly and accurately absorb information, make decisions and execute required tasks quickly and efficiently. AR displays in cars are a vivid example of this. This reduces the mental effort of applying information, reduces distraction and minimizes driver error and so on.

All this explains why AR is so powerful. There is no better GUI than the physical world around us. And when AR is used to enhance it by a digital overlay of relevant data.

### *Case Study-1*

A Newport News Shipbuilding USA, designs and builds U.S. Navy aircraft carriers. It uses AR during the last stages of its manufacturing process to inspect a ship. Traditionally, engineers had to constantly compare the actual ships with complex 2D-blueprints. But with AR, they can now see the final design super-imposed on the ship, which reduces inspection time by 96% (from 36 hrs to 90 mins only). It is observed that a time-savings of more than 25% are possible using AR.

### Case Study-2

Another company, Bosch Rexroth is a global provider of power units and controls used in manufacturing. It uses an AR-enhanced visualization to demonstrate the design of its smart, connected CytroPac hydraulic power unit. Now, the AR application allows customers to see 3D-representations of the unit's internal pump and cooling options in multiple configurations and how these subsystems fit together.

### Case Study-3

AccuVein, a medical device company uses AR technology to convert the heat signature of a patient's veins into an image that is superimposed on the skin. This makes vein's location easier. Also, it drastically improved the success rate of blood draws. It improves this working of company by about 45%.

### Case Study-4

Another company, at Boeing, provides AR training had a huge impact on the productivity and quality of complex aircraft manufacturing procedures. With the help of AR, trainees completed the work in 35% less time.

### Case Study-5

Reality Editor, is an AR app developed by the Fluid Interfaces group at MIT's Media Lab. It allows users to see a smart light bulb's control for colour and intensity and set up voice commands like **"bright" and "mood"** to activate them.

### Case Study-6

GE has already tested the use of voice commands in AR that has increased the productivity by 34%.

### Case Study-7

Another company Ford, is using VR to create a **'virtual workshop'** where geographically dispersed engineers can collaborate in real-time on holograms of vehicle prototypes.

### Case Study-8

U.S. Department of Homeland Security is going a step further by combining both—

[AR instructions] + [VR Simulations] → to train personnel in case of emergency conditions like explosions. This reduces cost and risk.

The challenge today is two-fold:

- The digital revolution.
- Explosion of data.

Hence, AR is emerging as one of the best solutions to these challenges.

Virtual Reality is a way that gives the user an experience to work or see things in a virtual environment.

In the 1950s, the invention of virtual reality experienced peaks and troughs. Sensorama was one of the earliest VR systems introduced in 1956. Ivan Sutherland, a computer scientist with his student Bob Sproull, created the first-ever HMD (head-mounted display) in 1968, but virtual reality started to popularize in the 1980s. In the mid-1980s, Jaron Lanier, founder of VPL Research, for the experience of virtual reality, began to develop gear like goggles. He also introduced the term 'Virtual reality.'

After this, VR began to get recognized for the upcoming year were the US military and NASA used it. In the mid-1980s at Ames Research Center NASA, Virtual Interface Environment Workstation (VIEW) system was coupled with an HMD (head-mounted device) with gloves to make a haptic device allow people to move around in the virtual space. In the back days, there were a couple of problems that VR was facing, which caused issues for worldwide acceptance of Virtual reality problems like the high cost, undeveloped systems, latency. The reason why these days VR is starting to get in the market and companies are doing development as the computer systems are more powerful, prices are also low as compared to the old days. So, VR evolution is possible now.

### 1.0.1 Applications of Virtual reality

Now globally, Virtual reality is used, and it is one of the hot topics that many companies demand due to its benefits and application in different fields. Some of the application are:

- Automotive Industry
- Healthcare

- Education
- Entertainment & Gaming Industry

If we talk about the Automotive industry, VR helps create models and designs for automobiles before making prototypes to increase profitability. Many companies use VR for easy configuration and reviewing of models like BMW, Jaguar. VR is helping this industry to reduce the cost of building prototypes. At the same time, VR is beneficial in healthcare, where it can train people not to work on a real body instead of practice in a virtual environment. VR is also very useful in the medical treatment of patients with PTSD and anxiety.

Nowadays, VR is used in education, also where the student can learn more competently. ImmersiveVREducation is building a VR classroom space with their 'Engage' product, where people/students can learn from lecturers worldwide.

You would know how Virtual reality is revolutionizing the entertainment and gaming industry. It has a very significant impact on the gaming industry that generated a revenue of $2.2 billion in 2017. Many consoles like PlayStation, Wii, Xbox and Nintendo are getting high income from virtual reality games. Many players or hardcore gamers are also willing to pay for expensive virtual reality gear also. Due to the increased processing power of the PC, VR gaming is possible now. Besides the gaming industry, theatre, museums, and music concerts use VR for a better experience.

## 1.1 INTRODUCTION TO AUGMENTED REALITY

AR i.e. Augmented Reality provides interaction with computer-generated objects in the real world through mediums like a mobile camera or any other device. People can interact with items or objects that are spawn in a real-world environment. AR systems consist of three things: a combination of actual and virtual objects, real-time interaction and accurate listing of virtual and real-world objects. For example, Pokemon GO.

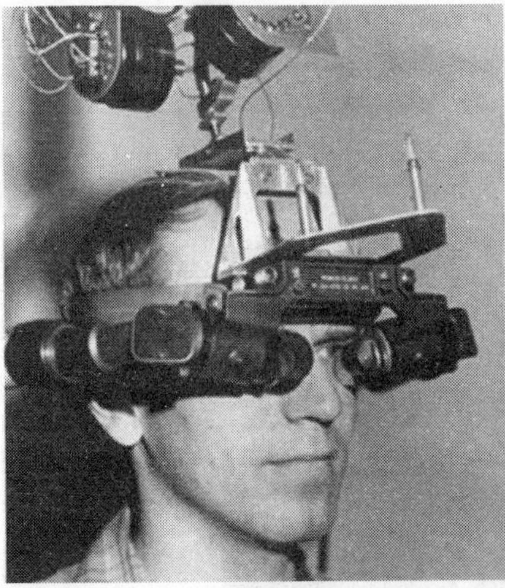

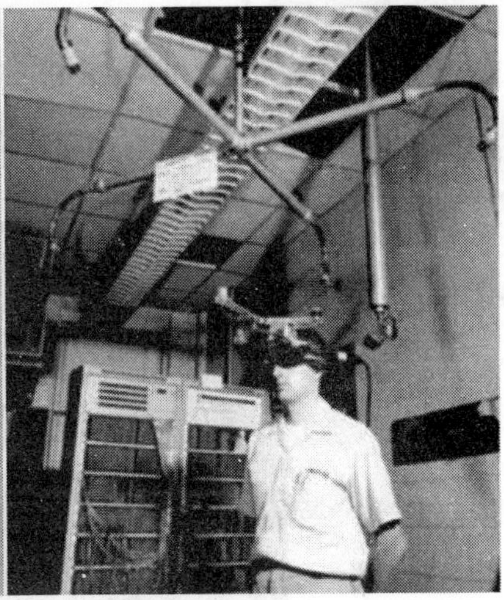

In 1968, Ivan Sutherland, a Harvard professor and computer scientist, created 'The Sword of Damocles' first HMD (head-mounted display). We can simulate virtual objects into the real world with the help of these devices. Many companies like Oculus, HTC are making these kinds of devices. In 2008, the first AR application was out in the market made in Munich by German agencies for advertising purposes, and many other companies also adopted the idea. 'Augmented reality' term was created in 1990 by Tom Caudell, a Boeing researcher.

AR and VR are different from each other. In VR, people experience the virtual environment like they are inside it, while in AR, virtual objects are spawn into the real world, and people can interact with it. The combination of AR and VR is called **Mixed Reality(MR)**.

## 1.2 APPLICATIONS OF AUGMENTED REALITY (AR)

Augmented reality has plenty of applications in retails, healthcare, entertainment media and other fields.

The gaming industry is making a significant profit from AR, while retailers are also using AR in their application to showcase their clothes in AR, which gives a plus point to online shopping. People can see how they look if they wear such clothes; not only the application but many malls and shops are planning to install an AR system to showcase these clothes.

In healthcare, AR is used to train and practice people on virtual bodies as in VR, which we talked about earlier. There are many other applications of AR used in Tourism, Education. A company named Sephora used AR in which people can check the different colours on cheeks and lips product on their digital face. So, AR is gaining acknowledgement from companies, and they are developing new things in it.

We can use different software to create VR/AR applications, either game, educational or any other app. Unity3D, the Unreal Engine software, provides you with a way to dive into this technology and work on it below; we will talk about using Unity3D to create such applications.

## 1.3 COMPUTER GRAPHICS

**Computer graphics is defined as the science and technology of creating, storing, displaying and manipulating images and objects.** It focuses on the mathematical and computational foundations of image generation and its processing. This helps in the generation of realistic models and representations of objects based on measurement data. **Please note that it is the combination of real data and imaged with techniques from computer graphics that is the current trend today.** So, computer graphics deals with the representation of objects and images, algorithms and techniques for generating and manipulating them. It is also about digital models for handling 3D geometric objects and 2D images, both. The objective is to achieve this all, in minimum time and memory storage requirements. In computer graphics, all images and pictures are considered to be a collection of discrete picture elements called as **pixels. A pixel is the smallest addressable unit on screen. The process of determining the appropriate pixel for representing pixels for representing objects like pictures is called as rasterization.**

**Also note that the process of representing continuous pictures as graphical objects is called as scan conversion.** Modern computer graphics is mainly concerned with the storage and manipulation of digital images (a 2D discrete signal).

## 1.4 REAL-TIME COMPUTER GRAPHICS

A real-time system is the one in which the correctness of computations not only depends on the computation but also upon the time at which the result is produced. If the timing constraints of the system are not met, system failure is said to have occurred. So, **time is the major factor here.** The output must be produced within specified time limit (deadline) else disaster can happen. An example of realistic real-time system is **Robotics which was coined by Sir Issac Asimov. Robot is benevolent and human-like machine.** Robotics is the study of robots. The study includes design, selection of materials of proper quality for the components, fabrication, study of various motors required for moving the components, design of electronic circuits, computers and computer programming and control of robots. They use sensors for measurements of position, velocity, force, torque temperature and other parameters.

## 1.5 VIRTUAL ENVIRONMENT REQUIREMENT

A trade-off exists between realism and interactivity of a VR system. **It has been observed that the more realistic a scene must appear, the longer it takes to render and the slower the virtual environment will update.** A VR system classically will include the following six main components:

- The virtual world.
- Graphics engine.
- Simulation engine.
- GUI.
- Inputs from users.
- Outputs from users.

Out of these, first four components are **internal components** to a VR software package while inputs and outputs are **external components.**

The **virtual world is a database that contains geometric representations and attributes for all objects within the environment. The graphics engine** generates the image for viewing. This naturally involves the use of the database and the user's current position, sounds, textures etc. to create a virtual impression. **The simulation engine** takes care of the dynamic of the environment like time. **The user interface** controls user navigation and interaction with this virtual environment. **Also note that it acts as a buffer between the virtual world software and huge number of input and output devices that may be used.**

## 1.6 BENEFITS OF VIRTUAL REALITY

It is the combination of AR and VR technologies that has helped us in education, healthcare and industries and has led to the new foundation for digital transformation. The entertainment industry is also exploring AR and VR content for an exciting cinema experience. Companies like Blue Star has applied AR/VR platform for inspection and manufacturing operations. Royal Enfield has applied it for marketing purposes. Also Volvo's manufacturing plants have deployed such a platform for engine quality control and assurance. VR can replicate the real environment using advanced processing, computing, sensing and display technology. AI and ML can help reduce human error rates through AR and VR simulations. Also, an AR display that uses AI image recognition can streamline complex maintenance in aviation. AI-based personalized shopping also utilizes VR devices. Light weight helmets and more powerful computers will provide deep ramifications into common homes.

## 1.7 HISTORICAL DEVELOPMENT OF VR

Virtual reality dates back to more than 40 years.

1. In 1962, Morgon Heilig invented **Sensorama Simulator** that was the first virtual reality arcade. This virtual reality workstation had three dimensional video feedback, motion, color, sound, aromas, wind effects and a seat that vibrated.
2. In 1966, Sutherland used two cathode ray tubes mounted along the users ears. Sutherland realized that he could use computer-generated scenes instead of analog images taken by cameras. He began to design such a scene generator. His work on "ultimate display" to the virtual world was not only limited to graphics but he also said that the sense of touch would be added to allow the users to feel the virtual object which they could only see earlier.
3. Frederick Brooks and his colleagues at University of North Carolina et. al demonstrated the ability to simulate 2D continuous force fields associated with molecular forces.
4. In 1981, NASA created the prototype of a liquid crystal display (LCD) which they named as the **Virtual Visual Environment Display** (VIVED). NASA (NATIONAL AERONAUTICS AND SPACE AGENCY) created the first VR system by incorporating a DEC PDP 11, a 40 host computer.
5. In 1985, Scott Fisher integrated a new type of sensing glove into the simulation. The globe was developed earlier by Thomson Zimmerman as a virtual programming interface for non-programmers.
6. By 1988, Fisher and Elizabeth Wenzel created a first hardware capable of manipulating up to four virtual sound sources. So, the original VIVED project became VIEW (Vitrual Interface Environment Workstation) and the original software was ported to a newer HP 9000 that had better graphics performance.
7. VPL Inc. was the first companto to sell VR products. They produced the first sensing glove called as **DataGlove.**

8. Then the game company, Nintendo introduced the much cheaper PowerGlovethat used ultrasonic sensors to measure wrist position relative to PC Screen.
9. In late 1980s, the first commercial head-mounted displays called as **EyePhones were introduced by VPL.** But it has high price.
10. In 1991, UK Division Ltd. Introduced the first integrated commercial VR workstation. It was called **Vision which was then followed by more powerful Provision 100.** The Provision 100 parallel architecture had multiple processors, 3D sound, hand tracking and gesture recognition. Again its price was very high.
11. In 1992, the Sense8 company developed the first version of its WorldToolKit (WTK) that is a library of C functions written specifically for VR applications.
12. Another famous toolkit was the Virtual Reality Toolkit (VRT3) developed in UK by Dimension International.

## 1.8 3D COMPUTER GRAPHICS: AN INTRODUCTION

This world is 3D i.e. three dimensional. So, to create a realistic model of this world we need a 3D model itself. Images were described in 2D but objects are described in 3D space. It requires the understanding of the shape of the object. Transformations are done. The construction of geometrical objects requires the use of geometrical and coordinate transformation. Reflection and perspective transformations are used in visual description of the objects.

Real world is composed of 3D images. 3D objects not only have height and width but also depth. Displaying 3D objects on 2D screen seems to be impossible job. Most of the engineering problems deal with 3D objects. A variety of patterns, shapes and techniques are used to create 3D object. Whatever method may be used, the 3D object is usually created in a 3D world coordinate system and then mapped onto 2D system of display. Manipulating, viewing and creation of objects image require the use of 3D object and coordinate transform. 3D transformation method is the extension of 2D transformation method by including the consideration for z-axis coordinate. In 3D transformation method, the coordinate of a point is represented by (x, y, z) and the homogeneous coordinate will be [x y z w]. **Note that the value of w for 3D transformation will be one.**

## 1.9 PERSPECTIVE PROJECTION

The centre of projection is located at a finite distance from the projection plane. When a perspective projection is defined then its centre of projection is explicitly specified, the centre of projection being a point, has homogeneous coordinates of the form (x, y, z, 1). **Please note that the visual effect of a perspective projection is similar to that of photographic system and of human visual system called as perspective foreshortening.** The size of the perspective projection of an object varies inversely with the distance of that object from the centre of projection. The perspective projection of objects tends to look realistic but it is not useful for recording the exact shape and measurements of objects. Distance cannot be taken from the projection. The perspective projection gives realistic image but loss of true dimensions. A perspective projection is mathematically described as follows:

1. **Centre of Projection (CP):** A point where lines of projection that are not parallel to projection plane, appear to meet. The eye of an artist generally acts as a centre of projection while an artist prepares realistic images of 3D objects.
2. **The view plane or projection plane:** The view plane is determined by:
   a. Reference point, R0 (X0, Y0, Z0).
   b. Unit Vector, $N = n_1 i + n_2 j + n_3 k$, which is normal to the plane.
3. **Location of an Object:** The location of an object is described by point P(x, y, z) located in the world coordinate system. The objective of perspective projection is to determine the image point P' (x', y', z') (on the view plane).

Perspective projections are characterized by the following:

a. **Perspective Foreshortening:** It is the illusion that objects and length appears smaller as their distance from the centre of projection increases. **Please note that the size of an object (d) varies inversely with the distance of that object ( r) from the centre of projection** i.e.

$$d \propto 1/r$$

b. **Vanishing Points:** The perspective projection of any set of parallel lines that are not parallel to the projection plane converge to a point called as **vanishing point.** In 3D, the parallel lines meet only at infinity. So, the VP can be thought of as the projection of a point at infinity. Therefore, there is infinity of VP's, one for each of the infinity of direction in which a line can be oriented.

**Also note that if the set of lines (projectors) is parallel to one of the three principal axis, the VP is called as axis vanishing points or principal vanishing points.** There are almost three such points corresponding to the number of principal axis cut by the projection plane.

**For example,** if the projection plane cuts only the z-axis that is normal to it then the z-axis has a VP because lines parallel to x or y axis are also parallel to the projection planes and have no VP. Perspective projections are categorized by their number of principal VPs i.e. by the number of axis the projection plane cuts.

## 1.10 3D CLIPPING

In 3D world, clipping is a well known phenomenon that contributes to the development of modern visualization tools. In 2D viewing, the windows introduced are now replaced by **viewing volume or clipping volume.** This viewing volume is generally a 3D box or a parallelepiped or a truncated pyramidal volume known as **frustum.** *A parallelepiped is used for parallel and axonometric projections while frustums are used for perspective projections.*

The objects within these volumes are visible while those outside these volumes are not. **Please note that objects that cross the boundaries of these volumes require to determine the visible and invisible portions and extending the discussions of 2D clipping to the 3D spaces.** The choice of the viewing volume depends on the projection.

c. **For parallel projection, the planes** are in the direction of projection extending from the edges of the window and form a rectangular box.

d. **For perspective projection, frustums are used** as the picture rays pass through the centre of projection forming a truncated pyramidal viewing volume.

**Also note that as compared to 2D clipping, in 3D space clipping needs to test the visibility, comparing the points against the planes of the viewing volume.** A 3D clipping requires comparing the point against six faces or planes in either case. Hence, the clipping in a 3D space reduces to the problem of finding the sides of the plane to which the point lies.

The general equation of the plane can be written mathematical as follows:

$$Ax + By + Cz + D = 0 \quad ...(1)$$

The visibility of the points $(x_1, y_1, z_1)$ about the viewing volume requires testing the visibility against the plane given by equation-1. If the point $(x_1, y_1, z_1)$ is on the plane then,

$$Ax_1 + By_1 + Cz_1 + D = 0 \quad ...(2)$$

On the other hand, if the point $(x_1, y_1, z_1)$ is not on the plane then it can be either side of the plane. The other two conditions are as follows:

$$Ax_1 + By_1 + Cz_1 + D < 0 \quad \text{and}$$

$$Ax_1 + By_1 + Cz_1 + D > 0 \quad ...(3)$$

In equation-3, note that—

a. the expression less than zero suggests that the point lies on one side of the plane.

b. The expression greater than zero declares it on the other side.

c. The point $(x_1, y_1, z_1)$ can be tested by applying the trivial tests of equation -2 and 3 successively against all six planes defining the viewing volume.

d. The method is simple and robust but the coordinates of the point must be known.

A well -known method is Cohen-Sutherland method. As in 2D, this method can be extended to 3D by using six-bit codes instead of four. The extended algorithm in a 3D- space clipping window boundaries defines 27 regions. The Left, Right, Bottom, Top, Near/ Front and Far/ behind **outcode** can be used to determine segments that are trivially visible, trivially invisible or indeterminate.

## 1.11 COLOUR THEORY

**A colour model is an abstract mathematical model that explains the ways the colors can be represented.** It may be represented as tuples of numbers like 3 or 4 values or color components. The set of colours is called as a **colour space.** A white light source like a bulb or sun, emits all wavelengths within the visible region. We know that when a white light is incident on a surface, some wavelengths are absorbed and others are reflected. This gives us the perception of the colour of an object. The dominant wavelength is called as the **colour or hue of the surface.** We can combine light from two or more sources with different intensities to produce a range of colours. **Note that if the two-colour sources combine to form a white light then they are complementary. For example,** red and cyan, green and magenta, blue and yellow are all complementary. We use three primary colours to produce a range of colours called the **colour gamut.**

## 1.12 SIMPLE 3D MODELING

3D objects have height, width and depth. Displaying 3D objects on 2D screen seems to be impossible task. If height and width are represented by x and y coordinates then how can the 3rd dimension, depth be displayed. This problem is solved by using techniques used by an artist and photographer in producing a realistic picture on a paper or film. The difference is that the computer uses a mathematical model instead of paint brush to create the picture. **Note that the complexity of mathematical model increases with the increase in the realism of a computer generated picture.** A 3D is created in a 3D world coordinate system and then mapped onto the 2D system of display. In 3D method, the coordinate of a point is represented by (x, y, z) and the homogeneous coordinate will be [x y z w]. The value of w for 3D transformation will be one. The facts used in 3D systems are:

Coordinates of original point, $[P] = [x\ y\ z\ 1]_{1*4}$

Coordinates of transformed point $[p'] = [x'\ y'\ z'\ 1]$

## 1.13 ILLUMINATION MODELS

Modelling the interaction of light with the surface of some object is known as a **lightning model.** The contribution from the light that goes directly from the light source and is reflected from the surface is called as a **local illumination model.** It takes into account all of the light sources in the active light list and that surface only. No other object is taken into consideration. Global effects such as shadows are ignored. On the other hand, a **global illumination model** adds to a local model the light that is reflected from other surfaces to the current surface. This model is more comprehensive, more physically correct and produces more realistic images. It is also more computationally intensive. Scan-line rendering methods use local illumination models only. Graphics systems like radiosity and ray tracing use this model. These produce more realistic images than scan-line rendering systems. **Please understand that illumination models model the interaction of light with a surface and range from simple to very complex.**

## 1.14 REFLECTION MODELS

**A transformation in which the direction of one axis is reversed is known as reflection.** In other words, reflection refers to a representation of the components of a coordinate system at an equal distance but in opposite direction about the axis.

**For example,** a point P (0,7) when reflected about x-axis becomes P' (0, -7) i.e. x-coordinate is transformed to its **negative value.**

Like other transformations, a reflection can be done about any of the axis or about the origin. For a matrix of transformation, if **the terms a or d is negative, it results in a phenomenon called as reflection about an axis. When both a and d are negaitive then it is called as reflection about origin.**

2D reflection is captured about a line in xy plane. But 3D reflections are captured about three principle planes i.e. xy plane, yz plane and zx plane.

Consider a 3D point having coordinate p (x, y, z) is reflected about xy plane. Reflected point we obtain is p' (x', y', z'). then **the coordinate of x and y remain unchanged whereas z coordinate changes to negative z.** Figure 1.2 shows reflection of a point about xy plane—

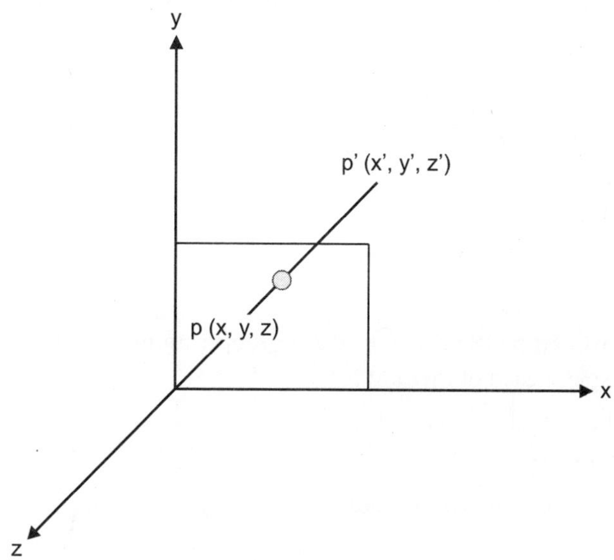


**Fig.1.2:** Reflection about xy-plane

The parametric equation of reflection is as follows:

$$x' = x$$

$$y' = y$$

$$z' = -z$$

These parametric equations we can write in matrix form also as follows:

$$[x' \; y' \; z' \; h] = [x \; y \; z \; 1] \begin{bmatrix} 1 & 0 & 0 & 0 \\ 0 & 1 & 0 & 0 \\ 0 & 0 & -1 & 0 \\ 0 & 0 & 0 & 1 \end{bmatrix}$$

Where the reflection transformation matrix = $M_{xy} = \begin{bmatrix} 1 & 0 & 0 & 0 \\ 0 & 1 & 0 & 0 \\ 0 & 0 & -1 & 0 \\ 0 & 0 & 0 & 1 \end{bmatrix}$

Note that this is similar to the scaling transformation matrix where $s_x = 1$, $s_y = 1$, $s_z = -1$.

## EXERCISE QUESTIONS

Q1. What are the four waves of transformation technologies?

Q2. How is computer graphics different from real-time computer graphics?

Q3. What are the VR environment requirements?

Q4. What are the benefits of VR and AR?

Q5. Explain the historical developments of VR.

Q6. What is perspective projection?

Q7. What are colour models?

Q8. What is 3D clipping?

Q9. What is 3D modelling?

Q10. What are virtual databases?

Q11. VR systems can be divided into three groups: immersive, non-immersive and hybrid. Explain each of them.

Q12. Explain the virtual world space.

Q13. Explain 3D clipping.

Q14. Write short notes on colour theory.

# 2 Geometric Modelling

## 2.0 INTRODUCTION

There are several factors that are involved in virtual object modelling. These include geometrical modelling, kinematic modelling (i.e. parent-child hierarchies), physical modelling and object intelligent behaviour. But as you know that the computational power is limited. Also, the need is for simulation of realism. All this needs the management of model size and complexity including level of detail and cell segmentation.

## 2.1 FROM 2D TO 3D

This world is 3D i.e. three dimensional. So, to create a realistic model of this world we need a 3D model itself. Images were described in 2D but objects are described in 3D space. It requires the understanding of the shape of the object. Transformations are done. The construction of geometrical objects requires the use of geometrical and coordinate transformation. Reflection and perspective transformations are used in visual description of the objects.

Real world is composed of 3D images. 3D objects not only have height and width but also depth. Displaying 3D objects on 2D screen seems to be impossible job. Most of the engineering problems deal with 3D objects. A variety of patterns, shapes and techniques are used to create 3D object. Whatever method may be used, the 3D object is usually created in a 3D world coordinate system and then mapped onto 2D system of display. Manipulating, viewing and creation of objects image require the use of 3D object and coordinate transform. 3D transformation method is the extension of 2D transformation method by including the consideration for z-axis coordinate. In 3D transformation method, the coordinate of a point is represented by (x, y, z) and the homogeneous coordinate will be [x y z w]. **Note that the value of w for 3D transformation will be one.**

**Please note that in general, moving from an n-dimensional space to an (n+1) dimensional space simply involves the introduction of an extra value fixing the data in the extra dimension. Also note that moving from an n-dimensional to an (n-1) dimensional space involves a projection like perspective projection.** The 2D shape is converted into a 3D lamina by assigning every vertex a zero z-coordinate. The final orientation of the lamina can be further controlled by manipulating the coordinate from 2D to 3D.

**Note:** An infinite range of orientation becomes possible by mixing different assignment combinations with sign changes and replacing the zero term with other numerical values.

## 2.2 3D SPACE CURVES

3D surface imaging technologies open new doors to the research field. Some of the applications of these surfaces are as follows: -

- Designing of automobile bodies.
- Designing of ship hulls.
- Fan blades, glassware and furniture designing.

A surface in a 3D space is an object definition that has width and breadth. It is represented by equations that has 2 free variables (or parameters). Surface may be represented in explicit, implicit and parametric forms. Out of these three, parametric form has more practical applications. **Also note that a solid surface is obtained by creating infinitely many copies of the curve and placing them next to each other without any gaps in between.**

**Bilinear surfaces** are curved surfaces that are fully defined by means of their four corner points. **Please note here that their four boundary curves are straight lines and the coordinates of any point on this surface are derived by linear interpolation.** So, here the shape in not complex rather it is highly curved. Also, it is found that if the four corners are coplanar, the **bilinear patch** defined by them is flat.

A ruled surface or a scroll is a surface swept out by a straight line as it moves through the space. For instance, a cylinder is formed by moving a straight line around a curve in a plane.

Surfaces are said to be **single curved or developable** when they can be created through ordinary bending of a planar surface without stretching, cutting or wrinkling the material. They can be flattened onto a plane. **These surfaces are useful as they allow round forms to be made out of materials like plywood, sheet metal or cloth. That is why they are used for ship building, tent sewing and fabrication of ventilation ducts etc. surfaces that bend in two directions at the same time and cannot be made out of a flat material are called as a double curved surface. For example,** sphere, a saddle. No double curved surfaces are developable. Ruled surfaces are constructed from straight lines. They are either developable or double curved.

In 1972, Pierre Bezier first of all described Bezier surfaces. A Bezier patch is a 3D surface generated from the cartesian product of two curves. A 2D Bezier surface is defined as a parametric surface where the position of a point, P as a function of the parametric coordinates u, v is given by-

$$\mathbf{P(u, v) = \Sigma\Sigma\, B_i^m\,(u)\, B_i^n\,(v)\, P_{i,j}}$$

where, i = 0 to m, j = 0 to n

## 2.3 THREE-D BOUNDARY REPRESENTATION

Different schemes for describing 3D surface boundaries can be represented as meshes of triangles. However, this process may be only an estimate of the original surface, the errors are normally small. Two such methods are as follows: -

1. Bilinear Surfaces.
2. Bezier Surface Patches.

1. **Bilinear Surfaces:** Suppose we want to develop a **surface skin** from four points $P_{00}$, $P_{01}$, $P_{10}$, and $P_{11}$ located in space as shown in figure 2.1.

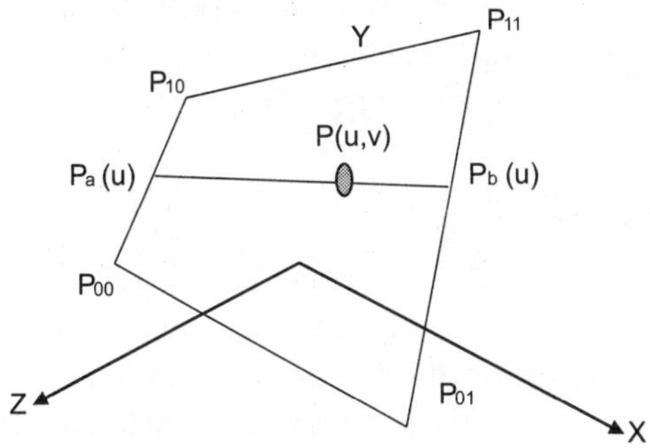


**Fig.2.1:** Surface skin from 4 points

There may be many ways of performing this task and that all will result in different surfaces. One method is to interpolate linearly the coordinate values of the points to create a bilinear surface. Any point on the surface can be accurately calculated by using the following analysis-

Any point along the line $\{P_{00}, P_{10}\}$ is given by the formula—

$$P_a(u) = (1 - u)\, P_{00} + uP_{10} \qquad \text{for } 0 \Leftarrow u \Leftarrow 1 \qquad \text{...(1)}$$

Similarly, any point on the line $\{P_{01}, P_{11}\}$ is given by the formula—

$$P_b(u) = (1 - u)\, P_{01} + uP_{11} \qquad \text{...(2)}$$

If a line connects the points $P_a(u)$ and $P_b(u)$ then any point $P(u, v)$ on this line is given by the formula—

$$P(u, v) = (1 - v)\, P_a(u) + v\, P_b(u) \qquad \text{for } 0 \Leftarrow u, v \Leftarrow 1 \qquad \text{...(3)}$$

From equations 1, 2 and 3 it is observed that this surface will be twisted and it can be converted into a **triangular mesh** by firstly computing a grid of points at regular intervals of u and v and then connecting them into triangles. **Please note that smaller the triangles are, the smoother the surface becomes.**

2. **Bezier Surface Patches:** An extension of Bezier curves and a better modelling tool is **Bezier surface patches.** ***Practically speaking, a model is built from Bezier patches that are then reduced to a mesh of triangles which are easily rendered in real-time world.*** Bezier surface patches may be quadratic, cubic, quadratic etc. In quadratic form, four control points are used to define the patch corners and five further points determine the surface geometry. One patch will not be sufficient to describe anything useful, so a mechanism is needed to construct multi-patch

objects. As during joining of two Bezier curves, slope continuity is must across the boundary in Bezier surface patches also. This slope continuity across the boundary is maintained if-

1. The control points at the boundary between the two patched are similar, and
2. The polygons formed by the control points at the boundary edge are coplanar for both patches.

## 2.4 GEOMETRICAL TRANSFORMATIONS: INTRODUCTION, FRAMES OF REFERENCE, MODELLING TRANSFORMATIONS, INSTANCES, PICKING, FLYING, SCALING THE VE, COLLISION DETECTION

Several application domains like navigation, missile tracking, robotics, biomechanics, architecture, CAD, education and VR require the knowledge of the real-time position and orientation of the moving objects within some **frames of reference.** To construct a VE, we need a **3D cartesian frame of reference** within which the objects and virtual objects are located. Objects are modelled relative to their own frame of reference, which will have an extra axes about which certain elements rotate. **Also understand here that the virtual object (VO) has its individual frame of reference that is used to capture the perspective projection of the virtual environment.** For simplicity and consistency, these three frames of reference are named as **the right-handed coordinate systems.**

> **Note:** Objects are first modelled within their Object Coordinate System (OCS) which can be visualized to be coincident with the World Coordinate System (WCS) representing the Virtual Environment Figure 2.2.

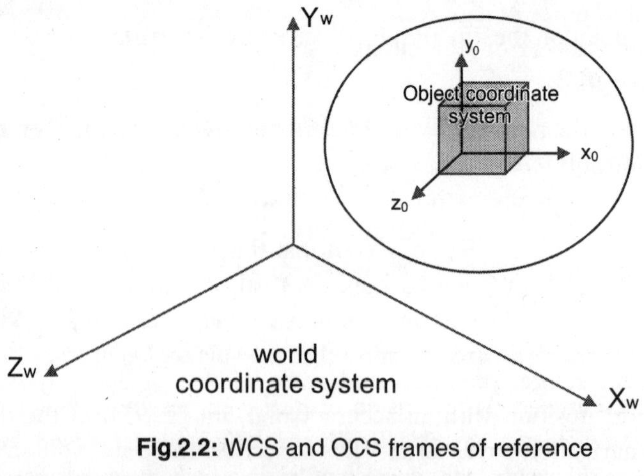


**Fig.2.2:** WCS and OCS frames of reference

Different modelling transformations like scale, reflection, rotate and translate are then applied to the objects to locate them in virtual environments. These transformations are usually expressed as matrices that can be concatenated to a **single transform matrix**. When a view of the virtual environment is rendered, this matrix is computed and applied to reveal the object's actual position in the virtual environment. Else the object is stored in the database in its original coordinate form along with its modelling transformations.

a. **Translation:** The translate transformation enables an object to be positioned anywhere within a virtual environment by specifying three offset values that are associated with every 3D vertex of the object. These offsets are held within a matrix associated with an object. Matrix is applied to reveal the object's true position (having these offsets) only when the object is required for rendering or for task like collision detection.

b. **Scaling:** This transformation alters the size of an object by scaling all of its coordinates relative to the origin of the Object Coordinate System (OCS).

c. **Reflection:** Say, a mirror is positioned in one of the planes associated with the principal axes, a reflection of an object can be computed by **reversing the sign of either the x, y or z coordinates. The rule is that if we reverse the sign of every x-vertex and leave the y and z coordinates untouched, the resultant object is a reflection of the original object.** Similarly, if the signs of the y-coordinates are reversed, a reflection occurs about ZX-plane and if the signs of the z-coordinates are reversed, a reflection occurs about the XY-plane. The result of reflection is that a polygon's vertex sequence is also reversed. This actually destroys any convention in use to maintain vertex sequences in a clockwise or anti-clockwise sequence. This can be corrected by reversing the relevant entries in the data structures supporting the vertex entries. We can reverse the x, y and z coordinates in one operation or any other combination. This could place the reflection in any one of the eight octants associated with the principal axes. **It is interesting to note that when an odd number of sign changes are made, vertices are reversed and when an even number of sign changes are made, the vertex sequence remains unchanged.**

d. **Rotation:** Direction cosines employ the cosines of angles formed between two frames of reference and are useful only when there is immediate access to these angles. A compound rotation can also be made by subjecting an object to a sequence of matrix operations. Rotations are non-commutative i.e. the chosen sequence generally leads to a unique result but a consistent sequence must be followed.

**Please note that these applications have different requirements of parameters like measurement range, precision and rates.** Global positioning system (GPS) transducers report position with an accuracy of 1-5m i.e. 95% of the time. This is quite ok for car navigation but as far as VR is concerned there are more strict accuracy requirements. On the other hand, the scale of measured distances for VR interactions is usually not larger than a room or a lab. A moving object in 3D space has six degrees of freedom—3 for translation and 3 for rotations. If the cartesian coordinate system is attached to the moving object then its translations are along the X, Y and Z axes. **Also note that object rotations about these axes are called yaw, pitch and roll respectively.**

These define a dataset of 6 numbers that need to be measured rapidly as the object may be moving at a very high speed also.

Geometric modelling means describing the shape of virtual objects like polygons, triangles, vertices, splines etc. as well as their appearance i.e. surface texture, surface illumination and colour.

**Rendering is defined as the process of converting the 3D geometrical models populating a virtual world into a 2D scene presented to the user.** This process has been pipelined in the last few years which means dividing it into stages and assigning these stages to different hardware resources. Graphics rendering has three functional stages that are pipelined: -

**Application stage → Geometry stage → Raster stage**

The 1st stage, the application stage is done by the software using CPU. It reads the world geometry database as well as the user's input. Depending on this input, this stage may change the view to the simulation or change the orientation of virtual objects.

In 2nd stage, the results of 1st stage are fed to the geometry stage which can be implemented either in software or in hardware. This stage consists of model transformations like translations, rotations and scaling, scene projections, clipping and mapping. Even lighting computations at this stage will shade the scene and give more realistic view.

The last stage is the rasterizing stage. It is done in hardware so as to achieve speeds. This stage converts the vertex information by the 2nd stage, like colour, into pixel information needed by the video display. It is at this stage that antialiasing is also done in order to remove the jagged appearance of the polygon edges. Antialiasing subdivides pixels into subpixels regions with an assigned color. These are summed up and thus they determine the R, G, B percentages in the resulting color assigned to the display pixel. **Also note that the more subpixels are used the larger is the computational load of the rasterizing stage and the better is the image quality.** To achieve better speed-up, the rendering pipeline stages themselves use parallel architectures.

Earlier the patient had to go several lengthy sessions are the doctor's clinic for certain therapies. With VR when these patients were made to perform 1.5 hrs of VR exercise daily for 3 weeks then they improved significantly in their hand motion and grasping power. Now patients keep their arms stationary during therapy and there was no arm-reaching motion. The point is that the comparative tests done on a **pick-and-place** task showed a great improvement.

The first stage of haptic (touch) rendering is **collision detection. It determines whether two or more objects are in contact with each other.** This can be considered as a form of haptic clipping as only objects that collide are processed by the haptics rendering pipeline. One such technique, approximate collision detection or bounding-box collision detection uses 3D extents/ bounding boxes. It detects whether two or more bounding boxes overlap in 3D space. If the two objects are in close proximity to each other, their bounding boxes overlap i.e. they collide.

**It is interesting to note that a virtual environment is not merely a collection of polygons.** A virtual environment is a **hierarchical structure** that finds out what a user can do. This structure contains the following—

- Geometrical descriptions of the VE.
- Attributes like lighting, colour, texture, sound, procedures for object building, procedures for finding out the size, orientation and position of different parts of articulated objects.

## 2.4.1 Instances

Modern design methods must reduce the number of different components used to construct an object. Using basic building blocks in different parts of a structure can result in drastic savings of manufacturing processes, storage space, assembly procedures and maintenance costs.

**For example,** consider the case of a chair that has four identical legs. A leg's geometry need only be stored once. Four references are made to this geometry in the chair's description, **It is interesting to note that the coordinates of the master leg are relative to the Object Coordinate System (OCS) whereas the chair's four legs require different positions and different orientations in the Virtual Environments (VE). Also note that the database can be organized such that the single leg is stored as a geometric entity with a collection of matrix transformations.** These are used to scale, rotate and translate this geometry to create the four legs in the correct position, orientations and sizes. Such geometric elements are known as **instances as they have no individual existence.**

There are two advantages of using instances as follows:

1. Geometric descriptions are minimized. This keeps the database size control.
2. If the attributes of the reference object like geometry, colour or texture are altered then they are automatically propagated throughout the Virtual Environment (VE).

On the other hand, if every object had a unique definition within a database, it will be difficult to make repeated identical updates and may lead to errors and inconsistencies. A simple chair might require only a top or four legs which means that we need to define the geometry of only the top and one leg.

**Picking:** Objects within the virtual environment are modelled in their local frame of reference and positioned within the virtual environment using modelling transformation like translate, scale, reflect and rotate. **Please note that by changing these transformations, an object can be moved about a virtual environment according to some set rules (procedures).** But if the virtual object wishes to move an object then somehow the transform associated with the VO's object must become associated with the object. Finally, the transform describing the object's new position and orientation must be consistent with the original definition as the virtual object may wish to interact with it again.

**Flying: The process of moving around the virtual domain that reduces the physical effort is known as flying.** This is obtained by **flying** through the virtual environment and requires the virtual object to indicate the direction of flight and instruct the system to fly in this direction until the command is terminated. Practically speaking, this is done by moving the virtual environment past the virtual object in the opposite direction to that indicated. As all motion is relative, the result is same. **Also note that the flying direction is specified using a 3D mouse or a glove and the distance moved at each frame update can be a system-defined parameter or the value determined interactively by the virtual object.**

**Scaling the Virtual Environment:** It is possible to scale up the virtual environment or down to obtain the new perspective. F**or example, by making it larger, the virtual object becomes smaller. By making virtual environment smaller the virtual object becomes larger.** For the virtual object to become usual to the rescaling operation it is effected over a period of second. **Please note that this implies that the scaling factor will be slightly less than or greater than unity. Also note that the scaling factor of 2 would double the size of the virtual environment at every frame update and create complex and big worlds very fast.**

**Collision Detection:** In VR, collision detection between objects is quite important. As virtual environment can be built from polygons, patches, particles etc. so different methods are required for each modelling modality. We need algorithms to make such schemes possible, so geometric data is extended with other artifacts like bounding boxes and bounding spheres. Collision detection between 2D shapes is effected by comparing the minimum and maximum x and y extents for two shapes. This is mini-max test for shapes. **If the x and y extents do not overlap,** neither can the reference shapes. On the other hand, **if the x and y extents do overlap then there is a possibility that the shapes intersect or touch. This must be tested by testing individual vertices of both shapes.**

Extending the mini-max idea to 3D creates the idea of a bounding box enclosing an object. **If the x and y extents do not overlap,** neither can the reference shapes. On the other hand, **if the x and y extents do overlap then there is a possibility that the shapes intersect or touch. This must be tested by testing individual vertices of both shapes.** Many methods are available to help in proving that an edge intersects a polygon.

Instead of enclosing an object within a box, it can be placed inside a sphere, the radius of which is adjusted to enclose all vertices.

## 2.5 GENERIC VR SYSTEM: INTRODUCTION, VIRTUAL ENVIRONMENT, COMPUTER ENVIRONMENT, VR TECHNOLOGY, MODEL OF INTERACTION, VR SYSTEMS.

In a generic VR system, there are four system elements to be considered-

- **The Virtual Environment** (VE) – covering model building, dynamic features, physical constraints, illumination and collision detection. VE can take many forms. Geometric accuracy is as much important as the attributes of colours, texture and lighting. You can even use 3D modelling software may be used to construct like environment showing architectural plans. Some environment may already exist as a CAD database so some form of conversion software is needed to translate it into a suitable format. Please note that the VE does not have any physical basis at all. For example, the virtual environment could be used to evaluate some physical simulation. Here, accuracy of physical behaviour is more significant than visual fidelity. In the scenario of simulation of the behaviour of molecules within electric fields, the behavioural dynamics of the atomic structures can be explored using simple models based on the coloured spheres, cylinders and twisted ribbons.

**Just remember the rule that states that " Whatever is the application, a geometric database must be built to represent the environment and stored such that it can be retrieved and rendered in real-time when required."**

Using virtual objects to build virtual worlds, many of the object's attributes must be stored in the database of VE like 3D geometry, colour, texture, dynamic characteristics, physical constraints and acoustic attributes. **Also note that a VR system provides a domain where a virtual world can be modelled, simulated, visualized and even experienced using immersive displays.** So, a VE consists of a collection of objects and light sources. Collision detection algorithms monitor collisions between specified objects. *The state of the VE is influenced by the input signals that come from the head trackers, hand trackers and speech channels. On the other hand, the outputs from the system are in the form of visual, audio and other data channels.*

Actually, objects in an virtual environment are of two types-

a. Static.

b. Dynamic.

- **The Computer Environment** – includes CPU configuration, I/O channels, VE database and the real-time operating system. **In general, a VR system needs a computing environment that can coordinate different inputs given by the user and output vital graphics and auditory data. Head data** is used control the dynamic behaviour of the virtual object within the virtual environment. Hand data provides the position and orientation of a 3D mouse or positions of user's fingers. There are two main output channels – graphics channel and **sound channel. Graphics channel** provides two independent images for the user's left and right eyes. This gives a binocular view of the scene. **Sound channel** provides the user with acoustic feedback with respect to the events taking place at a virtual level. The VE Database showing the virtual objects are stored on the hard disk and loaded into the main memory whenever required. Loading of data can take a few seconds only if the data is small but if there are, for instance, large number of texture maps the more time may be required. This process of copying of data is done on need basis.

Only required data is loaded at a time, the remaining data resides on the disk only. **The rule is to keep the active database to a minimum size. For example-1**, a panoramic display system is used in flight simulation.

**Example-2,** in a 5-channel system, the total field of view covers 200° (approx.). this means that it needs a 360° view of the virtual environment (VE) should always be resident in memory. This is must so as to adjust with sudden horizontal rotations, as found in helicopter systems. The objects will naturally be disturbed from their original positions during the session. **In some cases, it may be mandatory to reset the database to its original state so that an exercise can be repeated from a consistent start point.** In other cases, it will be mandatory to continue a session from a point reached in an earlier exercise. To achieve this, the user must have an option to save the database in its current state and recover it at later time. Some companies use open format for describing virtual objects, their formats (like physical properties, constraints, behaviour, geometry) and hierarchical relationships between the objects.

The real-time, run-time services are core to any VR system as they coordinate all other system components so that they can work coherently. The duties include the management of VE database, the I/O channels, collision detection, networking and CPU resources. This must be done synchronously to maintain real-time environments. To accomplish this, we run the services in discrete elements that run parallelly on multi-processor systems.

- The VR technology – covers the hardware used for head-tracking, image display, sound and hand tracking. It covers all hardware used by the user for a VR task. This includes head-mounted displays, 3D devices, headphones and 3D trackers.
- The modes of interaction – involves hand gestures, 3D interfaces and multi-participant systems. VR systems allows users to develop transparent interfaces. **Note that these systems are application specific. For example**, a virtual paint brush might not be a good tool to apply paint in free space, to create a painting effect. The design is VR interfaces is still a challenge.

A typical VR session begins by loading a virtual environment (VE) from disk into the host computers memory. **Please note that objects within the database will take up their default positions. Also note that the computer graphics display processor provides binocular views of the virtual environment.**

**Flying:** A head-mounted display (HMD) isolates the user from the real world and thus substitutes binocular views of the virtual environment. The display processor responds in real-time to the new viewpoint. Once it is oriented, the user inspects the virtual environment by moving his or head in different directions. HMD's cable is physically constrained in length so the navigation of the virtual environment is obtained by instructing the system to **fly the user's viewpoint in a specific direction. This is communicated to the operating system (OS) via the 3D mouse (or a glove) to**

**identify both the directions of travel and when to start or stop the object.** Note that even the simpler environments have to be navigated in the same manner.

**Flying** longer distances is time consuming and can be avoided by another technique of **teleporting.**

**Teleporting: It means identifying a new location in the virtual environment to which OS automatically transports the user without having to travel**. But the problem is in specifying the destination. **For example,** in air-flight simulation, the simulator is relocated to a new position by supplying the operating system with the longitude, latitude, height and heading.

Yet another method involves scaling the environment to a size whereby it can be viewed as a scale model. Here, the user identifies a new location by pointing to the model and is teleported there by the system.

**Object picking:** Objects that have been assigned dynamic properties can be interacted by the input devices like a 3D mouse or an interactive glove. **For example,** say in a VE contains a car then the car doors can be given dynamic properties. These doors are limited to allow them to rotate about their hinges through some angle. **Please note here that the user opens the door by moving the icon of the 3D mouse towards the position of the door's handle. Also note that when a collision is detected, the user confirms the selection of the door by activating a button on the mouse. This process is called as picking.** Actually, when the user's hand is moved to open the door then the system updates the rotation matrices associated with the door so that it can rotate. Furthermore, any attempt to rotate the door after the limiting angle (stored in the database) is prevented by the OS. If the door is closed now then a sound similar to a car's radio can be started at the point of impact.

If the virtual environment contains the objects that are not constrained then the user can **pick** them using the mouse icon. After the selection has been made by the user using the mouse button, it is our OS that arranges that from that point on, the object's motion is controlled by the position of the mouse. So, **the object goes wherever the user goes.** The user can release the object by selecting the required button. **At this junction, the object inherits the status of the last orientation and the position matrix of the user's mouse.** This might leave the object hanging in space or the object may fall downwards. **Note that any future response will depend on the simulation environment to which the object is subject.**

**Gesture recognition:** It has been observed that hand gestures are an excellent VR interface because you just have to track the user's hand position and finger joint angles and then give commands through an accepted vocal bury of signs. **But please note that all human gestures are not universal.** Whenever a user makes a gesture, a table of data is automatically scanned to find out what action to take. Practically, a hand gesture will be used to pick the objects and initiate or terminate an activity. Here, **neural networks** can also be used to recognize hand gestures.

**The User Interface:** The user interfaces used by conventional 2D windows system does not use and explore all such same tools (like menus, sliders, rulers etc.) for 3D VR interfaces also. New paradigm is now needed for virtual systems.

**Through-the-window systems:** Some engineers believe that **if a VR system is not immersive then it is not VR.** The systems in which the viewer's head position and orientation can be used to control the view-point of the computer-generated images that creates the impression of looking into a window, beyond which exists some volume of space, are called as **through-the-window systems.** These systems require just a graphics workstation and a simple head-tracker. So, now the user can interact with the VE using a spaceball, a 3D mouse or a glove. So, he can achieve everything that is possible within an immersive environment rather than experiencing the sensation of immersion.

**Many user systems:** Another challenge in VR systems is to network a group of people such that they can interact with one another in a virtual system. We need a highly distributed system model of computation that scales well to multi-user system.

**VR systems:** It is now clear that how a user interacts with a virtual database. **Please note that as VR technology evolves, newer system approaches will appear.** This may include multimedia interfaces, networks etc.

## SUMMARY

We have explored different aspects of graphics, geometric modelling techniques and geometric transformations. **We are now in a position to understand the basic building blocks for a generic VR system.** We have studied the central elements their roles and their coordination to work as a coherent system. The four system elements are also discussed for an immersive VR system.

## EXERCISE QUESTIONS

Q1. How can we move from n-dimensional state to (n+1) dimensional state?

Q2. Explain Bezier space curves.

Q3. Explain the relationship between the three frames of reference for the world, VO and the object coordinate systems,

Q4. Explain the following modelling transformations: -

a. Translate.

b. Scale.

c. Reflection.

d. Rotation.

Q5. What are the two major benefits of using instances?

Q6. What is picking? Explain.

Q7. What is flying? Explain with some examples.

Q8. How will you scale the VE?

Q9. What is collision detection? Explain the following tests: -

a. Mini-max testing for shapes.

b. Bounding boxes.

c. Bounding spheres.

Q10. With the help of a block diagram explain the basic building blocks of a generic VR systems?

Q11. Write short notes on:

a. I/O channels.

b. The VE database.

c. HMDs.

d. Teleporting.

e. Multi-user systems.

# 3 Virtual Environment

## 3.0 INTRODUCTION

The main challenge in computer animation comes from HCI (Human-Computer Interface). Computer animation provides **animator** with an alternative approach to the animation process. In cartoon animation, the **animator** simply draws line on paper. When sufficient frames have been produced they are animated as a **line test.** The process is complex, yet it is fully interactive and the animator is always in control. In 3D computer animation, animator works at the computer screen using several types of software tools. If a tool is not present, then the animator's job is to write some extra code. In VE, animation of objects show similar problems. **Please note here that the level of support needed to animate objects in a virtual environment varies from application to application. For example,** if we develop a virtual clock then its hands must rotate in synchronization with the current time. In many esoteric applications, the virtual human parts should look like real-world counterparts. Certain operators can be trained to handle it. The aim is to get highest possible realism in this simulation process though the final solution may be a compromise.

## 3.1 THE DYNAMICS OF NUMBERS

It is said that a virtual environment (VE) is a **complex numerical database** that animates physical or abstract attributes and involves **changing one number into another. Note that the numerical envelop of change as well as the derivatives at any point is significant here.**

For example, if we have to make a ball's simulation real then we must simulate its **downward acceleration** in a gravitational field and also its **deceleration** after it bounces and moves upwards. **Also note that to prevent the ball from indefinite bouncing, some loss has to be introduced to attenuate the ball's energy.**

## 3.2 LINEAR AND NON-LINEAR INTERPOLATION

To understand such ideas, the methods of linear and non-linear interpolation will be developed and then applied to various animation scenes. As per the Newton's law an object accelerates as it falls to the ground. A tossed coin, a swinging pendulum etc. will slowly lose its energy and come to rest. All these examples involve some sort of delay like **delay due to friction, generation of heat or noise or kinetic energy being converted into potential energy.**

Also we can linearly interpolate between two values using the formula as follows:

$v(t) = (1 - t)\, v_1 + v_2 + tv_2 \qquad (0 <= t <= 1)$

when $t = 0, v(t) = v_1$

when $t = 1, v(t) = v_2$

For intermediate values of t, v (t) is **linearly interpolated between $v_1$ and $v_2$.**

Consider the example of an object that is being moved from point $P_1$ to $P_2$. Further, say that this has to be applied non-linearly such that initially the object moved very slowly away from $P_1$, accelerated and then decelerated till it comes to a complete rest at $P_2$. One method of controlling this movement is to use a part of a cosine curve. **This is non-linear interpolation.** However, this method has some disadvantage also.

### 3.2.1 Disadvantages of non-linear interpolation

1. The cosine function that it uses, consumes a lot of time (particularly in real-time environment). To overcome this problem, use a **pre-computed cosine table and linearly interpolate between a pair of entries.** The object is **animated** by cycling a sequence of objects in prepared states. This cosine function can be used to control their orientation. At run-time, their movements will appear as desired.
2. It is not easy to make the acceleration part of the function different from the deceleration part. A function can be developed that provides the required asymmetry using **parametric interpolation.** This provides a wide range of controllable functions without complex calculations.

## 3.3 THE ANIMATION OF OBJECTS

All objects in real world possess *mass, potential energy and kinetic energy in form of linear and angular momentum.* Many object attributes like centre of gravity and moment of inertia are also talked about to predict the object's behaviour under different dynamic conditions. **Please note that Newton's laws of motion provide a useful framework to compute these predictions. Such scenarios can be simulated within a Virtual Environment.**

Let us now study a simple linear animation of objects.

## 3.4 LINEAR AND NON-LINEAR TRANSLATIONS

**Linear Translation:** It has been observed that **if the system's update rate is F Hz, then the time slice t between each update is 1/F. For instance,** if F = 25Hz, each frame is separated in time by 40ms. **Also note that if we now wish to show a virtual object moving at a speed S, it must be displaced a linear distance of (S *t) between each update.** Here the time, t is given by the formula:

$$\mathbf{t = actual\ time - previous\ time = t_{now} - t_{prev}}$$

The displacement of an object can be computed by the product of its component velocity ($V_0$) and the time, t , as given above. That is, ($t_{now-}$ $t_{prev}$) * $V_0$ . Say, an object is located at the VE's origin and assigned a speed $S_0$ representing the linear speed across the XZ plane, then to simulate this **sliding movement,** the x and z-coordinates of the object must be modified by the corresponding components of the vector, ($t_{now-}$ $t_{prev}$) * $V_0$. **Also note that to contain the object within specified boundaries, we can automatically compute the object's new velocity after bouncing off the boundary.** Figure 3.1 shows a plane view of XZ-plane.

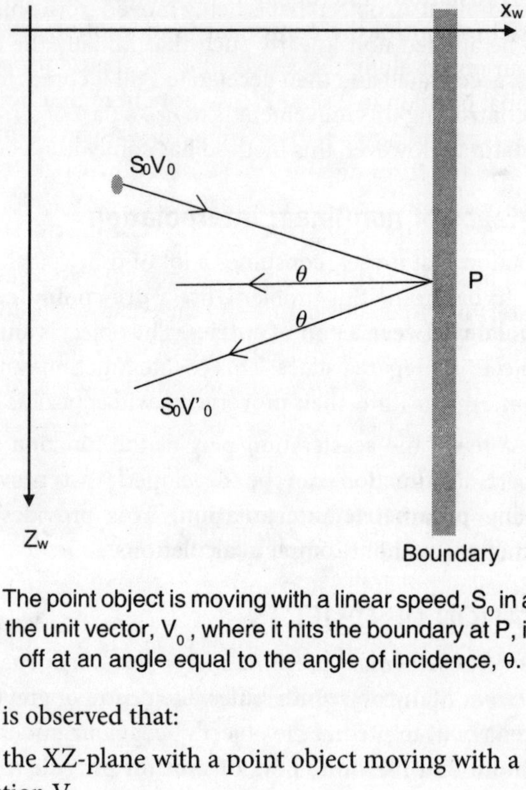


**Fig.3.1:** The point object is moving with a linear speed, $S_0$ in a direction given by the unit vector, $V_0$ , where it hits the boundary at P, it bounces off at an angle equal to the angle of incidence, θ.

From the figure it is observed that:

1. It shows the XZ-plane with a point object moving with a linear speed, $S_0$ and the direction $V_0$.
2. The point will collide at right hand boundary at P.
3. **Note that for simple elastic collisions, the angle of reflection equals to the angle of incidence, θ.**
4. The direction of point $V'_0$ after the reflection is given by ($-V_{ox}$, $V_{oy,}$ $V_{oz}$) where the sign of the x-component of $V_0$ has been reversed and the other two components are preserved. **Also note that the reversal of the x-component is only because the boundary was orthogonal to the x-axis.**
5. If the object's kinetic energy is required to decay with time, a parameter can be used to reduce the linear speed either by a constant amount or by a fraction of its current speed at each frame update.

In 1st scenario, the new speed $S'_0$ is given by the formula:

$$S'_0 = S_0 - \Delta s$$

Where $S_0$ is the previous speed and $\Delta s$ is the constant reduction. $S'_0$ must be prevented from going negative.

In 2nd scenario, the new speed is given by the formula:

$$S'_0 = k\, S_0$$

Where k is some suitable decay constant.

**Non-Linear Translation:** Interpolation techniques like quadratic, cubic and Hermite can be used to control the non-linear motion of objects. **For example,** it is required to move an object along the x-axis in 1 sec, pause for some time and then return it to its original position in 2 secs. **Please note here that both movements have to be non-linear and controllable. Also note that this can be simulated by computing the x-translation as a function of time.** If the real-time clock is in units of seconds then at time $T_1$ the translation can begin. At time $T_2$, i.e. $(T_1 + 1)$, the object pauses momentarily and then begins its return journey and at time $T_3$ i.e. $(T_1 + 3)$, it comes to rest at its original position. Furthermore, a parameter, t, (where $0 \le t \le 1$) is used to **control the two interpolations.** It is defined by the equations as follows:

$t = T - T_1$ (while $T_1 \le T \le T_2$)

$t = (T - T_1 - 1) / 2$ (while $T_2 \le T \le T_3$)

where T is the current time.

To control the non-linearity during the first slide two control values, $c_a$ and $c_b$ are used. And two further values, $c_c$ and $c_d$ are used on the return slide. **Also note that the values of** $c_a$, $c_b$, $c_c$ and $c_d$ should be chosen carefully to make sure that there is smooth acceleration and deceleration at the start and at the end of each movement.

## 3.5 SHAPE AND OBJECT INBETWEENING

**Shape inbetweening is defined as the process of speeding-up of creating networks in the cartoon industry wherein "inbetween" drawings are derived from the two key images drawn by a skilled animator.** These **key images** may show an object or character in two different positions called as *key frames*, which require extra inbetween images, if they have to animate animate properly. Instead of giving this task to the animator, the extra drawings are produced by an '**inbetweener**' who prepares them by interpolating between the two key drawings. **Please note that the number and positions of these interpolated image determine the dynamics of the final animation. For instance,** say that two simple key contours labelled as A and B are to be interpolated that is, contour A is to be animated into contour B by introducing extra inbetween lines. Then two cases arise:

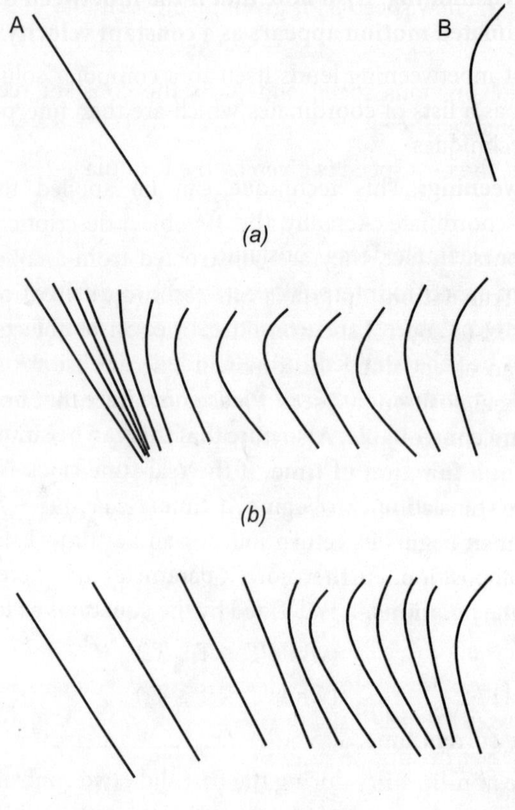


**Fig.3.2:** (a) two contours A and B to animate by inbetweening method; (b) Placing in between lines close to A creates an accelerated movement; (c) Placing inbetween lines close to B creates a retarded movement

> **Notes:**
> 1. If we use a quadratic instead of a linear interpolant, the lines would still be the same, but the interpolant would control their spacing.
> 2. This concept can be extended to work with contours having any number of vertices.
> 3. If they share the same number of vertices, it would be possible to interpolate open or closed complex shapes.
> 4. There is no need for the key shapes to share the same number of vertices.
> 5. Also note that a procedure can be made that maps a vertex of one shape to an equivalent position on the second shape.

**Case-1: Placing the inbetween lines close to A creates an accelerated movement.**

If the inbetween lines are drawn as shown in fig.3.2, and are animated then contour A will **transform** into contour B with an accelerated motion.

**Case-2: Placing the inbetween lines close to B creates a retarded movement.**

If the inbetween lines are drawn as shown in fig. c then A will still transform to B but the dynamic will be reversed. And the movement introduced into the final animation is called as **fairing** or **cushioning. Also note that if the inbetween lines are distributed evenly, then the animated motion appears as a constant velocity.**

This process of inbetweening lends itself to a computer solution now. Both the contours are stored as a lists of coordinates which are then interpolated using one of the mathematical techniques.

**Object inbetweening:** This technique can be applied to 3D contours by inbetweening the z-coordinate. Actually, the 3D object descriptions are not arbitrary collections of contours. In fact, they are constructed from a coherent set of surface elements. We cannot expect to interpolate between two different complex objects and expect that the inbetween objects are geometrically consistent. **For instance, a 4-sided tetrahedron cannot be inbetweened into a 6-sided cube without losing part of the surface geometry.** *It is possible to transform one object into another.*

**Parametric line inbetweening:** The techniques used above can be directly used on explicit shapes and objects. Same techniques can also be used to the control points of implicit parametric lines. **For example**, consider the case of a quadratic Bezier curve, the two end points and the associated control vertex could be inbetweened with a similar set belonging to a second curve. At each stage of the interpolation a curve can be computed from the status of the inbetween vertices. At the halfway point, the inbetween control points are halfway along their journeys joining A to B. They are used to develop the curve. **Please note that more complex shapes can be processes by employing piecewise curves.** Although curves with identical numbers of line segments are easier to process yet dissimilar curves can be processed by introducing phantom segments of zero length.

**Parametric surface-patch inbetweening:** It is the advantage of parametric techniques that its line based procedures can be extended to incorporate surface patch descriptions. For example, in case of Bezier surface patches, two sets of control meshes are inbetweened which involves two sets of 9 control points for quadratic patches or 16 control points for cubic patches. **Also note that even multi-patched objects can be inbetweened but a consistent level of patch correspondence must be maintained between the two key objects.**

## 3.6 FREE-FORM DEFORMATION (FFD)

**Free-form deformation is a technique of modelling and animating objects that works by surrounding an object with a 3D lattice of control points that can be used to deform an object by deforming the enclosed volume of space.** This can be understood easily by first considering its application to a 1D set of ordinates, then a 2D shape and finally a 3D object.

**Deforming 1D ordinates:** say, we have to alter the spatial distribution of the four ordinates $P_1$, $P_2$ $P_3$ and $P_4$. Then please understand that this FFD technique is to associate these numbers with a 1D lattice of control values which, when moved will disturb the positions of the original coordinates. This can be shown diagrammatically as in Fig.3.3.

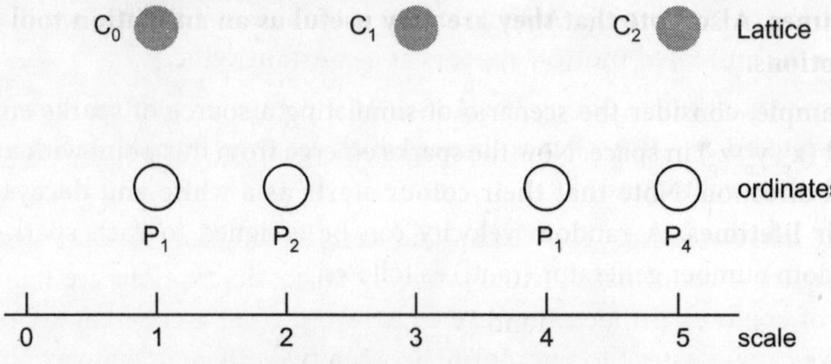


**Fig.3.3:** Deforming 1D ordinates

Fig. 3.3 shows four ordinates $P_1$, $P_2$, $P_3$ and $P_4$ with values determined by the button scale. The 3 control values $C_0$, $C_1$ and $C_2$ form a 1D lattice that can be used to alter the spatial distribution of the 4 ordinates. **Also understand here that if the Bernstein polynomials are associated with the control values then 3 control values effect a quadratic distribution while 4 vales effect a cubic distribution.** Also seen in fig.3.3 is that 2 control values $C_0$ and $C_2$ are positioned at $P_1$ and $P_4$ respectively while a 3rd value $C_1$ is placed half-way between $P_1$ and $P_4$. Now any ordinate P be moved to a new position P' by the equation given below:

$$P' = (1-u)^2 C_0 + 2u(1-u)C_1 + u^2C_2 \qquad \text{(for } 0 \le u \le 1\text{)}$$

Where the parameter, u is defined as follows:

$$U = (P - P_1) / (P_4 - P_1)$$

From fig.3.3, we observe that the 4 values of P' are identical to the original values of $P_1$, $P_2$, $P_3$, and $P_4$. This is because of the special values assigned to $C_0$ $C_1$ and $C_2$ .But if we change $C_1$ from 2.5 to 3.5, a new distribution is created. If, however, instead of moving the central control value, one of the boundary values are moved, the distribution of the original ordinates would become compressed or stretched. **Also note that it is now clear that the distribution of the original ordinates can be manipulated by altering any arbitrary number of control values.** If a greater degree of control is needed, a D lattice of four control values can be used to effect a cubic distribution.

This same idea can also be extended to control the family of 2D coordinates also with a 2D lattice of control values. In 3D case, a volume of space can be enclosed by a lattice of (3*3*3) control points. Moving one or more of the surface control points causes some deformation to the enclosed volume.

## 3.7 PARTICLE SYSTEMS

According to Reeves (1983), particle system is a very powerful technique that involves the modelling of fuzzy objects (like rain, fire, water and grass) from a very large numbers of discrete points or particles. Reeves used them for creating very realistic images of trees. **Please note that although their creative use produces photo-realistic images yet their discrete nature requires efficient anti-aliasing which leads to long**

**rendering times. Also note that they are very useful as an animation tool to show complex motions.**

**For example**, consider the scenario of simulating a source of sparks emanating from a point $(x_p, y_p, z_p)$ in space. Now the sparks emerge from this point with a random velocity and direction. **Note that their colour starts as a white and decays to blue during their lifetimes.** A random velocity can be assigned to each spark using a pseudo-random number generator (rand) as follows:

$$V = \text{rand}\,(V_{min}, V_{max})$$

where, $V_{min} \leq V \leq V_{max}$

Here, the direction of V is fixed by the angles θ and Φ where,

$$\theta = \text{rand}\,(0, 2\pi)$$

$$\Phi = \text{rand}\,(-\pi/2, \pi/2)$$

Also, the vector components of V are given by the expressions:

$$V_x = V \cos \Phi \cos \theta$$

$$V_y = V \sin \Phi$$

$$V_z = V \cos \Phi \sin \theta$$

And the positions of a particle after the elapsed time, t, is given by the formulas:

$$x = x_p + V_x t$$

$$y = y_p + V_y t - 1/2gt^2$$

$$z = z_p + V_z t$$

where g is the acceleration due to gravity.

The above parameters for each particle can be stored as a table that is updated on a frame-by-frame basis. When a **special effect** is initiated, the table is updated and rendered for each frame. **The values of** $V_x$, $V_y$ and $V_z$ **can be kept constant to avoid the evaluation of the sine and cosine functions. Also note that if this special effect is animated within a virtual environment, then one might want to consider the interaction of the particles with other objects.** With this concept, the particles will pass through other objects instead of bouncing them off.

## 3.8 PHYSICAL SIMULATION: AN INTRODUCTION

Entire universe is governed by different systems of laws. These laws describe the dynamics of objects, electromagnetic phenomena, atomic forces and cosmological models. Traditional animators depend upon a combination of visual memory and drawing skills to simulate different physical behaviours. **Please note that when a line test reveals that the animation is incorrect, it is redrawn and retested until it satisfies the animator.** However, such techniques cannot be used in real-time computer graphics. **Also note that if we want realism then we must rely on deterministic procedures that encode knowledge of the physical world.** These procedures may be based on either empirical laws or numerical techniques. But both have pros and cons too. Numerical techniques may be very realistic and efficient but may have limited application. On the other hand, empirical laws will accurately describe physical behaviour and enjoy a wide domain of applications but may require significant levels of computation. We cannot forget the Newton's laws when we study motion. **Newton's laws of motion provide us with the primary behaviours of theoretical particles having mass but no size. But these laws can be applied to describe the motion of very large objects without introducing significant errors.**

**Newton's 3-laws of motion** are as follows:

**Newton's first law of motion:** It states that **"the momentum of a particle is constant when there are no external forces."** This law explains us that an object moves in a straight line unless disturbed by some force. Different types of forces exist in thus universe like gravitational force, electric, magnetic or atomic. In general, it is only when we move away from the earth that the object begin to obey this law.

**Newton's second law of motion:** It states that **"a particle of mass m, subjected to force F, moves with acceleration F/m."** This law is also called as the **equation of motion of a particle.** It reminds us that work has to be done whenever an object is accelerated.

Newton's third law of motion: It states that **"if a particle exerts a force on a second particle, the second particle exerts an equal reactive force in the opposite direction."** This law is useful when considering collisions between objects.

## 3.9 OBJECTS FALLING IN A GRAVITATIONAL FORCE

From the school days, we have studied that when an object is moved away from the earth's surface, it is attracted back through a gravitational force. This force is known as the object's weight and is **equal to mg**, where m is the object's mass and g is the acceleration due to gravity. **However, please note that in general, g equals 9.81m/s², which is 0.3% smaller at the equator and 0.2% larger at poles.**

**Conventions: As the vertical y-axis represents positive offsets from the origin, upward velocities are defined positive and downward velocities negative.**

In general, if a particle has an initial vertical velocity of v and acceleration a, the distance d travelled after time, t is given by the formula:

$$d = (v * t) + 1/2at^2$$

If a particle has an initial vertical velocity of $v_0$ and is acceleration under the influence of gravity, then the distance, d is given by the expression:

$$d = (v_0 * t) - 1/2gt^2$$

Consider a particle that is positioned at point $P_0$ (as shown in fig.3.4) at a distance $h_0$ above the ground plane.

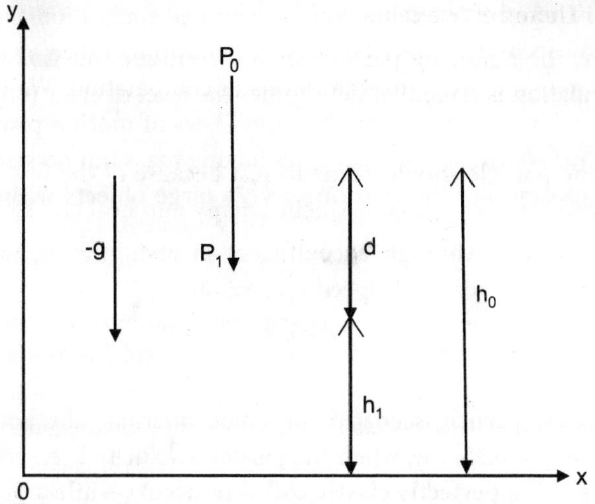


**Fig.3.4:** Particle p being dropped from a height, $h_0$

Fig.3.4 shows that of a particle P is dropped from a height $h_0$, after time, t, it will have travelled $1/2gt^2$ downwards. So, its new height, $h_1 = h_0 - 1/2gt^2$. How?

If a particle is allowed to fall under gravity, then after time, t, it will be at $P_1$ having fallen a distance d as follows:

$$d = -1/2\ gt^2$$

Its height $h_1$ above the ground plane is given by the formula:

$$h_1 = h_0 + d = h_0 - 1/2gt^2 \text{ (proved).}$$

Calculating $h_1$ above the ground plane is trivial. But if we want (say) to identify the point in time when the particle collides with the floor then further exploration is needed. If the status of the particle is sampled at different time intervals, the point of collision with the floor is detected when the particle's height is zero. Because of the sampling process we will not automatically discover the condition. It is more likely that the particle's height becomes negative and the point of intersection has to be computed. This can be implemented by maintaining a record of the particle's velocity and height at the previous sample.

**Temporal Aliasing:** With all discrete sampling systems, the problem of **aliasing** occurs. It occurs when any continuous system is discretely sampled. In this scenario, the simulation code computes parameters and different points in time. The display code may sample this data on a regular basis, which introduces **irregular temporal sampling**. Herein, the simulation code is evaluating a numerical model at a particular sample rate that varies with time. At any time, $t_n$, values of $v_n$ and $h_n$ are computed. The display code is updating the display processor with the latest version of the simulated model at a different rate. **Please note that even though this update is regular, the sampling process results in an inconsistent display of the simulation producing temporal aliasing. Also note that a practical way of minimizing this phenomenon is to increase the sampling rate of the simulation code.**

**Restitution:** There are two cases here:

Theoretically, the bouncing particle should continue indefinitely. It is the way the collision calculation is done that determines the level of error introduced into the model.

Practically, the particle should come to rest because of the imperfections in the physical system and the conversion of kinetic energy into heat and sound.

This can be effected through a coefficient of restitution e, which relates the separation speed $v_s$ to the approach speed $v_a$ as follows:

$$v_s = e\, v_a$$

where, $0 \le e \le 1$

In the bouncing particle scenario, we could alternate the bouncing cycle by introducing a value e = 0.95, say, when the particle's velocity is reversed. **Please note that by keeping e = 1, a perfectly elastic collision occurs while a perfectly inelastic collision is created when e = 0.**

Say, a particle strikes a smooth rigid surface with an approach speed $v_a$ at an angle $\alpha$ and a separation speed of $v_s$ at an angle of $\beta$. **Then it is observed that the component of its velocity tangential to the surface remains constant.** On the other hand, **the magnitude of the normal component is influenced by the coefficient of restitution.** This can be shown with the help of following equations:

$$v_s \sin\beta = v_a \sin\alpha \qquad \text{(i.e. tangential component)}$$

$$v_s \cos\beta = e.v_a \cos\alpha \qquad \text{(i.e. normal component)}$$

Note the factor 'e' in 2nd expression. So, we can say now that—

$$e \tan\beta = \tan\alpha$$

and that-

$$v_s^2 (\sin^2\beta + \cos^2\beta) = v_a^2 (\sin^2\alpha + e^2 \cos^2\alpha)$$

Hence,

$$v_s = v_a\, \mathrm{sqrt}(\sin^2\alpha + e^2 \cos^2\alpha)$$

$$\text{and } \beta = \tan^{-1}((\tan\alpha) / e)$$

## 3.10 ROTATING WHEELS

Say, we want to animate the rotational speed of a wheel in contact with some driving wheel. Fig.3.5 shows two wheels moving in opposite directions—one in anticlockwise and other in clockwise direction.

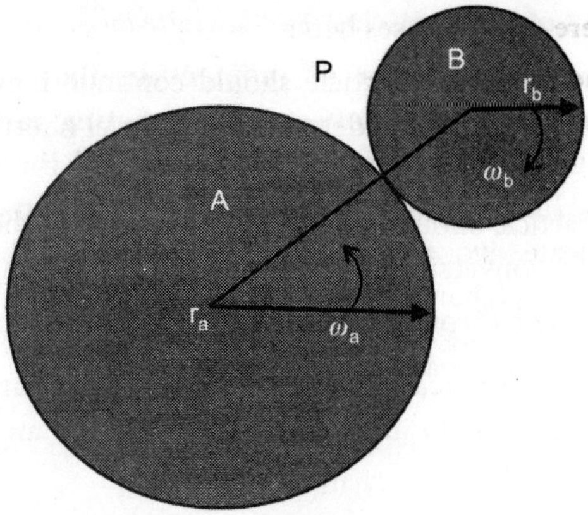


Fig.3.5:

Assume that two wheels, A and B, have radii $r_a$ and $r_b$ and rotational rates $\omega_a$ and $\omega_b$ rad/s respectively. At the point of contact, P, the angular speed of wheel A is $\omega_a r_a$, which must be same for wheel B. Furthermore, we assume zero slip between the two wheels. But wheel A is rotating anticlockwise while B is rotating in clockwise direction, so the following formula holds:

$$\omega_b r_b = -\omega_a r_a$$

and thus,

$$\omega_b = -r_a \omega_a / r_b \qquad \text{(rad/s)}$$

**Also note that if t seconds is the elapsed time from some reference time, wheel A will rotate $\omega_a$ t radians and wheel B will rotate $-\omega_a t r_a / r_b$ radians which can then be substituted into the relevant matrix used to rotate wheel B.**

## 3.11 ELASTIC COLLISIONS

Collisions between real objects of the world are complex physical interactions. These complexities may arise due to the following facts:

- Irregular boundaries of objects.
- Different coefficient of friction for individual surface.
- Their densities may be non-homogeneous.
- Objects may possess angular momentum.
- Objects may be travelling across an irregular surface which itself introduces non-linear frictional forces.

Note that it is possible to simulate (monitor) these phenomena.

Two cases arise here:

**Case-1: Direct impact of two particles.**

**Case-2: Oblique impact of two particles.**

**Case-1: Direct impact of two particles:** *Two laws are followed here:*

a. **Principle of the conservation of momentum that states that "when no external force acts on a system of several interacting particles, the total linear momentum of the system is conserved. The total linear momentum is the vector sum of the linear momenta of all the particles of the system."** The simpler collisions to simulate involves two imaginary particles with mass and velocity but no size. When two such particles collide, their new velocities are controlled by the principle of the conservation of momentum and the principle of relative motion. The momentum of a particle is the product of its mass and velocity. Given two particles with mass $m_a$ and $m_a$ and associated velocities $v_a$ and $v_b$ then it is said that–

$$m_a v_a + m_b v_b = \text{constant}$$

b. **Principle of relative motion** that states that **"the relative velocity after an impact equals the relative velocity before the impact multiplied by the coefficient of restitution."** So, if the respective velocities of the two particles after the collision are $u_a$ and $u_b$, then we may write—

$$u_a - u_b = -e(v_{a-} v_b)$$

where e is the coefficient of restitution.

**Please note that when two bodies collide, the interaction is assumed to take place during a short time interval.** The forces generated during the collision are assumed to be much larger than any external forces like gravity and wind resistance. Also note that any two particles are assumed to move **in the same straight line** connecting their centres. These types of collisions are called as **direct impact**.

Consider a particle A with mass $m_a$ and velocity $v_a$ striking particle B with mass $m_b$ and velocity $v_b$, travelling in opposite directions. Then their total momentum is given by the expression-

$$\text{Momentum} = m_a v_a + m_b v_b$$

Given $m_{a,} v_{a,} m_b$ and $v_b$ and using the relative velocities of A and B after the impact are $u_a$ and $u_b$ then–

$$m_a v_a + m_b v_b = m_a u_a + m_b u_b$$

Using the relative velocities for a perfect elastic collision we get:-

$$u_a - u_b = -(v_a - v_b)$$

Hence, $u_a$ and $u_b$ can be computed from these equations.

**Case-2: Oblique impact of two particles.**

When two particles A and B collide with velocities $v_a$ and $v_b$, at angles α and β to the line joining their two centres, the components of velocity perpendicular to the line are unaltered. **The tangential components are determined by applying the principle of the conservation of momentum.**

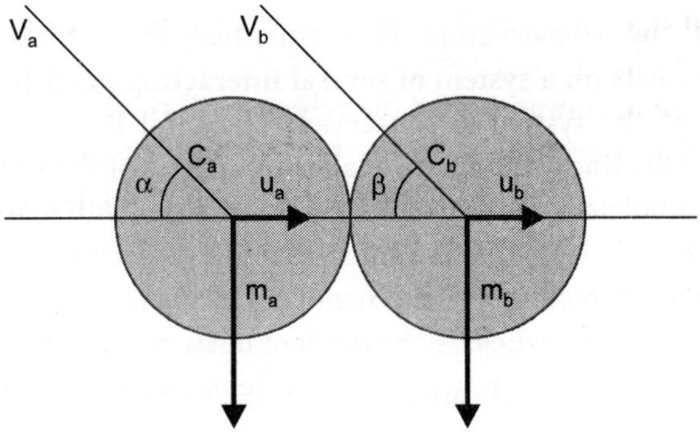


**Fig.3.6:** oblique impact of two particles.

Say, two particles A and B positioned at $c_a$ and $c_b$ at the time of impact. Also respective approach velocities are $v_a$ and $v_b$ at angles α and β relative to the line connecting their two centres. **Please note that the components of velocity perpendicular to the line $c_a c_b$ are unaltered by the collision. They are given by the expressions, $v_a \sin\alpha$ and $v_b \sin\beta$ respectively. Also note that the components of velocity parallel to the line $c_a c_b$ are subject to the conservation of momentum because the particle's masses are accelerated.** Hence, we can say that–

$$m_a v_a + m_b v_b = m_a u_a \cos\alpha + m_b u_b \cos\beta$$

By Newton's law of relative motion we have-

$$u_a - u_b = -e(v_a \cos\alpha + v_b \cos\beta)$$

where 'e' is the *coefficient of restitution.*

Note that the final velocity of each particle and its direction of motion is found from the perpendicular and parallel components.

## 3.12 PROJECTILES

Objects like shells, bullets, coin, stone or table are all associated with projectiles. **But please remember that an inflated balloon cannot be considered as a projectile** as its buoyancy and air resistance are vital factors influencing its motion. We assume that the frictional force due to air resistance is not important. **Also we assume that earth's gravitational force is constant at all heights.**

**Projectile motion:** We need to consider the free motion of a particle when it is projected in any direction in space. While considering this type of motion, we shall consider the following assumptions for simplicity:

- The motion of the particle takes place in a vertical plane.
- The acceleration due to gravity, g, is uniform and acts in the same vertical direction at all points of the path of the particle.
- There is no resistance due to air during the motion of the particle.

**Please note that when a particle is projected upwards with a velocity at an angle α with the horizon, the vertical component of the velocity will continually change whereas the horizontal component of the velocity will remain unchanged since the component of the acceleration, g. in the horizontal direction is zero.** Hence, the resultant direction of motion will continually change and the particle will describe a curved path. This path is a **parabola.**

Some definitions related to projectiles–

1. **Projectile:** A body projected in any direction in space is called as a **projectile.**
2. **Trajectory:** The curved path described by a projectile is called its **trajectory.**
3. **Velocity of projection:** The initial velocity with which a particle is projected in space is called as the **velocity of projection.**
4. **Angle of projection:** The angle which the direction of projection makes with the horizon is called as the **angle of projection.**
5. **Range:** The distance measured between the point of projection and the point where the particle strikes a given plane through the point of projection is called as its **range on the plane.** When the given plane is horizontal, we call it the **horizontal range.**
6. **Time of flight:** The time interval between the instant of projection and the instant when the particle meets a fixed plane through the point of projection i.e. the time for which the projectile remains in air is called as the **time of flight.**

To develop a general solution to the trajectory of a projectile, consider the scenario as shown in fig.3.7.

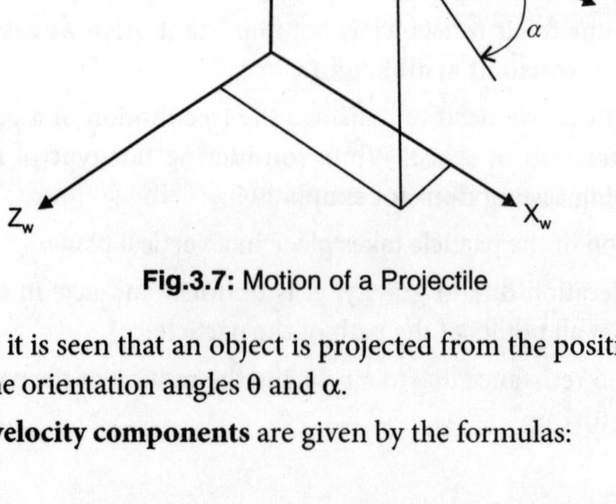


**Fig.3.7:** Motion of a Projectile

From fig.3.7 it is seen that an object is projected from the position $(x_p, y_p, z_p)$ with velocity $v_0$ and the orientation angles θ and α.

The **initial velocity components** are given by the formulas:

$$v_x = v_0 \cos\theta \cos\alpha$$
$$v_y = v_0 \sin\theta$$
$$v_z = v_0 \cos\theta \sin\alpha$$

**After time, t, after projection, the velocity components** are given by the formulas:

$$v_x = v_0 \cos\theta \cos\alpha$$
$$v_y = v_0 \sin\theta - gt$$
$$v_z = v_0 \cos\theta \sin\alpha$$

And the position of projectile (x, y, z) after time, t is given by the formula:

$$x = x_p + v_0\, t \cos\theta \cos\alpha$$
$$y = y_p + v_0\, t \sin\theta - 1/2gt^2$$
$$z = z_p + v_0\, t \cos\theta \sin\alpha$$

Using these equations, we can translate an object to position (x, y, z) as the elapsed time progresses. The resulting path is parabolic constrained within a vertical plane.

**Note:** The influence of a cross-wind can be introduced by defining the wind's speed and direction as a vector and adding the components to equations above.

**Collision with the ground:** If we maintain the status of the projectile at each sample, we can identify the precise moment in time when the **projectile's height becomes zero.** At this point, we can determine the impact velocity. Rather than repeating this analysis again, we will continue and consider the behaviour of the projectile if it bounces off the surface. As the ground plane is a specific case, an arbitrarily oriented surface will be used to derive the **bounce vector**.

## 3.13 SIMPLE PENDULUMS

**A simple pendulum shows approximate simple harmonic motion if it consists of a heavy concentrated mass suspended by an inextensible cord and restricted to a swing of up to +/−14°.**

Let us simulate this behaviour dynamically by analysing the forces as shown in fig.3.8.

It can be seen from the fig.3.8 that the mass of the pendulum, m, is supported by a chord of length, L. **Please note that if the mass is displaced from its upright position by an angle θ radians, a restoring force m sinθ will attempt to re-establish equilibrium.** The acceleration, a, produced by this restoring force is given by the formula:

$$a = (m \sin\theta) / (m/g)$$

$$a = g \sin\theta$$

If the angle of the swing does not exceed +/-14°, sinθ is approx. equal to θ radians. So, we can write now:

$$a = g\theta$$

But for these small angles:

$$\theta = d / L$$

Hence, a = g (d/L).

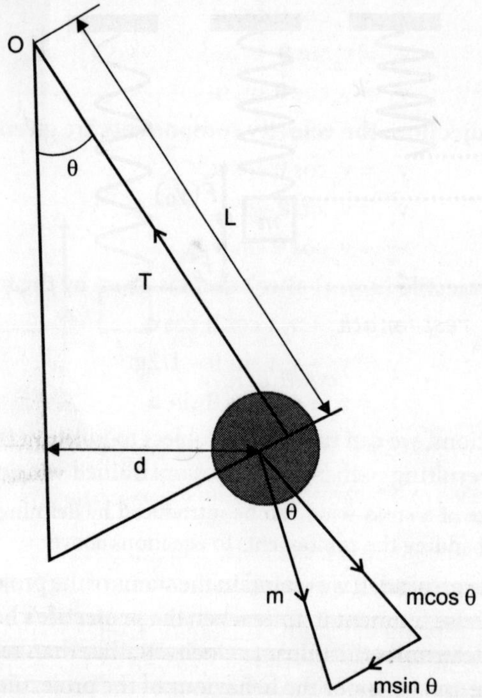


**Fig.3.8:** Shows a pendulum displaced by angle θ from vertical position

**Also note that at any point in time, t,** the pendulum has displacement d, velocity v and acceleration a. so, at time t + Δt the new displacement d' is given by the expression:

$$d' = d - v\Delta t$$

The acceleration is given by the formula:

$$a = g\,(d/L)$$

And the new velocity, v' is given by:

$$v' = v + a\,\Delta t$$

**Also understand that if the equations for the displacement, velocity and acceleration are iterated then the pendulum's motion is simulated.** And that the pendulum is animated by rotating the object description through and angle θ relative to the upright position, where θ = d / L.

## 3.14 SPRINGS

To simulate the motion of an object attached to a spring (or a piece of elastic), we have to analyse the dynamic forces acting upon the object.

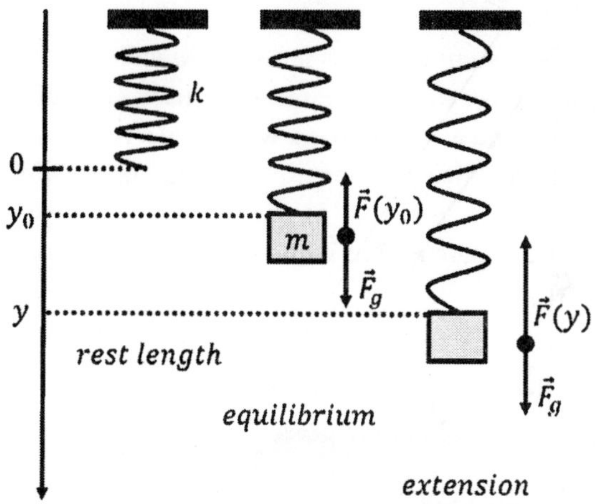


**Fig.3.9:** A mass m attached to a spring that oscillates with SHM

Let the length of the spring be = l, the force, F = ma, F(y) = T (tension), force due to mass, m = mg.

As shown in fig.3.9, a spring of length l is hanging from a rigid fixing. **Please note that if an object of mass, m, is attached to the free end of the spring, it will bounce up and down with simple harmonic motion (SHM).** Two laws are used to describe the active forces—**Newton's 2nd law of motion** and **the Hooke's law**. We have already studied Newton's laws. Now let us see what is Hooke's law.

**Hooke's law states that the tension, T, in a spring is given by the formula:**

$$T = \lambda\, e/l$$

Where 'λ' is the modulus of the spring, 'e' is the extension of the spring. While the object is moving up and down, its motion is controlled by:

$$ma = mg - T$$

where 'm' is the mass of the object, 'a' is the acceleration of the object and 'g' is the acceleration due to gravity.

If at any time, t, the mass has position y, velocity v and acceleration a, at a time t+Δt, its new position y' relative to the top of the spring is given by the formula:

$$y' = y + v\,\Delta t$$

The extension 'e' is given by:

$$e = y - l$$

Substituting this into this equation:-

$$ma = mg - \lambda\, e/l$$

The acceleration 'a' is equal to:-

$$a = g - \lambda\,(e/lm)$$

Thus, the new velocity v' of the mass is equal to-

$$v' = v + a\,\Delta t$$

We can put this value of v' in equation for y' to get a new value of y and continuously repeated, the trace of y is simple harmonic. Also the value of y can then be put into a matrix to subject an object to this motion. **One advantage of this method is that the model can be dynamically modified while it is running. Any of the above parameters can be interactively changed, resulting in an almost instantaneous change in the motion. Also note that as there is no loss in this model, the SHM continues indefinitely.** If the motion is required to decay to zero, a restitution term $k_d$ can be involved as follows:

$$v' = k_d v + a\,\Delta t \qquad 0 \le k_d \le 1$$

When $k_d = 1$, the motion continues unchecked,

But when $k_d < 1$, the motion decays away.

### *What are elastic structures?*

As studied earlier, free-form deformations (FFDs) are used by animators to form flexible objects. **But please remember that if elasticity has to be introduced into animation, the control points of the FFDs must be moved with suitable dynamics.** We can create and use the dynamic model of a spring to get this effect. This idea can also be used to model flexible objects like carpets, flags, curtains and table cloths. **Fabrics can be modelled as a matrix of mass points connected together in a mesh,** where each mass is connected to a neighbouring mass using springs. The forces acting on the springs can be related to the masses they act on using Newton's 2nd law of motion. Same ideas can be extended to 3D domain also.

## 3.15 FLIGHT DYNAMICS OF AN AIRCRAFT

We will develop a simple flight model that could be used to fly an aircraft within a virtual environment. **Numerical models** used to simulate the forces acting upon the frame of an aircraft are complex. On the other hand, **a mathematical model** may even include the dynamic behaviour of brakes, tyres and node-wheel steering system. The atmospheric model reflects the variation of air density and temperature with height. But please note that the mathematical techniques used to simulate such a complex system can only be an approximation of reality. The flying model makes many assumptions. To start, aircraft has no mass and it cannot rotate about any of its axes.

## SUMMARY

In this chapter, we have seen that the support needed to animate objects in a virtual environment varies from application to application. As an example, British Telecom are experimenting with behaviours associated with large multi-tier communication networks that may fail through random faults or sensitivity to network loads. Hence, a VR system is used to explore how software reacts to these faults by redirecting messages around failed nodes. To achieve these objectives, the methods like linear and non-linear interpolation are developed in this chapter. Also studied in this chapter is to simulate the motion of objects in a gravitational field, collisions with other objects and other simple dynamic systems.

## EXERCISE QUESTIONS

Q1. Distinguish between linear and non-linear interpolation.

Q2. Show how a point object moving with linear speed looks in an XZ-plane. What is its new speed if the object's decays with time?

Q3. What is shape and object in betweening? Show with an example of a contour.

Q4. What is parametric line in betweening?

Q5. What is free-form deformation?

Q6. State the following laws:

a. Newton's first law of motion.

b. Newton's second law of motion.

c. Newton's third law of motion.

d. Hooke's law.

Q7. If a particle P is dropped from a height $h_0$, after time t, it will have travelled by what distance downwards? What is its new height?

Q8. Define temporal aliasing and restitution.

Q9. Describe in details elastic collisions. Consider two cases:

a. Direct impact of two particles.

b. Oblique impact of two particles.

Q10. What are projectiles? How will you simulate the motion of a projectile?

Q11. Show how a simple pendulum shows SHM? Find its expression to show its displacement at any point of time, t.

Q12. Two laws are used to simulate a spring. Name those laws and explain them. Find out the expression to find a new velocity, v, of mass, m? How can you further get a very realistic motion?

Q13. Write short notes on:

a. Elastic structures.

b. Flight dynamics of an aircraft.

# 4 VR Hardware and Software

## 4.0 HUMAN FACTORS: INTRODUCTION

Can we think of those keyboard operators who work day and night on keyboard to do their job? These operators are now having the problems of repetitive strain injury (RSI). Similarly, computer screen have long time effects. Now, VR proposes a totally new interface for HCI (human-computer interface). An interface where the keyboard is replaced by interactive gloves and 3D mouse, head-mounted display. Please note that if VR has to be successful, then system designers cannot afford to ignore vital aspects of human physiology, details of which are available from any modern medical textbook. Also note that due to different reasons, designing and implementing an optimum VR system today may not be possible.

## 4.1 THE EYE, THE EAR, THE SOMATIC SENSES

**The eye:** An eye consists up of the cornea, the aqueous humour, the crystalline lens, the vitreous humour and the retina. Apart from the retina, they collectively provide an optimal element that reflects light from an external object. The refractive power of an optical element is measured in units of dioptres, where a 1 dioptre lens can focus a beam of parallel light at a distance of 1 metre. **The refractive power of the human eye is about 60 dioptres.** This means that its refractive power can be continuously varied by about 14 dioptres by tensioning or relaxing the ciliary muscle to its periphery. This is called as **accommodation or focusing**. It provides the mechanism for obtaining clear images from distant and close objects. As age increases, these lens become larger, thicker and less flexible. Sometimes the power of accommodation can be reduced to 2 dioptres at the age of 50 and zero at the age of 70. This is called as **presbyopia**.

When we focus on a moving object, an automated feedback mechanism tries to keep the image in focus by dynamically changing the refractive power of the crystalline lens. It has been found that the lens is permanently oscillating slightly upto 2Hz. This results in an image that moves in and out of focus continuously. Although we have extra skill to focus on objects at different distances, it is not exploited in HMDs. Our eyes has a clear focus on the items that are under field of view (FOV). Most HMDs, however, provide two images, permanently focussed between 2m and 3m. Now this is acceptable if the image content correspond to the spatial depth of field.

A similar type of problem also occurs in **panoramic displays used in flight simulators,** where the image is **collimated** such that it appears to be located many meters beyond the device. But these virtual worlds are local environments *like rooms*, so the conflict is not so acute. Also, **head and hand tracking in a VR system** provides the necessary **motion parallax cues** that one would expect between near and far objects.

**Iris and pupil:** The iris is a pigmented, opaque structure that is positioned in front of the crystalline lens. It contains a hole through which the light passes. **The hole is called as a pupil that changes in size under different conditions.** The size variation is between 1.5mm and 8mm (approx..) in diameter that gives an area ratio of 1:30. **Please note that an eye has a sensitivity to light in the order of 1000000 : 1, the pupil size has little effect on controlling the amount of light entering the eye.** The **main function of iris** is to increase depth of field for near vision by contracting, to confine incoming light to the central and optically best part of the lens by contracting and to maximize eye sensitivity by opening. **Also note that if the light level are low then the pupil size increases with a corresponding loss of depth of focus.**

**Retina:** It is the light-sensitive surface attached to the rear of the eye. It is several hundred microns thick and has 10 distinct layers. **Please understand that the light incident on the cornea passes through the aqueous humor, the lens, the vitreous humor and finally strikes the retina. Then it has to traverse 8 of the retina's 10 layers before it is absorbed by the rod and cone photoreceptors.** The rod photoreceptors are responsible for low-acuity, monochrome, night vision. While cones are for high acuity, colour, day vision. It takes 25ms to turn light into electrical signals which then have to be interpreted by the brain's visual cortex. This latency does not appear to cause any problems with everyday life, but there are occasions when this time delay prevents us from responding to certain events. **Highly sensitive central part of retina that accounts for the high-resolution portion of our field of view (FOV) is called as fovea.** The eye can be rotated by motor reflexes to capture on the fovea the light rays from a required point in space. **Fovea is only 0.1mm in diameter and contains the highest density of cones in the retina so only the centre part of our FOV is seen in high resolution.** The remaining image is projected on the surrounding retina which contains a mixture of rods and cones with a lower spatial resolution. **Also note that not only are the cones packed closer together at the fovea but they are finer than the cones distributed over the rest of the retina.** Also this contributes to the extra visual acuity of the fovea. **Fovea is quite small, so it accounts for only 1° of our field-of-vision (FOV).**

**Limitations:** As any other optical system, our eye also has some limitations. One of them is **visual acuity.** The eye's ability to distinguish between 2 external points of light is limited to 1.5-2mm (approx.) at a distance of 10m. *This measure of visual acuity is often specified in terms of the angle subtended to the eye by the light points.* For an average eye, this is about 40 seconds of arc and corresponds to a separation of 2 microns on the retina.

**Light and dark adaption of eye:** The luminous sensitivity of the eye is automatically adjusted by the slight changes in concentration of the photosensitive chemicals in the rods and cones. We observe this phenomenon when we move from bright sunlight into a dark room. **Although we appear to become accustomed to the new ambient light quickly, it can take as long as 40 mins before we can completely adapted. This is called as dark adaption.** On the other hand, **moving from a dark room back into bright sunlight (reverse) is called as light adaption.**

**Note:** The relative change in eye sensitivity through adaption is in the order of 25000:1.

Rods can take in excess of an hour to adapt fully to a high sensitivity whereas cones cease adapting after several minutes. So, when we do on an HMD, we quickly adjust to the new light level.

**Peripheral vision:** The retina is not just a passive photosensitive surface. Its structure like the connectivity of the rods and cones to the ganglion cells, provides us with a range of useful image processing functions. **For example**, some ganglion cells are excited by changes in light intensity that helps us to direct our attention to the moving objects in our visual field. This feature is available across retina. Although image resolution is poor at the periphery, anything that moves in our peripheral vision is very much noticeable. **Note that as the distribution of rods is much higher at the periphery,** their extra sensitivity, which is 300 times greater than that of cones, complements the detection of movement with extra visual sensitivity. **Also note that by the time signals are travelling along the one million axons down the optic nerve they encode the attributes of colour, motion, shape and retinal stimulus derived from the 100 million photoreceptors.** It is the job of visual cortex to place some sort of visual interpretation on this data as well as integrating it with similar data from the other eye.

**Persistence of Vision: The electrochemical nature of the retina** introduces a reaction time into the visual process such that when a very short pulse of light is observed, the rod receptor potential reaches a peak in 0.25secs (approx.). **Cones react about four times faster.** Their combined action introduces the phenomenon of **persistence of vision.** This persistence of vision is at the core of display technology including VR systems. Ability to integrate a rapid succession of discrete images into a visual continuum takes effect at the **Critical Fusion Frequency (CFF)** that can be as low as 20Hz. It depends on the image size and brightness.

**For instance,** TV images are refreshed at rate of 50Hz for UK, 60Hz fields for USA, cinema uses a frame rate of 24 frames per second.

### 4.1.1 The ear

Earlier scientists believed that the substance named **the lumeniferous ether** enabled light to be propagated over any distance. Later, Michelson and Morley said that **ether did not exist** rather light was an electromagnetic phenomenon. Today we assume that light can also be thought of as particles called as **photons** that have no mass and travel at about 300,000 km/sec. on the other hand, sound does not require any transmission media whether it be a gas, liquid or solid. Air is our medium of sound transmission. **Note that sound is a compression wave that propagates through a medium so its velocity is sensitive to the medium's density.**

In case of air at 0° C, sound travels at about 331 m/s while at 20° C its speed increases to 344 m/s (approx.). **Also note that it can be shown that the velocity of sound in gas varies inversely as the square root of its density. The velocity of sound varies dramatically in pure gases. For instance,** in $CO_2$ its velocity is 257 m/s and in hydrogen it is 1286 m/s. **Also note that a liquid transmits sound much faster than a gas and like a gas, the velocity is sensitive to density and temperature.** A typical value for the sea is 1453 m/s at 1° C, varies with altitude and salinity. The speed of sound in solid (like cast iron bar) is about 3500 m/s. Hence, it is not possible to talk about the speed of sound without specifying the nature of the medium accurately. Also we know that the range of frequencies related to human hearing is 20Hz-20KHz. This range reduces with age.

If we assume the velocity of sound = 344 m/s then,

At 20 Hz, the wavelength, $\lambda$ = 17.22m,

At 1KHz, the wavelength, $\lambda$ = 34.4 cms,

At 10KHz, the wavelength, $\lambda$ = 3,44cm.

This range is very significant in the designs of theatres, big halls etc. as unwanted reflections and standing waves can compromise on the sound quality. Our bodies interact with the pressure wavefronts. **Such interference has an important effect on the quality of sound in concert halls when the hall is empty or full. Also note that with very high frequencies, say $10^{12}$ Hz, sound waves can be used to scatter light. As the corresponding wavelength is very small** (like light) **it can be described as a particle called as a photon.**

Recently, **ambisonic techniques** have been considered to provide 3D sound stages for VR systems, using either loudspeakers or headphones.

**Somatic sensations:** These are associated with how we sense surface roughness, vibrations, and movements against the skin, position, pressure, pain and temperature. Sensations that arise from different parts of our bodies can be put under four categories:

a. **Deep sensations:** These provide us the information about the status of joints, bones, tendons, muscles and other tissues. **Receptors within these structures are activated when muscles are contracted and relaxed.**

b. **Visceral sensations:** The sensations that we experience from the organs like abdomen, chest, and intestines, liver are in form of pain.

c. **Proprioceptive sensations: They encode the physical state of the body like its** position, equilibrium and muscle sensations, standing on floors, on bed or leaning against a wall.

d. **Exteroceptive sensations:** These are the touch sensations that we feel over our body surface.

**Role in VR:** The sensations explained above, show an incredible range of receptors that are used to monitor the body's response to touch and position. **Please understand that we will never be able to simulate with total fidelity, similar physical responses to virtual objects.** The haptic interface to the virtual domain presents an incredible technological problem. If we ignore the idea of recreating a virtual equivalent of the real world haptics then we can develop suitable interfaces. Today, many gloves are available that feedback pressure cues to the user's fingertips. These gloves can be used to complement a variety of visual and audio cues like touch conditions. **For example, force feedback joysticks, force-reflecting exoskeleton hands and robotic arms with force feedback have also been used.**

## 4.1.2 VR Hardware

Introduction, Sensor hardware, Head-coupled displays, Acoustic hardware, Integrated VR systems

### *Introduction*

If we see the history of computers, we can see racks of hardware full of meters, valves, switches, lights and electrical cables. There used to be operators who used to take care of all these machines. Current day computers are not of that type. They may be as small as the size of your pocket or as large as your room. Today, processor speeds are advancing at both the ends of the processor spectrum. This also implies that any problem in VR systems due to processor's performance are temporary and hence will be quickly resolved.

**Sensor hardware:** A virtual environment requires various sensors and transducers to monitor user's actions and feedback signals that reflect the status of something within the environment. **For example,** an interactive glove must be tracked in 3 dimensions—finger positions may be monitored and the glove may even incorporate pressure pads that inflate when a virtual touch condition is detected. **Please note here that sensors are needed to monitor the glove's position as they provide the x, y and z coordinates relative to some physical frame of reference, which is complemented by the orientation angles such as yaw, pitch and roll. Also note that the pressure pads must give a tactile stimulus when activated.** That is why, these sensors must be reliable, accurate, portable, fast safe, robust and cheaper.

Let us now study some of the sensors that are being used in present day's VR systems.

a. **Tracking sensors:** the core requirement of any immersive VR system is the perfect tracking of the user's head with respect to its position and orientation. In literature, several methods have been researched for head-tracking like ultrasonics, low frequency a.c. electromagnetic fields, pulsed d.c., electromagnetic fields, mechanical coupling, optical, image processing and the earth's magnetic field. **For instance, the user's hand is also tracked using the identical sensor technology. Also note that in case of glove, the sensor is attached to the back of the glove while a 3D mouse has the sensor embedded within the device.** The task is to provide accurate spatial and angular reference information. A good tracking system must operate in real-time. It must provide 50 updates per second.

One major problem in real-time system is latency. **Latency** is defined as the time delay between when the sample is taken and when data is available for processing. **Please note that a system updating at 100Hz makes a sample every 10ms but if there is a 100ms system latency before the information becomes usable, the high update rate contributes in very small to real-time tracking.**

**Range: It is a measure of the active tracking distance for determining translation and orientation within the operational specification.** *Both range and linearity of a.c. electromagnetic systems are influenced by conductive metals like stainless steel and aluminium within tracker.* **Also note that this is due to the eddy currents that are induced by the alternating electromagnetic fields. This in turn set up new field patterns that distort the original field.** Ferrous metallic structures in the fabrication of floors, walls and ceilings are also a problem. On the other hand, an alternative approach is followed to employ d.c. magnetic fields which do not cause these continuous eddy currents. **In general, trackers work reliably up to a radius of 2-3m in a perfect environment but practically speaking, this range is reduced by local electromagnetic noise and metallic objects.**

> **Note:** Translational accuracy is in the order of 2.5mm and translational resolution is 0.8mm. Angular range covers +/-180° of yaw and roll and +/-90° of pitch with an accuracy of 0.5° (approx.).

Some trackers are like Logitech head tracker, spaceball 2003, BioMuse etc.

b. **Force feedback sensors:** If it is a simple touch response then that can be generated by a low-frequency electromagnetic transducer which is small and lightweight. But when large torques are involved, careful design is needed to minimize the weight of the actuators and not to interfere with the natural movements of the user. Hence, the system must be light. **For example,** Touch Master, Force feedback master, PowerStick etc.

c. **Glove-like Advanced Interface (GLAD-IN-ART project): A research project to** control manipulative and explorative procedures in artificial realities. **The objective of the project is the development of an advanced interface system capable of replicating forces to the human operator's hand.** It uses the ARTS glove that is capable of recording all the movements of the fingers and wrist, an **arm exoskeleton and a hand exoskeleton, for the replication of forces at the level of the human arm and hand respectively. Also note that the system also includes proprioceptive and force feedback interface software modules. The arm exoskeleton** is a force-replicating device attached to the user's arm. The hand force feedback system is a set mechanical exoskeleton structure covering the fingers. Each exoskeleton is capable of recording the movement of each joint of the finger and exerting forces in correspondence of the central part.

**Head-coupled displays:** HMDs or head-mounted displays are developed for military pilots so that navigational and tactical data can be integrated.

a. **Military HMDs:** A military pilot is not able to wear any headgear. So, any display system must have optimal impact on the weight of the pilot's helmet. **Note that the**

**pilot needs high resolution information to be displayed on an optically accurate and rugged display.** Today, cockpit-mounted displays along with pilot's helmet are preferred along with flexible, coherent fibre optic cables. These displays are of full colour with a horizontal resolution of at least 1000 lines. Then, the computer generated images are superimposed over the pilot's view of the real world. A typical specification provides a field of view (FOV) of 60° **horizontal**, by 55° **vertical** and with about 45° **binocular overlap. Also note that the specification also addresses features like minimum aberrations, peripheral vision, exit pupil, eye relief, optical transmission, scene collimation, chromatic correction, interocular adjustments and optical mapping functions.** But high performance HMDs are costly. They cannot be considered for non-military applications.

b. **General purpose HMDs:** A lightweight, monoscopic, stereoscopic HMD that can fit into the user's forehead without interfering with normal vision is **General Reality's CyberEye. Please note that when gazing upwards into the HMD, the user sees a collimated view of the displayed images. Also understand that for increased degrees of immersion, the display is lowered into the natural gaze direction of the user.**

For example, **n-vision DataVisor HMD** that employs a pair of miniature CRT displays fitted with liquid crystal shutter devices. The shutters are electronically switchable. They are light filters that allow only one primary colour to pass at any instant of time. **This process of synchronizing the shutter with the miniature CRT, RGB components of each full-colour frame are displayed in rapid succession to produce full coloured images inside the HMD. Also note that these shutters and CRTs are balanced at ear level. They project high contrast polarized images into HMD relay optics.**

Technical dimensions of Datavisor includes—

- Infinity -focussed exit pupil 12mm in dia with FOV = 50°.
- Interocular distance is adjustable between 58mm and 75mm.
- Video formats supported are—(1280 * 960) at 30Hz, (800 * 600) at 55Hz and (640 * 480) at 60 Hz.
- Even stereo headphones are included with the HMD system.

Other types of HMDs: MRG2, VIM, VISETTE 2, VR4 etc. also exist.

c. **Boom Devices:** BOOM is a monochrome device. It is a stereo that uses CRT technology only. There are 6 joints in the supporting counter-balanced arm. This enables us to move the BOOM within a sphere of approx.. 2m radius. Sensors are there in the arm joints that enable the position and orientation of the BOOM to be computed. **Also note that there are 2 buttons mounted on the ends of the handles that can be programmed to perform any task in any VR application.** In fact, Fakespace Ltd. Supplies three BOOM devices namely, BOOM, BOOM2C and BOOM3C.

d. **Virtual Screens:** Private Eye is a compact display device attached to the user's head. It can be viewed by one eye. Its technical specifications includes- adjustable viewing distance to 25.4 cm, display resolution is (720 * 280) pixels, that can be formatted as 25 lines with 80 characters per line. Its application is when computer-generated information like manuals, e-books or remote displays is required.

### *Acoustic Hardware*

Some companies like Crystal River Inc, provides special support in 3D sound with their devices like convolvotron, beachtron, acoustetron alphatron etc. **Concolvotron** is a digital audio signal processing sysem. It can be controlled from any RS-232 interface. **Beachtron** is configured for PCs. It creates 2 independent virtual sound sources at a rate of 22Hz. **Acoustetron** is an integrated 3D audio workstation. **Alphatron** plays back 2 sounds/ wavefiles and allows user to locate them anywhere in 3D space.

### *Integrated VR systems*

Traditional VR systems have no comparisons with present day's VR products. Today, anyone who wants to explore an application for VR can either buy **a fully-immersive development system or different combinations of VR toolkits working on PCs. Please note that are all said to be integrated as they provide a coherent system where a virtual world can be created, simulated, visualized and experienced through immersion.**

**For example,** PROVISION 100 SYSTEM by Division Ltd.

## 4.2 VR SOFTWARE

Introduction, Modelling virtual world, Physical simulation, VR toolkits, Introduction to VRML

### *Introduction*

For a computer to work, three things are very important:

**Hardware + Software + Graphical User Interface (GUI)**

VR systems use off-the-shelf technologies as their basic building blocks to configure a system. Some of these include: -

a. Workstations, PCs and graphics boards that provide a good range of real-time hardware platforms.

b. HMDs that explore LCD elements from the TV and camcorder markets.

c. VR software explores two decades of CAD and graphics development and also

d. Tracking hardware is based on well-established electromagnetic techniques.

**Please note that the weakest link in the system chain is the GUI that will evolve as VR is applied in different application domains.** The main challenge comes in implementing these in a real-time system. **Also note that minimizing latency and**

**maximizing update rates are the main factors considered by a system designer.** Both of the parameters will decide whether a VR system will serve a useful task or not. But the role of software is much more even in VR systems. Some of the functions of VR software systems are as follows: -

- Software determines the overall framework for coordinating events within the processing envelop of the hardware.
- Software is helping parallel processors to work in real time systems with more reliability.
- Software performs ultimate integration.

We must also analyse the VR software environment and study the modelling tools for building virtual worlds, simulating physical behaviours and how this environment is supported in real-time systems.

**Modelling virtual worlds:** VR system modelling do not follow any hard and fast rules. It varies from application to application. A simple environment model (like for a room) can be constructed from **polygon objects only.** Complex applications like an airport requires models to be viewed over distances ranging from a few meters to several Kms. Hence, in this scenario objects must be modelled at different levels of abstractions (detail) that are automatically selected depending on their range. **Note that this is the reason as we will never find an interactive modelling environment to satisfy for all of these different applications and modelling. Also note that it is possible to import models.**

**Importing models:** Model formats like AUTOCAD, 3D Studio, Wavefront, Alias, Mutigen, ProEngineer and Computer Vision can be easily imported into most of the VR systems saving lot of **re-building time. Also note that it is not possible to import models that exploit all of the modelling system's features. For example,** models have to be sometimes manipulated and rendered in real-time. Some models like polygon models pose lesser problems and hence they can be converted into other formats too.

### *Features/ characteristics of Modelling Toolkit*

Some of the features of a modelling toolkit are as follows:

a. **Libraries:** Modelling systems must provide the user with a set of several tools to select **shaped and objects from a system library** (just as MS WORD provides). **Please note that a shape library holds parametric definitions of arcs, circles, parabolas, ellipsis, squares, rectangles and polygons while an object library consists of cubes, cuboids, boxes, spheres, cylinders and cones. Also note that interactive commands are available to delete or insert vertices, reverse a vertex sequence in a facet or delete a facet.** Standard tools like **extruding and sweeping** are also used to construct more user required objects. **For example. Superscape's VRT system** has an *extensive library of virtual objects* that includes tools for building an office, a house and other outside environments.

b. **Object Sorting: The process of speeding up of the rendering process to make the modeller determine the rendering sequence of the objects is known as 'n'**

**object sorting.** So, at rendering time, the renderer is not engaged in any form of sorting process to determine visibility.

c. **Surface Attributes:** Objects may be coloured too. One colour can be assigned to an entire object or each facet could be given a different colour. **Note that even vertices can be coloured and interpolated when it is rendered.** Even a facet can be given 2 colours-one for each side. It could even be given a **degree of translucency.** Facets can be **decorated using texture maps scanned from photographs. Also note that this may require positioning, scaling and orientating.** Some rendering systems may be able to process a nest of texture maps called as **mip maps,** to adjust with bigger viewing ranges.

d. **Lighting: VE systems need to be illuminated also by a mixture of ambient light and individual light sources.** These could be directional, point or spot lights. **Please note that it may be that a light source is held by the user and used to explore the virtual system environment.** Also we can imagine a design application where a user needs to adjust interactively every parameter associated with lights. **Also note that lights may be used to illuminate the entire environment or specific objects.** To prevent the use of virtual light sources, the virtual world can be prelit by colouring objects with colour intensities that suggest a directional light source. **For example,** to simulate a ceiling light, all surfaces pointing towards the ceiling are made bright while others are made darker depending on their vertical orientation. **Please understand here that if a radiosity model is used to illuminate the environment, then illumination levels can be integrated into a database. There is no need of any extra lights.** But it means that the renderer must be able to cope with this hybrid mixture of geometry and illumination.

e. **Dynamic Vertices: The Superscape System** supports **dynamic points** that allows vertices to be animated between two extremes. At the modelling stage, the modeller identifies the points that remain static and those that will move. **Please note here that an inbetweening procedure finds out a sequence of inbetween shapes which when rendered in sequence, creates an animated effect.** This is useful for animating levers and instruments. It doesn't involve any geometric processing.

**Physical simulation:** The need is to simulate physical behaviours and for arbitrary geometric databases, designing good interfaces is a big challenge. **Many animation systems like Wavefront, Alias and Softimage** take this type of problem in their stride as it is their domain. On the other hand, a VR system should work in real-time and will not be able to support every type of physical behaviour used in stop-frame animation. This can become better, however, if the CPU performance improves. The VR system designers are including procedures (in software) that animate the virtual environment (VE) with credible simulated behaviours.

For instance-1, **Division's Ltd. dVISE environment** employs the concept of **actors** (servers) that are responsible for different system activities. Like there are actors to support collision detection, audio tracking and image generation. A **physics actor** is responsible for implementing an extensible group of physics-based functions. **Please note here that the physics actor uses Newton's second law of motion (i.e. F = ma) to**

**calculate the forces acting upon an object and how the object's behaviour changes, especially in collisions.**

**Note:** All computations use SI units only like length (meters), time (seconds), mass (kilograms), force (newtons), torque (newton meters) and angles (radians).

**Rigid bodies:** The physics actor implements a **Newtonian model involving rigid bodies. Deformable models** are to be included when processor performance can support their simulation in real-time.

**Mass: Homogeneous, symmetric objects** are represented as **a point mass,** *where the object's inertial mass is assumed to be concentrated at a point.* **Please note that if this model is used for non-homogeneous, irregular objects then the physical simulation is far from accurate.** And this dVISE physics actor supports **point and extended masses,** where the latter simulates distributed mass.

**Forces due to fields: A pseudo-gravitational field** is supported by the physics actor. It always creates **a vertical downwards force in a Cartesian from of reference. Also note that the force due to the earth's gravitational field should take into account the spherical nature of the earth, by accelerating the objects towards the earth's centre.** This is the reason as to why dVISE refers to it as a pseudo-gravitational field. Practically speaking, for most of the simulations the error is negligible. Objects can be subjected to forces derived from other fields, which are accumulated to derive a resultant force.

**Forces due to direct intervention:** External forces can also be applied to an object at any point. In its frame of reference, together with torques about an object's centre of mass. **Note that the forces that don't pass through the origin of a frame of reference cause a torque about that origin.**

**Forces due to collisions:** The physics actor implements **simple reflective collisions using a coefficient of restitution to simulate energy losses. The conservation of momentum calculations also ensure the correct distribution of energy.**

**Dead reckoning:** Dead reckoning information consists of an *object's linear position, velocity and acceleration, angular position, velocity and acceleration and a scale factor.*

**Collision Detection:** The Physics actor supports different types of collisions that involve interactions between polygons, edges and vertices. **All the interactions are subject to a user-defined tolerance levels. Please note that a collision of a polygon against a polygon implies that one or more coplanar polygons of one object intersect with a group of coplanar polygons from another object. When this occurs, the point of collision is taken as the centroid of the plane figure. A collision of an edge with a polygon implies that the edge lies in the plane of the polygon and the point of collision is taken as the centre of the edge. Also note that in a collision between a polygon and a vertex, the collision point is the location where the vertex lies within the polygon. A collision involving two edges creates two possible collision points:**

1. When the edges are coincident, the point of collision is taken as the centre of the line segment common to both edges.
2. Else, it is where the edges intersect.

**A collision with an edge and vertex creates a precise point of contact along the edge. Finally, two objects collide vertex against vertex.**

**Steady-state behaviour:** As the VR session starts, the physics actor is initialized and then exhibits a steady-state behaviour. It involves **steps** like **locking** the database, **extracting** all information in which actor is interested, updating the local copies, **unlocking** the database, **simulate** the physics for the next time step, simulating the collision detection code, **reporting** the change in collision to the rest of the database, **rewinding** the simulation to the time of the change in collision state, to **adjust** the physics model to account for the change in collision status, **recalculate** the remainder of the time step, repeat these steps till the entire time period is used up, **check** the dead reckoning positions of all the objects with changed local positions to see if they are still within an acceptable tolerance of the current positions. If not, **update the positions in the database** for those objects that have unacceptable dead reckoning positions.

**The physics library:** It provides a wide range of functions **to set an object's physical properties.** This includes inertial mass, centre of mass, inertial tensor, translate tensor, gravitational mass, gravitational field, restitution, mass and external forces.

For instance-2, **Jack is a general purpose interactive environment for manipulating articulated geometric figures.** One of its applications includes importing into Jack a geometric database from a CAD system and then to introduce an articulated human figure to explore the database for fit, reach, movement, strength and view. **Note that Jack includes a wide range of articulated figures with revolute and prismatic joints. Also note that a general purpose constraint engine uses iterative inverse kinematics to manipulate the points into different positions and a behavioural control regime manages the articulation and constraint envelopes.** As the software includes **goal-directed (AI) animation procedures,** commands like 'move arm', 'place hands' etc. can be issued interactively to produce human-like behaviours. One big advantage of Jack is its ability to explore in real-time the physical behaviours of articulated figures. The key features of Jack include articulated hands, ability to reach and grasp, collision detection, collision avoidance, scaling, walking behaviours, balance control, field of view, joint torque and sensors. Another benefit of Jack is that this system shows great potential concerns of the modelling of the figure's interior. This has been created with a level of accuracy that opens up all sorts of applications for medical training.

For instance-3, **Superscape's VRT** can be given a range of dynamic features that depicts the dynamics of objects in the real world. This includes gravity, fuel, climbing and falling, friction, restitution, driving velocity, external velocity, maximum velocity, angular velocity and whether an object can be pushed or not. **Time can be defined in terms of absolute time or based on the scene update rate. Also note that apart from these physical attributes, Superscape's VRT includes facilities for animations, bending, viewpoints and paths.** An object is animated by preparing a sequence of cels that show the object in different states, during modelling stage. **At run time,** these are activated at a specified rate, resulting in **smooth animation. Sequences** can include a linear pass, a cyclic repeat, a bounce, pauses and mixed mode combinations. **Bending**

**alters the position of vertices in an object, which in turn influence the position of facets. The bend is made about an existing point and is affected by selecting a collection of points in the object and specifying the bend angle.** The object can be bent about one of its vertices to create new shapes as follows:

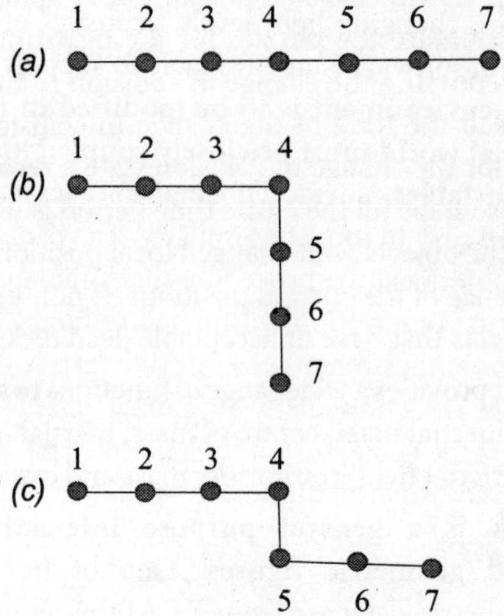


**Fig.4.1:**

Figure-a shows the original object, fig. b shows the bending pat of the object about vertex 4 and fig.4.1(c) shows the bending part of the object about vertex-5. These figures show, how the group of vertices are **rotated** and how a **second bend** is introduced.

**Viewpoints:** The virtual observer is treated as an object in the virtual environment and controls the viewpoint, it is a simple process to attach the viewpoint to any other object.

**Viewpoint paths:** A viewpoint can be moved through a virtual environment along a predefined path. The path is a closed loop, defined by a few set positions of key frames. **Please note here that the viewpoint moves between the key frames at a speed set by the number of frames between them.** At the end of the sequence, control returns to the beginning again. **Each key frame can define the position of the viewpoint, its rotation or both.** Position may move along a straight line between key frames or they may follow a smooth curve through them. **Also note that rotations may be set relative to the rotation of the object to which the viewpoint is attached or looking forward along a defined path.**

## 4.2.1 VR TOOLKITS

Computer graphics involves drawing of lines, circles, polygons etc. even animation involves another factor of **time.** Achieving synchronization is a serious problem. High level computer graphics library is also helpful. Integrated computer animation kits are also available that enable modelling and animation of objects is done in one environment only. **But please remember that a VR problem is more complex as it is 3D, animated, and interactive and runs in real-time. Also note that virtual reality (VR) is not just related with moving about a virtual environment to gain a different view of a model rather VR is about the interaction that can occur with all aspects of the virtual domain.** This may involve touching of the objects, moving objects to new positions, measuring angles, changing light levels, acoustics or shadow events. And such things cannot happen if software is not available to support them. **It may further be pointed out that if an environment is to be modified in real-time by the user commands, then the virtual world must be closely coupled to the system software. Vertex, edge and polygon tables, surface normal and texture maps must all be immediately accessible and easy to modify.** Similarly, if a virtual object is supposed to behave like its physical counterpart, the procedure that simulates this behaviour must be able to modify the virtual description without introducing **excessive latency.** To achieve these objectives, VR toolkits have become commercially available and provide us with a **coherent software environment to support a wide range of virtual reality applications. Also note that the core concept to these toolkits is the control language used to support aspects of interaction, animation and physical simulation.**

We are now in a position to explore such systems to understand the level of programming support for a VR system.

## 4.2.2 Division's dVISE IDE

dVISE is a **virtual world simulation and authoring tool.** It is based on a **simple model** in which the virtual world is composed of a number of objects, each with user-defined features like colour, movement restrictions, behaviours and audio characteristics. Actually, objects can be designed using a range of commercial CAD and modelling systems and then animated using dVISE.

**Some of its salient features include:**

1. dVISE provides two modes of authoring (i.e. authoring a world). It has a 3D interface that facilitates a user to modify virtual objects while immersed in a virtual world. Also it has a conventional 2D window interface where objects are represented iconically and controlled using a mouse and a keyboard.
2. dVISE is an ASCII text file that may be edited using a simple text editor.
3. Commands are available to control collision detection, illumination, acoustics, update rate and the size, orientation and orientation of objects. **For instance,** for an object to be picked up, COLLIDE command must be activated.
4. **The main objective of the design of dVS was to create a distributed model for VR simulation. Please note that this stemmed both from the need to simplify the process of defining complex VEs and also to optimize the performance.** A parallel model of the 3D user interface helps to control the complexity of the resulting system. The **distributed model** employs different servers or actors can mediate different elements. **Actors** have many functions like **sensing** of the real environment like tracking of the head, hand and body attributes, **control** of the

virtual environment like movement of objects and sounds and **display** of the virtual environment like visual and acoustic rendering of the virtual environment. This is shown in fig.4.2.

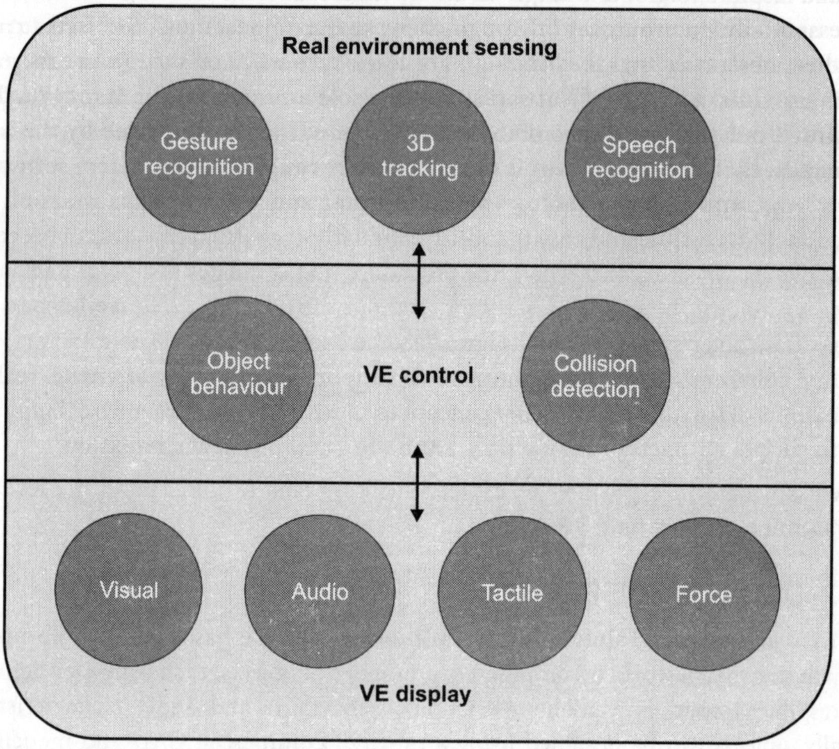


**Fig.4.2:** shows activities of visual, audio, tactile and force actors in a system and their sensitivity to events like collision detection and object behaviour.

From fig.4.2, it is clear that there exists a relationship between different actors. Also it shows how they are charged with controlling a specific part of the real and virtual environments. **Also note that the 'visual actor' provides a visual display, an "audio actor" provides an acoustic display, a "collision actor" provides collision detection services and a "tracker actor" provides 3D positions.**

5. **Shared data space:** If you are given a model in which different elements of the overall user interface are provided by **separate servers (actors),** it is necessary to create an efficient **infrastructure through which these servers can communicate.**

   **In traditional/conventional client-server architecture,** a set of messages are defined to encapsulate all possible server functions. Then the client addresses the server through either local or remote procedure class.

   On the other hand, this does not scale to a **multi-server system,** in which different parts of the interface are handled by different servers. **Also note that it does not adequately address the needs of multi-user systems in which multiple servers need to arbitrate state changes to maintain consistency.** So, dVS adopts a **more**

**abstract model. Please note that instead of each actor establishing direct connections to other actors, a *shared data space* is created into which actors may place shared objects called as *elements.*** Different actors monitor these elements and respond to **global changes** in the environment. **Also understand that actors essentially communicate through these shared objects and the structure of these objects defines the functionality of the system. Access to the environment is provided by a library of access routines called as virtual library (VL).** This provides low-level functions to create, delete, extract and update elements and instances. **The environment is the virtual library (VL) database.**

6. The **overall functionality of the system is defined by the elements that an environment contains.** Although the VL database is totally general and can maintain any element yet there are a set of **standard elements** that are supported by the **standard actors** which form a part of the **VS run-time release. These elements are essentially the components of a virtual environment (VE).** The standard elements include VCObject, VCLight, VCAudio, VCVisual etc.
7. The user application actually communicates with the run-time system through the VL database.
8. **VCToolkit: It is a collection of high-level C routines that create and manipulate virtual objects.** It allows the programmer to create visual objects and to arrange these within a **spatial hierarchy. Please note that these routines are provided to manipulate the visual, acoustic and physical properties of the objects.** There are functions to create, delete and modify all standard elements. Also there is a flexible **callback system** to process events which result from VL updates made by actors within the dVS run-time.
9. Another tool kit is Sense8's WorldToolKit (WTK) is a **library of C functions that can be used to write C programs for developing and interacting with virtual worlds.** The user writes a C program referencing the functions, which then becomes a WTK application. A typical program consists of an **initialization phase followed by a simulation loop. Initialization** consists of setting up the interactive and tracking sensors, identifying the objects, configuring the illumination, initializing the viewpoint etc. On the other hand, **the simulation loop** supports an interactive virtual reality session. **Please note here that the update rate of the display depends on how many times the simulation loop is evaluated per second.** WTK uses a collection of WTK objects where the class objects includes-

    a. 3D objects.
    b. Sensors.
    c. Lights.
    d. Animation sequences.
    e. Paths.
    f. Polygons
    g. Windows.

Any WTK program begins by a call to the function **WTuniverse_new** which performs an initialization job. **Also note that initially 3D objects are known by name** but in order for them to be manipulated by WTK functions, a pointer is required. Similar pointer functions are available for sensors, lights, animations etc.

10. We can also construct a number of **parallel universes.** Also we can move from one to anther using a WTK **portal. Portals are defined as doorways in space that connect the currently displayed universe with another universe. Please note that only one universe is ever displayed at a time.** And crossing a portal causes the connected universe associated with the portal to be displayed. Each portal is associated with a **polygon** at the time of creation. **Also note that when the current viewpoint is moved through the plane of the polygon concerned with a portal then the connected universe for that portal is automatically loaded.**
11. WTK includes a library of parametric objects like a block, cone, cylinder, sphere and hemisphere. Other objects can be imported using the Autodesk's DXF format, Wavefront's OBJ format etc.
12. In WTK, the front face of a polygon is the side of the polygon is the side of the polygon for which vertices are ordered **anticlockwise. Also it is the side from which the surface normal points.**
13. Models can be arranged in hierarchies to create articulated structures.
14. 3D objects may be static or dynamic. The objects that can move, may be tested for intersection with other objects in the universe using some function calls (**like WTuniverse_intersect). The object's bounding box (rather than its polygon) is tested against the polygons of the other 3D objects.** This function returns either 'true' or 'false' then another function can identify the polygons involved in the collision. Functions like-
    - WTuniverse_intesect: identifies only the possibility of an intersection.
    - WTpoly_intersectpoly: can determine whether the two polygons intersect or not.
15. The system's update rate **will be affected** if the functions were applied to every polygon.
16. In VR world, sensors has to take care of different positions, motion and orientation of objects. Software support is provided for a mouse, head tracker, joysticks etc.
17. WTK also includes a networking capability where applications can asynchronously communicate over Ethernet between many PCs and Unix workstations. **Also note here that the time it takes for a change in the distributed simulation to propagate through the entire simulation is a function of the number of nodes in the simulation, the current packet traffic, the frame rate of the slowest node in the net and the network's communication bandwidth and latency.**
18. Another integrated VR system comprises of several editors. **For example, Shape Editor and the World Editor. The Shape Editor provides interactive tools for building polygon objects.** On the other hand, **the World Editor arranges**

**the construction of virtual worlds from these objects.** Many other editors are available for customizing screen layouts, editing texture and sound, controlling menus and dialog boxes.

19. **Visualizer** can be used to display the world, move around it and interact with it. When used as a **desktop VR system, a Spaceball is used to control the picking of objects.**
20. **To control the objects within a VE, performing actions not undertaken by other functions, a Superscape Control Language (SCL) is used.** It is very much similar to C language. **Note that each object can have its own attached SCL program, which is executed once per frame.** Some simple methods are provided to allow SCL programs to continue execution over several frames.
21. Simple animations can be implemented in SCL by a series of individual textures. Such textures may be photographs of real scenes, drawings etc. like if the animation shows a cartoon moving on the screen then the sequence is prepared in form of **still frames.** Then SCL activates these textures and displays them over any period of time and even cycles them as a **closed loop.** This sequence is activated by initiating some event like pressing of a button or collision with an object.
22. SCL can be used to construct 3D objects also using some procedures. **For instance, a flag could be built from a mesh of triangles using SCL procedures and then modulated by a sinusoidal function. Also note that if a function includes a phase delay, the wave function could be made to move across the flag.** By storing several frames of the flag in different **cels, SCL can animate the flag at run-time by cycling models.**
23. **SCL programs that are associated with object are executed once per frame,** with the frame redraw occurring after all of them have finished executing. And to split the execution of a program over several frames, SCL has commands like **waitf and resume.**
24. **Waitf suspends execution until the next frame, storing the position in the program and data.** Hence, SCL procedures on other objects can then execute.
25. **Resume,** (on execution) **resumes execution** at the last **waitf,** restoring the stored information. It continues as if nothing has happened. **Also note that in the meantime, the VE has been displayed and SCL code on other objects has a chance to be executed.**

### 4.2.3 Introduction to VRML

VRML or Virtual Reality MarkUp Language is a Universal language for specifying multi-user, interactive simulations:

- 3D display
- interaction
- networking through Internet/WWW
- VRML Version v1.0 allows

- static 3D models (worlds)
- WWW links to other VRML models, HTML, and MIME.

- Browsers support
  - loading models
  - navigation
  - selecting links

### Example Browser for VRML

- WebSpace Navigator v1.0

### History of VRML

- Spring 1994, First WWW Conf., Geneva: Need expressed for common language for 3D scenes with WWW links ("HTML for VR"):
  - VRML (Virtual Reality *Markup* Language)
- Mailing list created. Moderator Mark Pesce announces intent to have draft spec ready for Fall 1994 WWW Conf.
- Decision not to extend HTML, but to adapt existing format.
- Choose SGI Open Inventor ASCII File Format:
  - Select subset
  - Extend for networking.
- Gavin Bell (SGI) adapts file format, Paul Strauss (SGI) develops parser to be released by SGI.

### Language used:

- Node: Container for objects.
- Scene graph: Ordered hierarchy of nodes
- Scene graph has state: Earlier nodes can affect later ones

### Syntax used:

- File header
- #VRML V1.0 ascii
  - Must start every file
- Comment
- #
  - All chars until next NL or CR are ignored (except if # is in string)
- Node definition (unnamed)
- objecttype { fields children }
  - **objecttype**: node type (e.g., cube, sphere, material, separator)

- **fields**: optional parameters (e.g., sphere radius)
- **children**: optional child nodes if node is a *group node*.

Exactly *one* node definition follows the header.

The designers of VRML usually discuss about virtual reality and virtual worlds. A graphical simulation of three-dimensional spaces and objects with restricted forms of interaction. The motivation of VRML was to connect such worlds over the internet and let several users simultaneously interact with the objects in these worlds. VRML should be **platform independent and extensible.** Also it should work with **low bandwidth connections.** *In summary, VRML is a file format to encode interactive, animated 3D objects and scenes as part of the WWW.* In the WWW data and services of the internet appear as a huge, cross-referenced document, which the user can browse through. Using VRML the data and services of the internet will appear as a gigantic room, a huge universe, which the user can move through- the cyberspace.

### *Please remember the following points regarding VRML*

1. VRML stands for **Virtual Reality Modelling Language and is pronounced 'vermil'.** It is a standard for delivering 3D picture on the net, just like HTML is a standard for web pages. VRML is a subset of the Open Inventor standard developed by SGI for their graphics workstation.
2. It has a way of describing geometry which creates objects and spaces in which you can move around, as well as light, texture and sound which can be approached and viewed from whatever angle. **The files are called 'worlds' and have '.wrl' extension and .wrz (compression).**
3. In order to see VRML worlds, we need to **install a VRML browser**. Internet Explorer comes with a default VRML browser, and almost all other internet browsers can install one.
4. Applications include:- Architecture, Training, Medicine, Engineering and Design, E-Commerce, Entertainment, Manufacturing.
5. VRML file contains Nodes that describe the scene. A **Node** is defined with several Fields › Each line give the field, the type of the field, the name and the default value. #VRML V2.0 utf8 Node WorldInfo { field title "Example 1" } DEF FBOX Shape { appearance Appearance { material Material { diffuseColor 0 0.5 0 } } geometry Box { } }
6. A ROUTE wires two events together. TouchTouch NodeNode SoundSound NodeNode Touch timeTouch time Start timeStart time DEF SENSOR TouchSensor { } DEF SOUND Sound { } ROUTE SENSOR.touchTime TOROUTE SENSOR.touchTime TO DEF SENSOR TouchSensor { } DEF SOUND Sound { } ROUTE SENSOR.touchTime TOROUTE SENSOR. touchTime TO RouteRoute
7. There are several types of sensors in VRML: › Time Sensors › Visibility sensors › Collision Sensors › Proximity Sensors › Touch Sensors › Sphere Sensors › Cylinder Sensors › Plane Sensors

8. Capacitive sensing on a table Sensors on a PDA Software developed for weather Forecasting (signaled from satellite)
9. In the beginning there was VRML 1.0. › It was the first attempt at an internet 3D language. , VRML 2.0 replaced VRML 1.0 and add many features (animation). Version 2.0 was submitted to ISO for standardization, the outcome was VRML97 which is almost identical to VRML 2.0.
10. 1.Shapes › Geometry › Appearance 2.Transformations 3.Lights 4.Groups
11. Each Shape has a geometry field that contains a geometry node and an appearance field that contains an Appearance node. Ex:- Shape { appearance <some appearance> geometry <some geometry> }
12. Basic types › Box › Sphere › Cylinder › Cone › Text Box › defined by its size field Box { size 2.0 2.0 2.0 } Sphere › defined by its radius field Sphere { radius 1.5 }
13. Cylinder › defined by its height and radius fields Cylinder { height 2.0 radius 1.0 } Cone › defined by its height and radius fields Cone { radius 1.3 height 1.8 } Text › defined by the string and the font geometry Text { string ["Hi!"] fontStyle FontStyle { family "TYPEWRITER" style "ITALIC" } }
14. Defines the look of some piece of geometry › Material combination of ambient colour, diffuse colour, emmisive colour, shinines, transparency, specular colour. › Texture defines a picture to paste to the object supports movies › TextureTransform defines how the picture is applied to the object
15. Material › Shiny Material ambientIntensity 0.3 diffuseColor 0.1 0.7 0.2 specularColor 0.6 0.8 0.6 shininess 0.6 › Dull Material ambientIntensity 0.1 diffuseColor 0.1 0.7 0.2 shininess 0.0 › Transparent Material diffuseColor 0.1 0.7 0.2 transparency 0.5 Colour components defined in RGB (red, green, blue triplets)
16. Define the positions of objects in 3D space:- XY are the plane of the screen , Z is towards the Viewer Transformation basically contains › rotation › scale › translation , Rotations follow "right-hand" screw rule X Y Z
17. Provide illumination in the scene › DirectionalLight › PointLight › SpotLight 1.DirectionalLight › light rays travelling in parallel lines e.g. sunlight DirectionalLight { direction -1 -1 -1 intensity 0.8 }
18. PointLight › radiate in all directions , SpotLight › radiate only in certain directions, and with volumes of different intensity
19. Real animation must include some sort of programming. VRML accepts two kinds of programs: › JAVA. › JavaScript. The script node can receive and send events very easily.
20.
    i. Platform Independence–the viewer is still platform dependent, but the simulation will run on all types of platforms, since it is an ASCII language.

ii. Extensibility–the first draft of the language runs in concurrence with HTML, not over it.

iii. Low bandwidth requirements–it runs as fast as your machine will allow it.

iv. Open Standard–refined be the collective wisdom of expert user community

v. Widely supported–static file VRML file import and export in most 3D packages and visualization tools.

vi. ASCII encoding -> many possible developer interfaces › GUI Editors › Text Editors › Translation programs (Java or Perl) › combinations of the above

vii. Motivating–3D graphics, audio, media files, immediate feedback, visual debugging.

viii. Gradual exposure to programming–modeling -> animation -> interaction -> scripting -> programming

21. Object-Oriented concepts–objects (nodes), fields, input/output interfaces (routes), abstraction and inheritence etc. Other applied concepts–data structures (trees, stacks, etc), 3D math, linear algebra, etc.

## SUMMARY

This chapter deals with every aspect of a VR system application, ranging from the definition of a single polygon, to the storage of a **quanternion** from a tracking sensor. We have seen in this chapter that even a VR system requires a clear system specification before it is constructed and implemented. Again even the design of a VR system must be failure-free as in software engineering. This is so because VR systems are quite complex so anything can go awry. For instance, objects may not move, collision detection may be ignored, more latencies may be observed. Such errors need to be corrected and located as done with any program. Many VR tool kits have also been explained in this chapter that simplify these tasks.

## EXERCISE QUESTIONS

Q1. Explain how VR models are created? Throw light on some of the modelling toolkit features.

Q2. Explain how Superscape's VRT helps in animations, bending, viewpoints and paths identifications?

Q3. Write short notes on VR TOOLKITS.

Q4. Explain Division's dVISE environment.

Q5. What is a shared data space? What is its need?

Q6. With the help of a neat diagram show how visual, audio, tactile and force actors are responsible for specific activities in the system?

Q7. What do you mean by parallel universes?

Q8. What are shape editors and world editors? Distinguish between them.

[**Hint: Shape Editor**–uses vertices and facets to create 3D objects that can thus be coloured, replicated, transformed and animated. A bounding cube is always associated with an object. It is used to sort object in a VE.

**World Editor**–uses object descriptions from the Shape Editor to build virtual worlds arranged in form of a tree of objects. An object may contain other objects as its siblings (children). Their positions are not actual rather they are relative to their parent's origin. This implies that moving the parent will move all the children with it. This editor is also used to assign the physical attributes like velocity, fuel, gravity, climbing and restitution. It also arranges the animation cels that are so obtained from the shape editor into animation sequences that will occur when the scene is rendered. VRT detects collisions using bounding cubes or collision boxes. Bending, viewpoints, viewpoint paths and moveable objects are also controlled by the World Editor. Automatic replacement of objects as their distances from the observer increases.]

Q9. What are SCL programs? Explain the following SCL commands:

a. Waif.

b. Resume.

Q10. Write short notes on:

a. Imported models.

b. Object sorting.

c. Lighting.

d. Jack.

e. The physics library.

f. Viewpoints and Viewpoint paths.

g. Actor concept in VR.

h. VCToolkit.

i. Universe of objects.

j. WTK networking.

k. Shape editors.

l. World editors.

m. SCL.

n. Procedural models.

o. Frame waiting and its commands.

p. VRML.

# 5 VR Applications

## 5.0 INTRODUCTION

Virtual environment can be subjected to –Finite Element Analysis (FEA techniques) or to other mathematical procedures that can be used to predict its behaviour under different physical conditions. Earlier we have studied these methods in computer graphics but now they are being used in VR environment also where parameters can be adjusted in real-time environment. Even users are the part of this environment now. **Note that all applications don't demand that the user be immersed within a virtual environment. Total immersion will have some benefits in some areas while partial immersion in others.** Once a virtual object exists, it can be subjected to many forms of procedures. The dimensions can be adjusted to satisfy optimum layouts. The user can explore the environment. **Also note that the ramifications (depth) of this approach to design many options for stage designers, interior designers, lightning designers, animators and car designers.** Models play a vital role in different industries. But there are several reasons that can be explored to find out as to why virtual models should be used for visualizations, simulations and new manufacturing techniques.

The applications of VR have been put under four categories:

- Engineering.
- Entertainment.
- Science.
- Training.

a. **Engineering:** Virtual systems are not new to us. They range from 2D CAD systems to 3D CAD systems used to design PCBs and ASICs in industries. This is possible as computers are very flexible. **Geometric information** about these objects can be used and the process of **stereo-lithography** may be used to create a real physical representation. Herein, the virtual systems have been a framework for storing descriptions of 2D and 3D objects. The workstation screen is a simpler projection space to view them. **Please note that VR provides another role for these computers wherein the virtual domain becomes a 3D space that can be explored by the user.** All those engineering components that were considered as lifeless drawings of static projections only, can now be visualized as animated objects. This is great!!! **Also note that VR has opened new doors to a virtual**

**engineering domain where objects can be manufactured, inspected, assembled, tested and subjected to all types of simulations (monitoring).** The full potential of VR is still to be explored. **For example,** removing an engine from an airplane is a complicated task. But it can be simulated in a VR environment easily. A VE engineer will open the door bay, positions it and jacks the trailer to a proper height. With the help of **virtual tools,** the engineer removes the bolts. Some benefits of VR SYSTEMS INCLUDES- LESSER MOCK-UPS AND PROTOTYPES AND EARLIER DESIGN TESTING AND OPTIMAL COSTS. A sequence of polygon optimization programs are written to improve the speed of **virtual models.** Many more functions were then written to colour objects or their parts. The feasibility study terminated with a successful demonstration of the VR system. Still the research is going on. As another example, flying through a virtual submarine was unrealistic method of moving about the environment. There was absence of 3D tracking systems. The use of VR tools is being done now.

**Architectural design:** Earlier 2D CAD systems were very popular. CAD systems play a vital role in many major architectural practices and provide us with plans, sections, elevations, interior as well as exterior views. The use of integrated databases, data exchange and scheduling tools are a must now in an interactive multi-user environment. **Please note that it is the combination of form, function and space [FFS] that dictates the success of any architectural project.** Today most of the CAD systems provide complex diagrams and visualization of any data related to the project in hand.

On the other hand, **VR systems** work with interactive workstations. So, VR is a natural technological progress that brings us closer to virtual designs. **Also note that immersive displays will provide much better method of assessing the success of their designs.** They will be able to walk through their buildings in real-time.

**Illuminations:** Lighting of building's internal is also very important in VR designs. **Radiosity** is a tool of architects. It is now familiar **global illumination model** in graphics. Such VR systems already exist that are capable of exploring complex interiors that incorporate precomputed **radiosity levels.** Modern algorithms are bringing radiosity into the real time domain. **For instance, The Real Light Software System** is a radiosity-based renderer that is easily integrated into a VR system. Hence, it will be possible to explore a virtual environment and adjust internal light fittings for position and intensity levels. **Therefore, there is no reason as to why** a virtual light meter should not be used to measure the new illumination levels.

**Acoustics:** It is very important to consider the acoustic properties of buildings. Architects use several mathematical tools for determining reverberation times, acoustic effects of reflections, decay profiles and how electronic audio systems can be used to balance the frequency characteristics of a large auditorium.

**Human factors modelling:** The main challenge today is to develop interactive environments where a fully jointed human figure can be used to evaluate virtual

3D worlds. One system known today is **JACK.** It was developed by the Centre for Computer Graphics Research at University of Pennsylvania. Jack is a virtual 3D human model that incorporate 68 joints. Joints can be positioned by **translations and rotations** within some predefined constraints. Limbs possess attributes like **centre of mass and moment of inertia. Please note that with these qualities, the model can be subjected to dynamic simulations to show its behaviour under changes in velocity.** Jack is animated using inverse kinematics. It has various motor reflexes like grabbing, reaching and also maintaining balance, directions and re-orientation behaviours. This it does by adjusting its centre of gravity. When grabbing an object, collision detection is used to ensure that Jack's hand does not penetrate the object being grasped. The entire body should adjust to accommodate the wheel's new orientation when the wheel is turned. When Jack is placed inside a virtual environment, it is possible to explore human factors like field of view (FOV), load and collision. Collision avoidance is a property where Jack moves automatically to avoid being hit by a moving object. Jack can be set to walk and also to avoid obstacles like walls or any solid object. With the help of **force fields** even a hidden object behind a wall can be searched with visual sight. **Also note that the hidden object emits an attractive field while obstructing objects emit a repulsing field.** Jack has also been used to train military. When projected onto large video screen, Jack is animated in real-time to show patterns related with weapon handling. Thus, we can say that virtual humans will play a vital role in VR application systems.

b. **Entertainment:** In addition to single user, immersive VR systems, even motion theatres are a good candidate for VR. VR technology will continue to stimulate new game formats while single and networked users will compete with one another and complex motion theatres will provide another experience. Computer animation and VR are different. In computer animation, sequences are generated on frame-by-frame basis. On the other hand, VR is a real-time environment where animated movement is a natural feature of experience. Earlier, when developing a 3D cartoon character with human-like behaviour like walking, hands gestures etc. non-VR systems used to solve these problems using **inverse kinematics** for walking and running. On the other hand, VR approaches couples the animator directly to the real-time virtual domain, instead of writing software procedures. Many such systems have been developed like CyberTron, wherein a player wears an HMD and then plays by flying if they find an obstacles, tunnels or mazes. This system can be networked to support multi-player games.

c. **Science:** Another well-known domain of computer graphics is **scientific visualization** wherein different types of data are interpreted using images. It addresses the complex, multi-dimensional data sets being created by simulations. **A true real-time VR system simply makes the user a natural part of the computational process and not a passive observer. It means that the user is one who interactively modifies parameters and observes the results.** Several potential candidates have been identified where VR science has been applied like computational neuroscience, visualization of complex spike in cerebellar Purkinje cell and many more. The main focus of these projects has been to explore the use of low-cost VR systems as a visualization tool. Molecular modelling, phobia handling, ultrasound echography and telepresence (remotely controlled vehicle) used by NAS are all its applications today.

**Molecular Modelling:** The traditional approach to molecular modelling includes the use of workstation and an interactive graphics system. **Please note that the aim of VR is to immerse the user so that he can directly interact with the graphical representation of the molecule.** Physicists, chemists are all using this technique today to study atomic particles and valency bonding in these molecules. The objective is to design systems using existing stereo imaging facilities that can be developed to use VR systems. Lab. Staff will now be able to use better GUIs of VR systems to study the structure of macromolecules and their functions. Three molecular modelling systems may be developed:

- A system for building models of macromolecules that satisfy low resolution experiments.
- A protein visualization system for accurate analysis of protein structure.
- A system for exploring the similarities between molecules.

Also note that this will provide a better exploration into the space configurations that effect the ability to engage new atoms into a molecular structure.

d. **Training:** Training can be done based on many things like using a computer, driving a car etc. but training with real thing is what is desired. Training simulators are used for planes, submarines, power plants, tanks, helicopters, ships, trains, surgery and air traffic control. **Please note that such simulators use a replica of the real operational environment and real-time computers to model its dynamics. Also note that training through simulation provides more benefits as compared to other methods.** Many simulators use computer-generated images during the training process. Immersive VR systems provide new training paradigm for existing and new training applications. **For example,** the Fire Service College, UK, is using Superscape's desktop VR system as a training tool. In conjunction with the VR system, the college is using the VIRTUAL EGRESS ANALYSIS AND SIMULATION (VEGAS) software system developed by Colt VR Ltd. VEGAS provides a means of modelling human behavioural response under different emergency conditions. This software can handle many parameters like the physical size of the occupants, pushing and resiliency during escape, toxic fumes exposure limits etc. in flight simulations, again virtual domain has many benefits as follows:

1. **Accuracy:** Airport models can now be built with greater accuracy as they are based on plans and CAD data repository. They can be easily updated also.
2. **Interaction:** collisions with other objects, pilot's need to know when the simulated craft touches the runaway and interaction related to runway landing lights etc also need better interactions.

3. **Animations:** VE can be animated to include other planes, ground vehicles etc. **Animated sequences** are used to show rotating radar dishes, lowering of sea gates.
4. **Weather:** It was earlier impossible with physical scale models to simulate weather effects. But now in this virtual environment, it is possible to recreate rain, snow, lightning, cloud, foggy conditions etc. with effective realism.
5. **Time:** By simply changing a few parameters in the database it is possible to alter lightning conditions, say, from bright sunlight to dusk. Texture maps may be used to show seasonal changes.

Presently, VR technology creates the possibility of developing training simulators where surgeons can develop surgical skills without harming animals or human beings. Real world images are overlaid with 3D datasets that are derived by real-time scanners. Fields of medicine like colonoscopy, laparoscopic simulator are using VR technology today. Image fidelity, accurate virtual anatomical models, realistic physical models and force feedback need to work coherently in a real-time system.

Training means transfer of skills. Computer based training is very common now a days. Total control of training means repeatability, reliability, accuracy and confidence in information so obtained. **It is believed that the virtual domain will eventually be able to offer all of the realism associated with the real domain. Also note that the virtual domain is repeatable, interactive, 3D, accurate, reconfigurable and networkable. For instance,** application of VR in infantry training, military simulators and stinger missile training simulator based trainings are being done.

As an another application of VR, recently the Research and Development division of Electricitie de France (EDF) has installed a VR system to investigate a range of applications for designing and testing of the operating procedures of a nuclear power plant. EDF has built a VE to model the interior of the nuclear reactor building that includes all of the major reactor components, piping and ductwork, multi-level scaffolding, control points etc. also a radiation plan complements the reactor model to simulate the **radiation dosage received per second** in any particular part of the building. So, using a complex model, the maintenance engineer enters the virtual reactor building, with the help of a 3D mouse, the engineer moves around the virtual building. During this movement in the virtual world, the system regularly computes the radiation level that the engineer would have experienced in real time actual operation. **Please note here that with the help of this virtual radiation dosage information, operators can plan a safer and more efficient procedures.**

Another company, Volvo Ltd. UK used VR for an accident simulation for one of their cars. In short, in a realistic 1.5 secs, the entire accident is simulated accurately, from the realistic noises of the crash to the displacement of the driver's seat.

## 5.1 INTRODUCTION TO UNITY 3D

Unity is a cross-platform game engine used for making games and other applications. Unity was created by Unity technologies Inc. and released at Apple Inc. worldwide developers conference as Mac-OS exclusive software. Unity3D has extended to many platforms, including Windows, Android and other console gaming platforms like Playstation, Xbox. Unity is not only used in the gaming industry but also in film making, automotive and construction. Unity3D is easy to understand for beginners as compared to the Unreal engine.

Where Unreal engine is right for PC games, Unity3D is better for Mobile games. If we compare the graphics of both the gaming engines, they stand at the same place as the developer, which is a better option for them.

Unity3D is written in C++, which uses C# (C-sharp) as a scripting language. We can use Unity for both 3D and 2D development. Unity is free to use; Unity has a paid pro and enterprise version for an intermediate developer with additional features. Now there are also many more Unity products that can be used for core development.

Fall guys and Pokemon Go are some of the popular games made on Unity3D. Unity is perfect to start with VR and AR development.

For VR development, Unity recommends using XR management, as explained below.

## 5.2 GETTING STARTED WITH VR USING UNITY3D

For VR development, Unity provides XR management, which is a package provided for simple XR-plugins. XR Management will help us to manage supported platforms like Oculus, Windows Mixed reality. For third-party platforms like Google VR and openVR, SDKs are available, which have to be downloaded and added manually.

Before starting VR development, we need to configure VR development settings in Unity3D, as mentioned below.

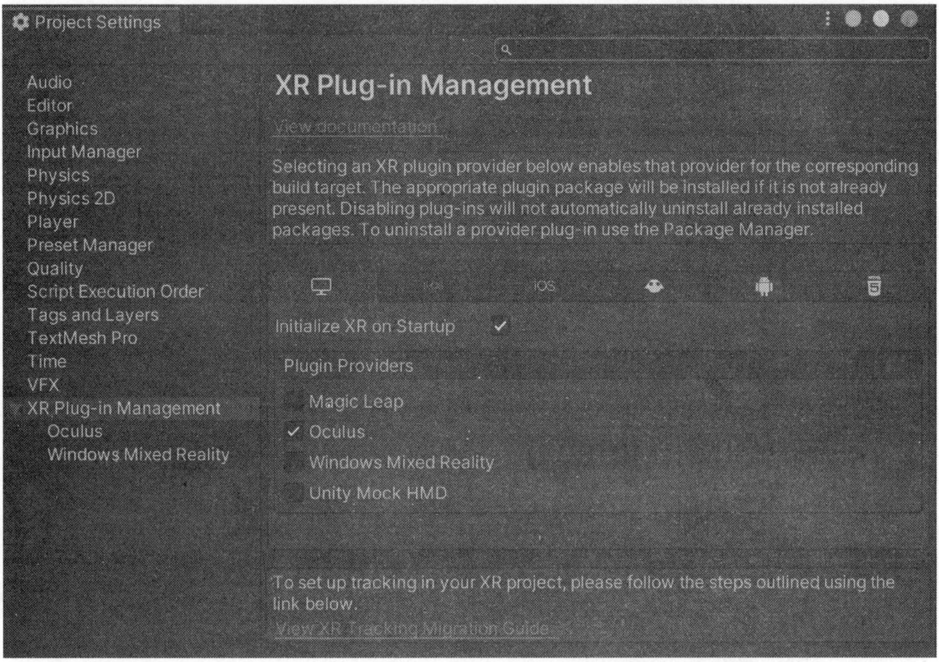


- Open Project settings that are present in the edit option.
- You will see the XR Plug-in Management option, and you can select the platform you want.
- If you don't have XR Management, you can download it from the package manager.

  After this, you will see your packages installed by XR management, as shown in the figure. You can use the XR Rig to set up tracking. In the hierarchy view, make a game object, then add the XR rig component to it.

**Note: Implicit camera tracking, used in Unity versions before 2019.3, has been removed in the new XR plug-in framework.**

- Create a New scene and tag the only camera in the scene to the main camera. Be sure there is only one camera in the scene.
- Create a GameObject and add XR rig Component to it, allowing the scene to support the XR framework correctly.

**Note: Main camera should be the root of the hierarchy.**

If you face any problem, you can search for the official documentation of Unity. If there is no error, you can develop a VR game using an input system for VR and Raycasting. You can also switch platforms like Android, IOS.

**Note: You need the necessary gear to play VR games or test them.**

As VR gears are costly for a new developer, it is good to go with Android and IOS VR development for a start.

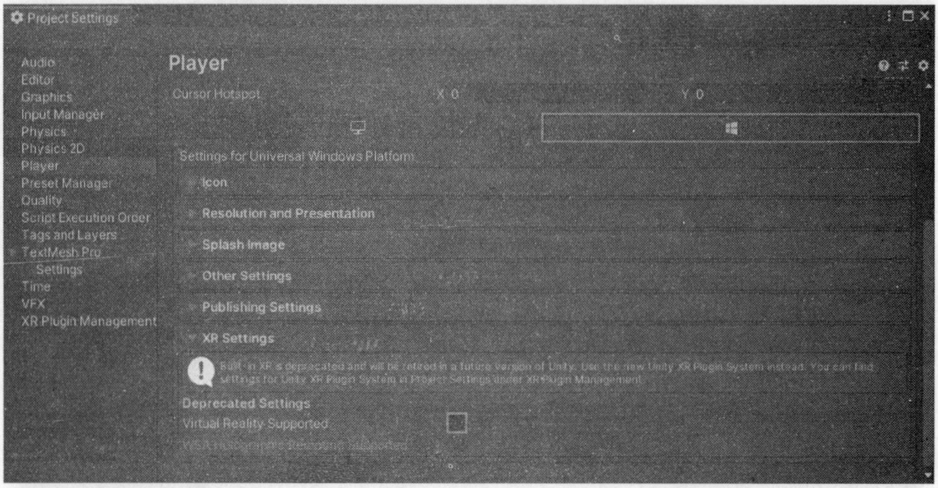


For a simple VR game, you can use the old version like unity 2019. In this, you can select virtual reality support after selecting it. You can choose a platform, as shown in the above fig. After that, your Android or IOS will work as a simple VR camera shown in the figure below.

**Note:** This option is not available in Unity 2020+ versions.

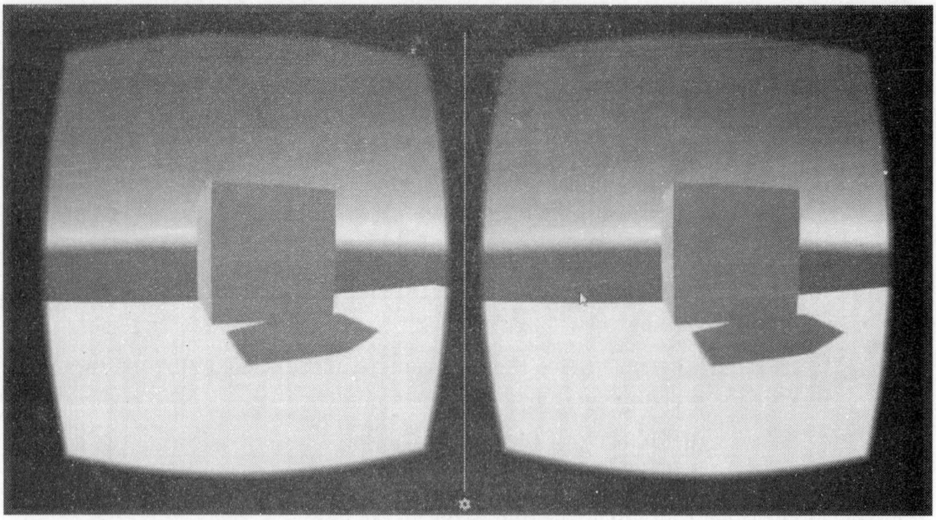

To make things interactable, you can use raycasting—raycast cast a ray, which will return true if the ray collides with a game object. You can use raycasting for detecting objects in the scene by the point the camera points to the objects.

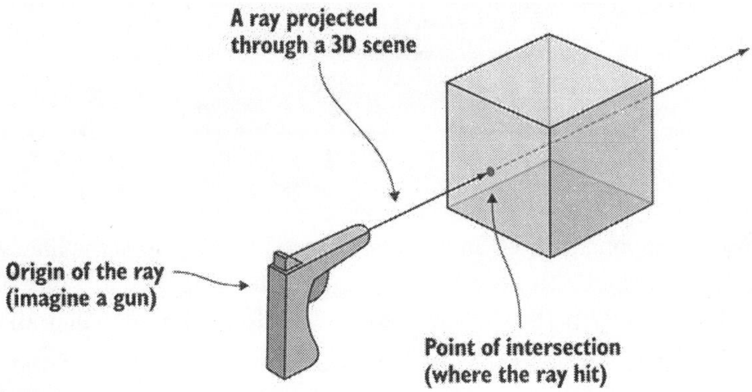


With the help of a ray cast, you can make a VR scene intractable.

**Note:** You can use budget-friendly gear like VR Box for android to test your VR game, which is suitable for beginners. For PC, XR management use is preferred.

## 5.3 GETTING STARTED WITH AR USING UNITY3D

For AR development, you can use Unity ARFoundation. ARFoundation is a package made by Unity technologies for the support of AR development. This package combines the packages and features of Google ARCore for Android and Apple ARKit for IOS.

- First, you have to download ARFoundation and ARCore and ARKit packages from the package manager.
- After install, you can use ARFoundation components like ARsession and other features for easy AR development.

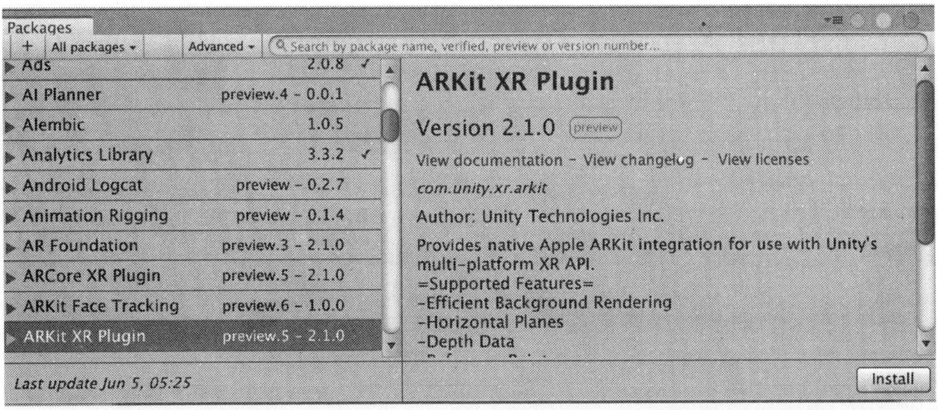


Or you can also use XR management for AR development. By adding ARCore and ARKit plug-ins. ArFoundation automatically selects the package according to the platform.

After adding these packages, set up the scene for AR by adding ARsession and ARsession origin components in the scene.

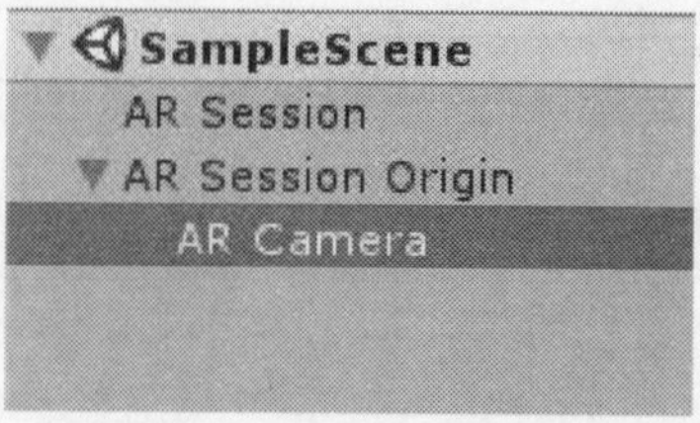


ARsesson components hold an ARsession script that controls the life cycle of the AR scene. It's also responsible for downloading and checking the necessary libraries in your phone like AR services by Google needed in Android phones to play an AR game.

ARsession Origin is responsible for tracking the transform of the trackable features, and also it allows you to modify the virtual objects in your scene like their scalability, transform.

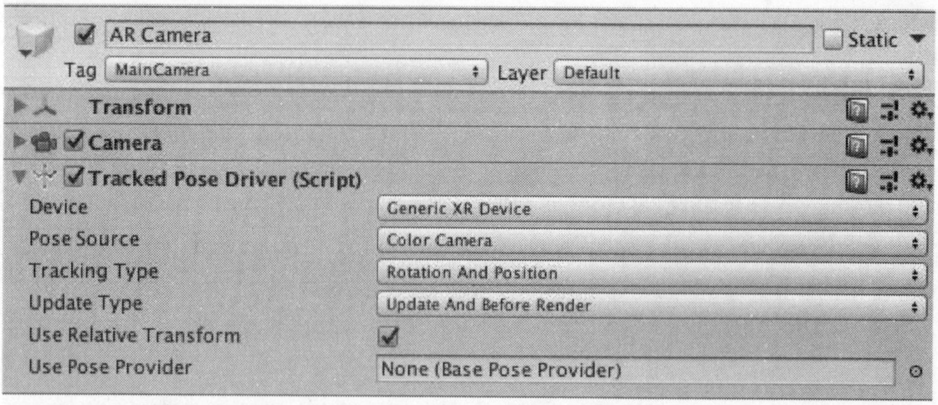


AR Camera used as the mobile camera or device in this you can see Tracked Post Driver, which used to track the local position and orientation of the parent components, which is the camera in this case.

There are other components like ARRaycast Manager, Meshing Manager and AR Camera manager available in the ARFoundation package. In ARFoundation there is a script called AR Plane Manager, which is used to detect the horizontal and vertical planes.

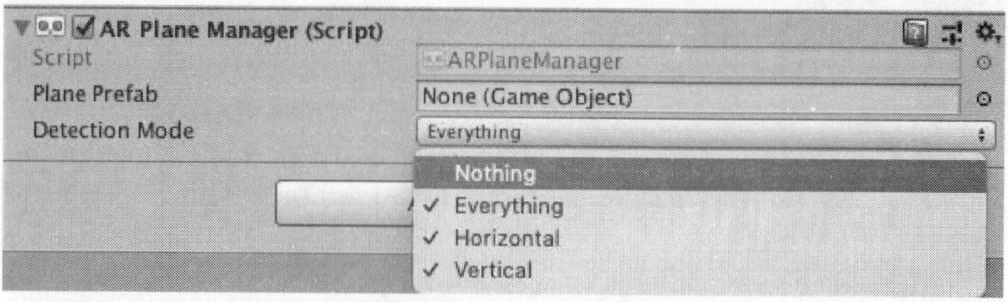


With the help of the plane manager script, we can place objects on the detected planes as it tracks all the detected planes. Using these components, we can easily create a simple scene.

With the combination of these components, we can create an interactive AR game. For a more realistic experience and an enhanced experience of Augment reality, there is a Depth estimation API provided by Google ARCore and ARKit, which provides data of the depth of the scene in the form of depth maps. The Depth API also allows colliding with real-world objects. There is also light estimation, which affects the appearance of the virtual game objects due to light in the real world, which adds more reality to the scene.

## 5.4 THE UNITY INTERFACE

In this section, we talked about the user interface or workspace of unity. Below is a pictorial representation of the **Unity 2019 interface.** The Unity interface is quite simple for beginners. We can use Unity3D to create different applications on different platforms. We can use it for animations, environment building.

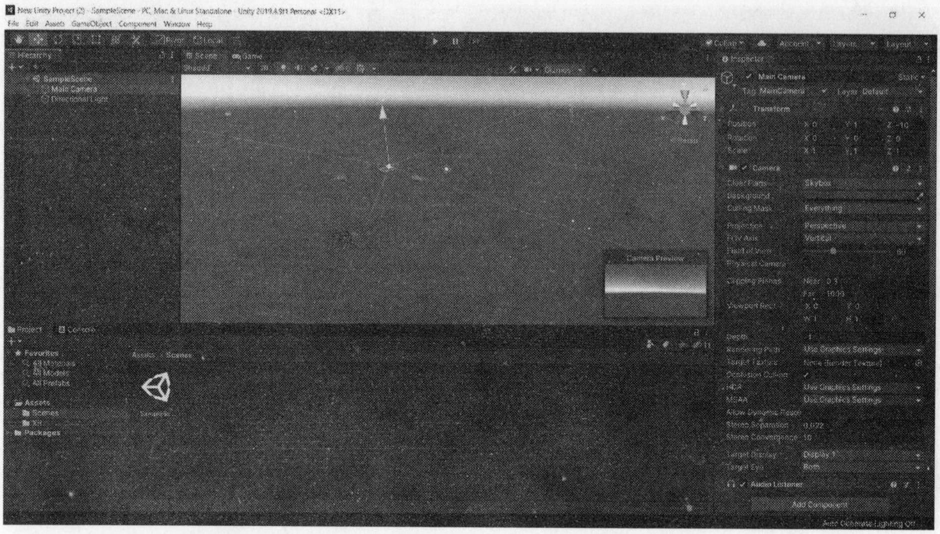


As we can see above, there is the **Scene** panel that shows all the components present in your game. You can move them, rotate, and scale according to your need. The **Game** panel, however, indicates what the user will see when your game will run at the left, **Hierarchy** panel where all the components of the games are listed, like the main camera, directional light in the above picture. The **Inspector** panel on the right will show all the properties of a game object.

At the bottom, you can see the project panel that is your file directory. You can see all your files, prefabs, scripts saved on your pc. The console panel is where you can see all the warnings, errors, and logs.

In the scene, the **Main camera** is used as the user's eyes, or we can say what the user will see on the screen. **Directional light** here acts as a sun. It illuminates the whole scene.

## 5.5 SCRIPTING IN UNITY

Unity supports three scripting languages **C#**, **Unityscript** (also known as **JavaScript**), and **Boo**. Visual Studio is the default scripting IDE that would install during the installation of Unity.

You can also switch the IDE by going to the edit option on the toolbar and then preferences. You will find the external tools option where you can select your IDE, and then unity will automatically open your IDE when you create or modify any script, as shown in the picture below.

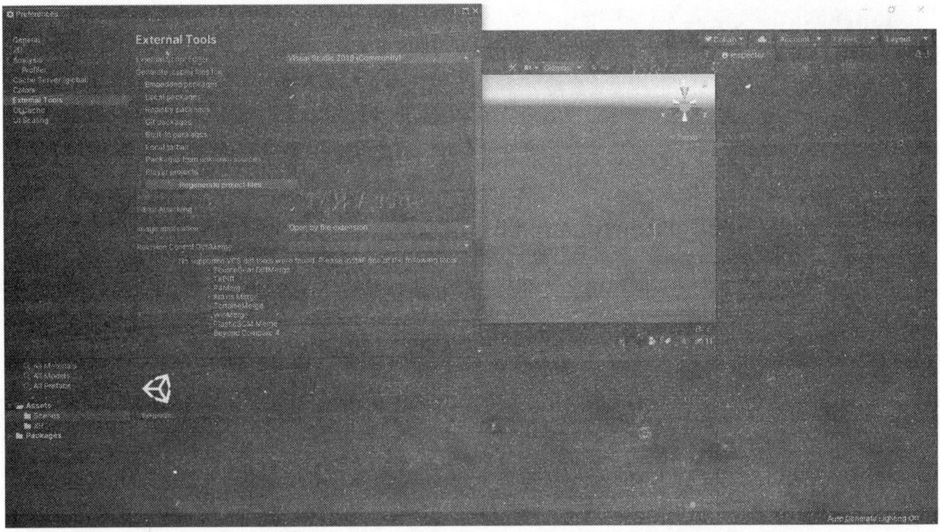


Scripting is easy in Unity. To perform something, you can write code and then drag-drop the script on to the game object. Scripting is essential to take input from the user or achieve graphical effects and custom **AI** behavior for your game objects. All the C# scripts must inherit MonoBehaviour class. It contains the functions definition of **Start()**, **Awake()**, **Update()**, which will be discussed later in this chapter.

**Note:** Unity also supports JetBrains Rider and Visual Studio Code for scripting.

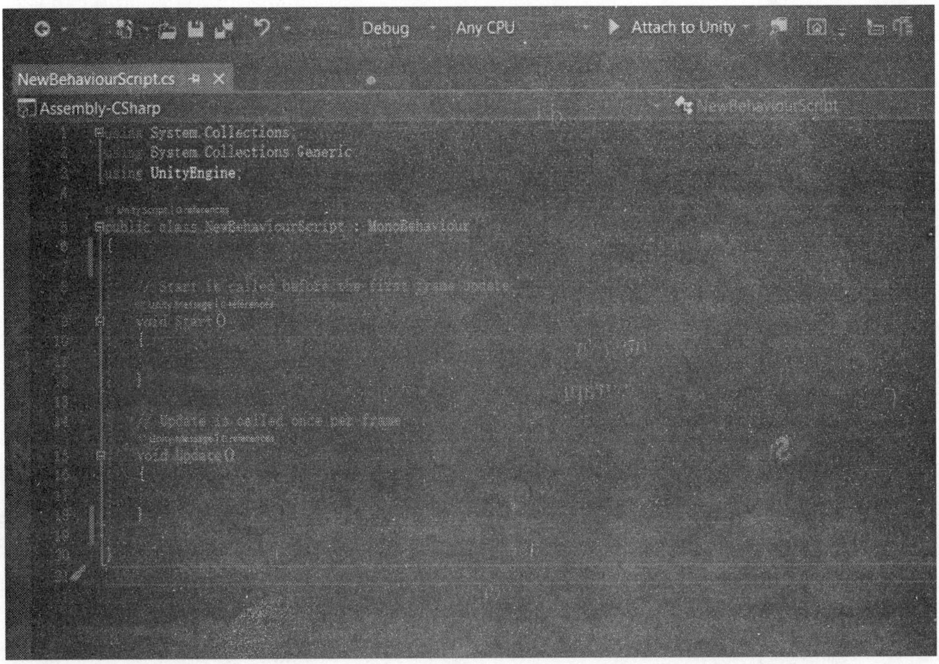


When you make a script and start the coding, you should know some functions like a **Start()**, **Update()**, as you can see above. You can see the class has inherited

**MonoBehaviour** class, which is inherited by every C# script as it contains all the definitions of functions. This class doesn't support the null-conditional operator (?.) and the null-coalescing operator(??).

**Start()**–When the script is called Start function is run first. It runs before the Update function and any other function excluding **Awake()**. The Awake function is called even before the start function. We can initialize everything in Awake, so everything is in order before the start function runs.

**Update()**–This function is called every frame like a loop. The Update is used to check or update things in your game.

**FixedUpdate()** is used for physics logic like movement as FixedUpdate calls at a fixed rate.

**LateUpdate()** is called at every frame after all the Update functions.

There are more functions in MonoBehaviour like **OnGUI()**, **OnDisable()**, which you can learn by seeing the official documentation of Unity3D.

## 5.6 ANIMATIONS IN UNITY

Unity is also used for animations and creating models. For animating a model, you can go to the animation panel as shown below in the picture.

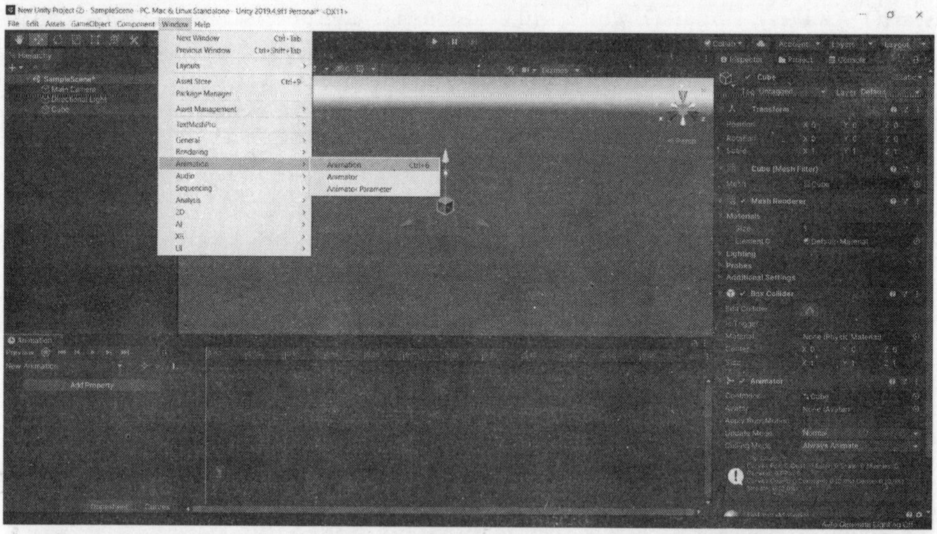


To animate something, you need to select the game object, and then in the animation panel, you will create a **.anim** file. After that, you see something like in the picture.

You can animate any property/Component of the game object by adding it into the animation by clicking the **Add Property**. To animate, you have to press the red button to start animating. Whenever you change something like the value of speed or the game object's position, it will create a Keypoint. This Keypoint refers to the exact position when the value will change to the one you applied.

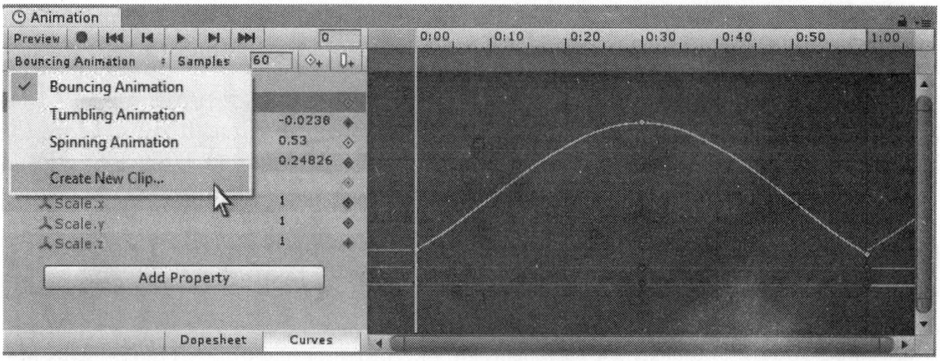


Or you just start the animation by clicking the red button, and at that time, whatever you will change will be indicated by the red color that means the value will be altered at a particular keyframe when you change it.

## 5.7 THE ANIMATOR PANEL

The **Animator** panel is an interface to control the mechanics of the animation of a particular game object. **For Example,** a third-person control when you press 'w' should play the animation for moving forward and moving left animation by pressing 'a' and so on that can be controlled using an animator.

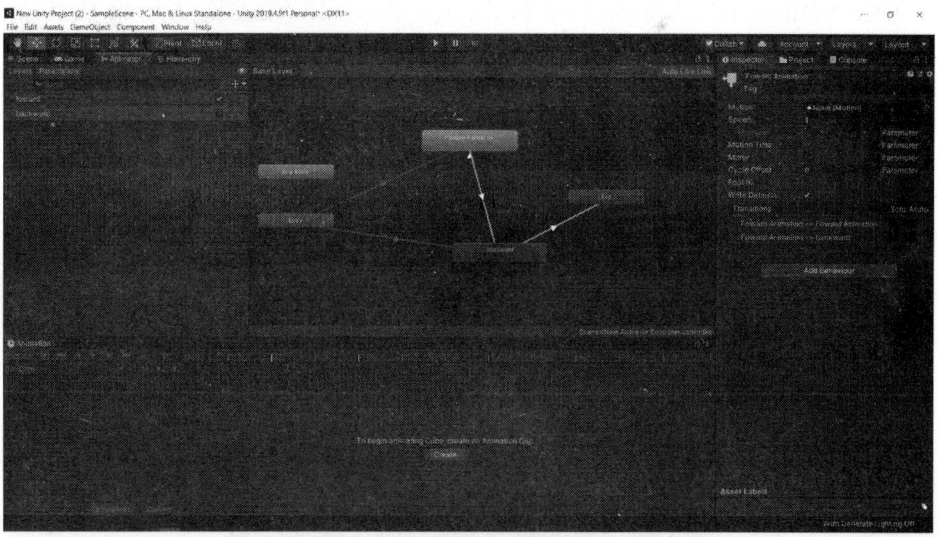

To use an animator, first, you need to create an animator controller. After making the animation controller, you can add the animator component on the game object to which you can animate like a person model or something else. Then you will drag and drop the animation controller on to the controller option. You can make different parameters as shown in the above picture like forward, backward, they are **Bool,** but you can select **int, float, trigger,** and more as your requirement. Now using the reference of an animator, you can easily handle animation by script. Animator makes handling multiple animations easy. You can also use other software to create animation and then import the animation in unity.

## 5.8 ARTIFICIAL INTELLIGENCE (AI) USING UNITY

Unity has inbuilt A.I components like Navmesh, Navmesh Agent. For creating A.I game objects which can follow your player or move to a particular place.

**Navmesh**–Navmesh is referred to the specific area where the A.I object could move.

**Navmesh Agent**–It is the agent that moves on the navmesh (A.I objects).

So, to make a navmesh, you first need to open the **Navigation** panel. To go into the windows option in the toolbar that you will see AI from that select Navigation.

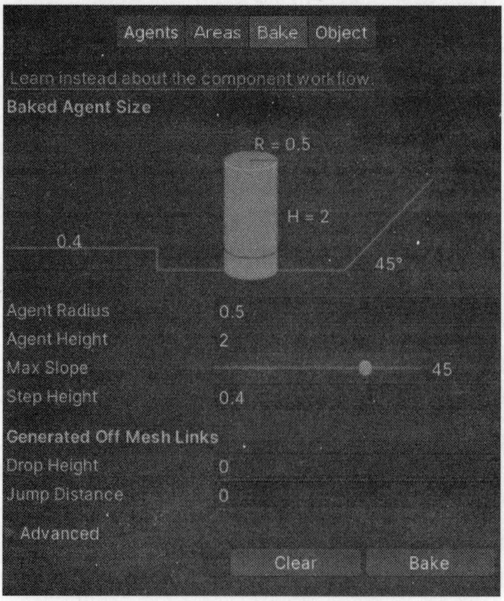

Now, select the plane or game object which you want to use as a platform for your agent to move. You will see something like the picture on the left. Here are all the options to determine the agent size and radius of the agent.

When done with these settings, click on bake that will create navmesh data in the navmesh folder. You can make a different A.I agent according to your needs.

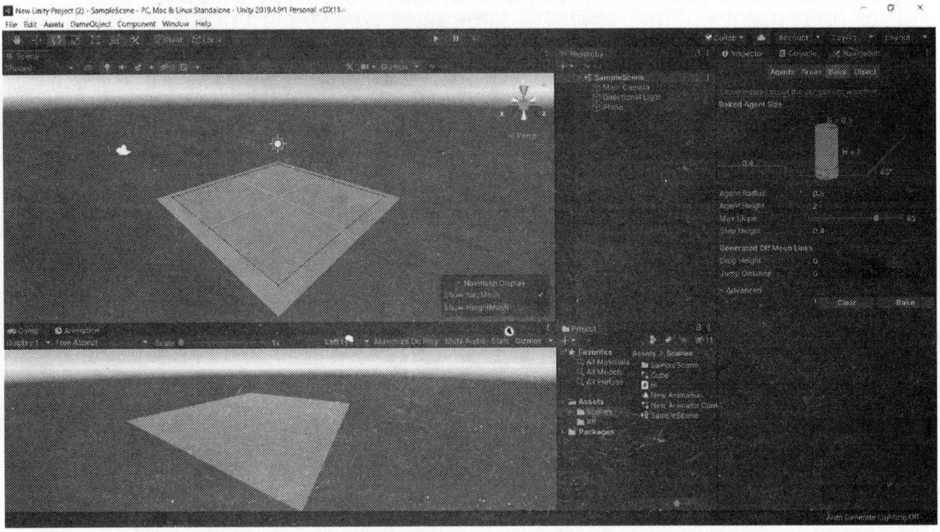

After baking, you will see a blue area, which refers to the walkable area for your Navmesh agent. If you give the agent instruction to move out of the blue, it will not move as you need to provide it with a correct position inside the blue area, or it will never reach the place you mentioned.

A Navmesh agent could be anything like enemy troops, any model or structure to make an agent. You have to add the Navmesh agent component to the game object, as shown in the picture below.

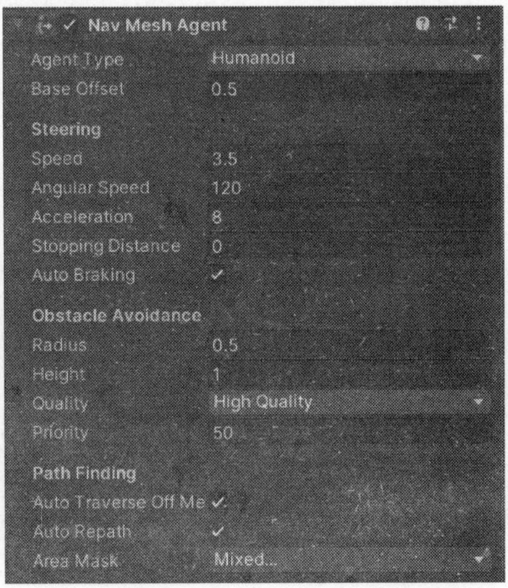

Navmesh agent is compulsory to make A.I work. Here, you can see all the settings like speed, acceleration, radius depend on these settings, and your agent will act according to those settings. For example, a bigger size of agent cant moves across a small door. So, be precise with your settings. You can use multiple agents in a scene, and you also need to bake the platform according to the navmesh agent. So it works properly. You can add various agents by going into the agent's option in navigation and add any other agent and then apply the same agent type you just made.

To move the navmesh agent from one place to another, you can use a script, and there is an inbuilt function that will work. To use the A.I function, you need to import the UnityEngine.AI library, which contains the definition of these functions.

```
using UnityEngine;
using UnityEngine.AI;
public class FollowDestination : MonoBehaviour
{
public Transform target; Vector3 destination;
NavMeshAgent agent;
void Start()
{ }
agent = GetComponent<NavMeshAgent>();
destination = agent.destination;
}
}
```

As you can in the above example when the script runs, we set a destination for the agent, and then the agent will move to that location using the shortest path algorithm to reach the destination. Agent variable refers to the game object in the scene, which has a navmesh agent component attached to it using GetComponent. GetComponent will return the component that is attached to the game object on which this script is applied. If the component is not attached to the game object, you will face a null exception.

**Note: Unity Navmesh uses A* algorithm to find the shortest distance.**

There is one problem in this strategy that you need to bake the area to make A.I work, but what if the area is dynamic and moves constantly or changes randomly.

For this, there is two option that you can use first is to use **NavMeshSurface** components that you have to download it manually from GitHub you find the link on the internet. You can also watch a unity video on Runtime Navmesh for better understanding. In these components, you will provide a bunch of features. One of them is the function **BuildNavMesh()** that can bake the area on runtime.

On the other hand, you can use the Navmesh Obstacle component. If you apply this to any game object, it will work as an obstacle, and the area will not be walkable, but as long as the obstacle is moved or removed, the area becomes walkable.

## 5.9 MULTIPLAYER AND NETWORKING IN UNITY

Unity provides multiplayer services to the developers to make a 3D multiplayer game. Unity used **UNet**, which is free and gives a couple of features for developers like lobby management, Hosting. Still, UNet doesn't satisfy many game developer's needs so, it slowly becomes deprecated. Now instead of UNet, unity is working on a new multilayer system to fulfill developers' needs. They called it **Connected games**.

Unity is working with Google to make these connections. Till then, we can use other platforms for multiplayer services. You can use PhotonEngine services for multiplayer services. Many built-in functions and callbacks can be used in unity, making multiplayer game development easy. To use PhotonEngine multiplayer, you need to download the PUN (Photon Unity Networking).

You can use a dedicated server that is provided by PhotonEngine. For free up to 20 people, which means your game can connect 20 people at a time, and the key feature is that you can at any particular time, you can increase server capacity. This helps many developers to publish the game. This allows the beginner also to test their application.

## 5.10 BLENDER SOFTWARE

In this section, we will talk about Blender, which is software that is used **for making models and animations.** Unity also provides **ProBuild and ProGrid,** which can be used to make models in unity, or you can use Blender Software as blender offers many features.

Blender is used for modeling, rigging, animation, simulation, rendering, compositing and motion tracking, video editing, and 2D animation pipeline. Blender was first introduced in 1998 and is written in C++ and Python.

You can make a model that can then be used in unity.

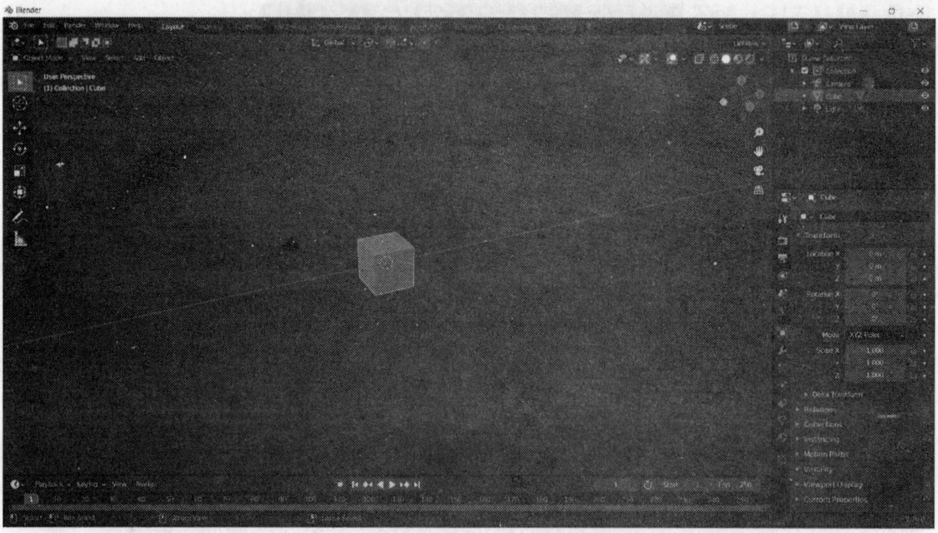

After creating a model, you can import that into unity very easily. You can also use other software rather than Blender like **Zbrush** and more that depend on the developer. People use such applications as it is easy to make animations and models compare to unity.

## 5.11 THE FUTURE: VIRTUAL ENVIRONMENT, MODES OF INTERACTION

**Virtual Environments:** 3D VEs have been around us for many years now. These represent architectural projects that interacted on frame-by-frame basis. Even CAD systems were not sufficient for that. The simulation industry is also performing modelling, displaying and updating VEs in real time. **Note that the training simulators for ships, aircrafts and military vehicles use the same VIRTUAL ENVIRONMENT (VE) as a substitute for the real working environment.** VR provides the same option to explore every angle of virtual design before it is manufactured. VEs will be used to train doctors, soldiers, police, firemen as well as children. Surgeons can practice on virtual limbs and bodies too with the help of VR.

**Modes of Interaction:** The basic, core quality of a VR system is its **flexibility in building virtual representations of anything from atom to airport, applied sciences to computer science displays like screens, displays, mouse, HMDs.** That is why we say that VR is an open-ended future. The industry can today find out the advantages of using VR by using VR toolkits. **Even a dedicated VR system** may be used here.

## SUMMARY

We have studied in this chapter that VR can be applied to almost all exciting application areas like plastic surgery, education, AI, Robotics, simulations, art, fashion, information retrieval, museums and so on. Many Universities and companies are working together to achieve these objectives.

## EXERCISE QUESTIONS

Q1. What are the tangible benefits of using VR systems?

Q2. Explain with an example how submarine design could be done using VR?

Q3. What is JACK? How it works?

Q4. Explain the role of VR in the entertainment field.

Q5. List some game systems that are based on the VR technology.

Q6. What is scientific visualization? Give some applications where VR has been used in this field?

Q7. Write a note on molecular modelling.

Q8. How phobias are being handled by VR?

Q9. Can VR be used for trainings? Explain with examples.

Q10. How can VR help in flight simulations?

Q11. How VR helps in the field of medicine?

Q12. Explain how VRs are helping in-

  a. Nuclear industry.

  b. Accident simulations.

Q13. Throw some light of the 'future of VR'.

Q14. The key quality of VR systems is its flexibility. Explain what it means.

Q15. Give a small introduction to UNITY 3D.

Q16. How do you work with VR using UNITY 3D?

Q17. How do you work with AR using UNITY 3D?

Q18. Explain the GUI of UNITY.

Q19. Can we do scripting in UNITY? If so, how?

Q20. How animations are done in UNITY?

Q21. Explain the animator panel?

Q22. How can you achieve AI using UNITY?

Q23. What platform does UNITY provide for multiplayers and for networking?

Q24. Explain the role of Blender software. Can you name any other such software?

# Appendix: Deep Learning with Virtual Reality

## A PROJECT: SELF-DRIVEN CAR

1. Requirements
2. Driving decisions and actions
3. Vehicle Hardware
4. Vehicle Software
5. Case Study
6. Safety Hazardous and Assurance of Safety
7. CARLA Simulator
8. Taxonomy
9. Kinematic Modelling in 2D
10. Vehicle Actuation
11. Longitudinal Vehicle Control
12. Lateral Vehicle Control
13. Longitudinal and Lateral Trajectory
14. Sensors used for vehicle estimation
15. Interpreting the Objects
16. Kalman Filter
17. Calibration of Sensors
18. Vehicle Visual Odometry
19. Camera Sensor
20. Stereopsis
21. Image Filtering
22. Convolution Neural Networks
23. Output Layers and Loss Function
24. Application of CNN in current scenario
25. Semantic Image Segmentation

26. Occupancy Grid
27. High-Definition Road Mapping
28. Mission Planning
29. Dynamic Object Interaction
30. Time of Collision
31. Behaviour Planner
32. Trajectory Rollout Algorithm
33. Planning the Lattice Using Python
34. Velocity Profile Generation
35. Output
36. References

## 1. REQUIREMENTS

Automated driving in cars has to fulfil some major requirements to reach different levels of automation. The task of driving does not only depend on the brakes and accelerator. It is much more than the mechanical controls of the vehicle. Apart from the proper control of speed, acceleration and steering, the vehicle should also take into account the static and dynamic objects in the path of driving. These objects like traffic lights, road signs, speed breakers, zebra crossings, lane dividers, or other vehicles driving with the automated vehicle play a major role in a safe autonomous drive. Not only this, the vehicle should decide the long and short term plan of the driving task, all of which will be discussed in detail below.

### 1.1 Driving Task Requirements

#### *1.1.1 Lateral Control / Steering*

Lateral Control of the autonomous vehicle defines the control of the area to the left and right of the vehicle. It includes the vehicle changing the lanes and monitoring the direction of the vehicle during the turns, intersections or overtaking. Thus, proper lateral control is one of the major factors which defines proper functioning of an auto-driving vehicle.

#### *1.1.2 Longitudinal Control / Braking and Accelerating*

Longitudinal Control of the autonomous vehicle defines the control of the area to the front and back of the vehicle or essentially the longitudinal motion of the vehicle, for example, its longitudinal velocity, acceleration or its longitudinal distance from another preceding vehicle in the same lane on the highway. The throttle and brakes are the actuators used to implement longitudinal control[1]

A very familiar example of longitudinal control is the standard cruise control system available on most vehicles today. With a standard cruise control system, the driver sets a constant desired speed at which he/she would like the vehicle to travel. The cruise control system then automatically controls the throttle to maintain the desired speed. It is the driver's responsibility to ensure that the vehicle can indeed safely travel at that speed on the highway. If there happens to appear a preceding vehicle on the highway that is traveling at a slower speed or is too close to the ego vehicle, the driver must take action and if necessary apply brakes. Application of the brakes automatically disengages the cruise control system and returns control of the throttle to the driver.

### 1.1.3 Object and Event Detection Response / Detection and Reaction

Object and Event Detection and Response is one of the major requirements for driving task of an autonomous driving vehicle. It is used to detect the static and dynamic objects on the road while travelling in highway or urban area. The static objects include road markings, traffic lights, curbs, road signs or construction signs, etc. while the dynamic objects also include vehicles (2 wheelers, 4 wheelers) and pedestrians.

The OEDR also includes responding to the event or object detected by the sensors while driving on a highway or urban roads. The vehicle can respond by increasing or decreasing speed, stopping or honking, etc. Some of the test cases and appropriate responses to them are listed below:

#### Case 1: Stray animals on the road.

If there is a stray animal near on the road the vehicle is driving on, the sensors and camera should detect it and accordingly act on the event by decreasing the speed, stopping immediatelyand honking on the animal to get it out of the way.

#### Case 2: Speed limits as road signs

As soon as the vehicle reaches near the road sin, it will detect the sign and read it to then limit the speed under the limit according to the road sign.

### 1.1.4 Short Term and Long Term Planning

The planning is what essentially completes the automation of a vehicle. It is of two types: short term planning and long term planning.

#### Short Term Planning

It includes the planning and decisions on the following factors:

Speed changes required according to the traffic lights, road signs, time limit to reach the destination and number of vehicles on the road. While calculating the time required to reach the destination, the average speed of the traffic should be taken to take into account the vehicles driving with the autonomous vehicle on road [2]

The lane changes required to overtake vehicles in order to drive faster with safety.

#### Long Term Planning

It includes the planning and decisions on the following factors:

The calculation of shorter route with minimum congestion to reach the destination on time.

The calculation of number of turns, intersections and traffic lights to be crossed on the optimum route chosen.

The driving behaviours required to be fulfilled by the vehicle. They include proper signalling and using of horn while turning or changing lanes on the road or taking a U-turn and requesting new routes from route planner when tackling an unpredicted even like road block [3] .

The motion planning of the autonomous vehicle while driving, taking turns, changing lanes or overtaking another vehicle. There has to be proper planning and decision to get the perfect trajectory and path of the vehicle which takes the velocity of other vehicles into account to reduce any possible chances of damage or accidents.

## 1.2 Requirements of Perception

To fulfil the behavioural requirements of an autonomous vehicle, it must first be able to adequately localize its position and perceive the surrounding environment. Since there may be areas of poor GPS coverage, the surrounding road coverage and legal lanes of travel must also be sensed. Finally, the vehicle must be able to perceive all obstacles in its path and appropriately classify obstacles as vehicles. [3]

For each perception requirement, multiple sensors are required to achieve the highest levels of accuracy and reliability.

- The Localization component determines the vehicle position and orientation in the world.
- The Road Detection component determines a road coverage map as well as the position of each lane in nearby segments.
- The Object Classification component detects obstacles and classifies them as either static or dynamic. A dynamic obstacle is any obstacle that is capable ofmovement, so a stopped vehicle would be classified as a dynamic obstacle with zero forward velocity.

### *1.2.1 Static Objects*

The object detection along with the object classification module will classify an object as static if its fixed and does not change its position with time. There can be a lot of static objects on a road while driving which need to be classified as static by the autonomous vehicle so that the vehicle can respond to that object accordingly. The most common static objects encountered by a vehicle include:

#### *1.2.1.1 Road and lane markings*

The vehicles on the road often come across road markings like lanes dividers, zebra crossings, stop signs, Bus lanes, and more. These static objects need to be detected as soon as the vehicle comes in a range of these road markings. The vehicle also needs to respond to the static object detected according to the particular road marking.

#### 1.2.1.2 Curbs (off-road)

The road is surrounded by the footpath for pedestrians to walk on, and it is separated by the curbs. The vehicle must identify the curbs (end of a footpath) to stay in the limit of the road it is driving on. Since it is illegal to drive on footpaths and curbs are important for the safety of pedestrians walking on the footpath, they should be accurately identified by the vehicle.

#### 1.2.1.3 Traffic Lights (off-road)

The traffic lights are one of the most important elements of driving on the road. Not only is it illegal to not obey the traffic lights, it can be fatal in most of the cases. So the vehicle should identify any and all traffic lights on the road and respond to the traffic light glowing. The vehicle must slow down and/or stop when it detects a red / yellow light and should indicate to the vehicle around on the road.

#### 1.2.1.4 Road Signs (off-road)

The road signs are important as they inform the driver about what they're approaching ahead. So, as soon as the vehicle reaches near the road sign, it will detect the sign and read it and then accordingly. In case of a speed limit, other sign that requires speed to be controlled, it will get the speed of the vehicle under control, if it's stop sign, the vehicle should come to a stop.

#### 1.2.1.5 Construction Signs

The road is always near some construction or under repairs which entitles the workers to put up construction signs. These signs are important as they inform the driver to be careful about it. So, as soon as the vehicle reaches near the construction sign, it will be careful about the construction area.

### 1.2.2 Dynamic Objects

The object classification module will classify an object as dynamic if it changes its position with time (like vehicles, pedestrians, etc…). There can be a lot of dynamic objects on a road while driving which need to be classified as dynamic by the autonomous vehicle so that the vehicle can respond to that object accordingly. The most common dynamic objects encountered by a vehicle include:

#### 1.2.2.1 Vehicles (on-road)

There are a lot of vehicles on the road at a particular moment and are moving at their different velocities which must be taken into account along with the predictability of where these vehicles are going to, thus making the driving of the vehicle smoother and incident-free.

#### 1.2.2.2 Pedestrians

There are many pedestrians crossing roads, moving towards footpaths or walking down the road where the vehicle is driving. Thus the vehicle must modify their route, speed, and acceleration according to any pedestrians that walk in front of the vehicle while driving.

### 1.3 Ego Localization

The vehicle ego-localization task is one of the most important technologies for an autonomous vehicle driving on the road. Obtaining an accurate vehicle position is the first-step to supporting driver safety and comfort. In particular, ego-localization near intersections is important for avoiding traffic accidents. The Ego Localization thus essentially means positioning the vehicle on a map to check the further traffic, possible jams, road accidents or shorter routes. A global positioning system (GPS) is generally used to estimate a global vehicle position. Recently, in-vehicle cameras for the ego- localization have been put to practical use. Meanwhile, aerial images have become readily available, for example from Google Maps [4].

However, standard GPSs for a vehicle navigation system have an estimation error within about 30–100 meters in an urban area. Therefore, a relatively accurate position is estimated by matching information, such as a geo-location and an image taken from a vehicle, to a map. Among them, map-matching is one of the most prevalent methods. This method estimates a vehicle position by matching a vehicle's driving trajectory calculated from rough estimations using GPS to a topological road map.

### 1.4 Challenges of Perception

To be a level 5 automated vehicle, there are many challenges that a vehicle has to overcome in terms of it's perception of objects in the road in daily life. These challenges in perception include sensor uncertainty, occlusion, reflection, illumination, lens flare, weather, precipitation and others [5]. The developers and engineers are trying their best to tackle these issues for a smoother and accident free rides.

## 2. DRIVING DECISIONS AND ACTIONS

### 2.1 Planning

As stated previously, planning is an important part of the process and is essential for deciding how to reach the destination. The process of planning can be categorized into 3 types on the basis of time taken in planning. They are:

#### *2.1.1 Long Term Planning*

How to reach from starting place to destination?

#### *2.1.2 Short Term Planning*

Can I change my lane to the lane right of me? Can I pass this intersection and join the left road?

### *2.1.3 Immediate Planning*

Can I stay on track on this curved road? Accelerate or brake, by how much?

## 2.2 Taking Decision

Consider an example that the vehicle is turning left.

A simple maneuver of a left turn at an intersection requires a series of decisions and planning, then the whole process will require a lot of planning (both short term and long term).

## 2.3 Type of Planning

### *2.3.1 Reactive Planning*

In reactive rule based planning, we have rules that take into account the current state of ego and other objects and give decisions.

**Examples:** If there is a pedestrian on the road, stop.

If speed limit changes, adjust speed to match it.

### *2.3.2 Predictive Planning*

Make predictions about other vehicles and how they are moving. Then use these predictions to inform our decisions.

**Example:** That car has been stopped for the last 10 seconds. It is going to be stopped for the next few seconds.

Pedestrian is jaywalking. She will enter our lane by the time we reach her.

# 3. VEHICLE HARDWARE

## 3.1 Sensors

Sensors are sophisticated devices that are frequently used to detect and respond to electrical or optical signals. A Sensor converts the physical parameter (for example: temperature, blood pressure, humidity, speed, etc.) into a signal which can be measured electrically. Sensors are the most important part of the autonomous vehicle's hardware because they measure the parameters of the vehicle and environment surrounding it to make decisions for smoother and safer ride.

There are two types of sensors used in autonomous vehicles:

**Extroceptive Sensors**: extero means surroundings. Thus, exteroceptive sensors measure the changes in the surroundings of the vehicle and help it to act accordingly.

**Proprioceptive Sensors**: proprio means internal. Thus, proprioceptive sensors measure the internal changes of a vehicle.

### 3.2 Types of Sensors

- **Camera**
- **LIDAR:** Light Detection and Ranging RADAR–Radio Detection and Ranging Ultrasonic
- **GNSS/ IMU:** Global Navigation Satellite Systems and Inertial measurement units Wheel Odometry

## 4. VEHICLE SOFTWARE

The vehicle hardware collects data using sensors and the software is thus needed to compute and instruct the vehicle to perform the next task accordingly[6]. The autonomous vehicle software decomposition can be done into:

- Environment Perception
- Environment Mapping
- Motion Planning
- Controller
- System Supervisor

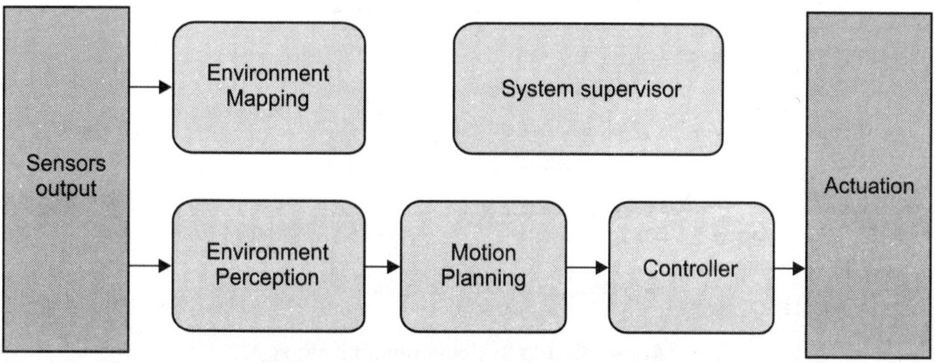


**Appendix.Fig.1:** Autonomous Vehicle Software Decomposition

### 4.1 Environment Perception

This is the step which perceives the environment surrounding the vehicle and performs the following steps on the data obtained from the hardware:

- Localization of the vehicle (detects the location of vehicle on the map)
- Dynamic Object Detection (detecting vehicles or pedestrians on the road)
- Static Object Detection (detecting objects like traffic lights or curbs on the road) Thus, after detecting dynamic objects, the software needs to track the object to avoid collisions and predict its motion to thus change/maintain the vehicle's path effectively [6]. The whole configuration of Environment Perception is shown in a block-diagram below:

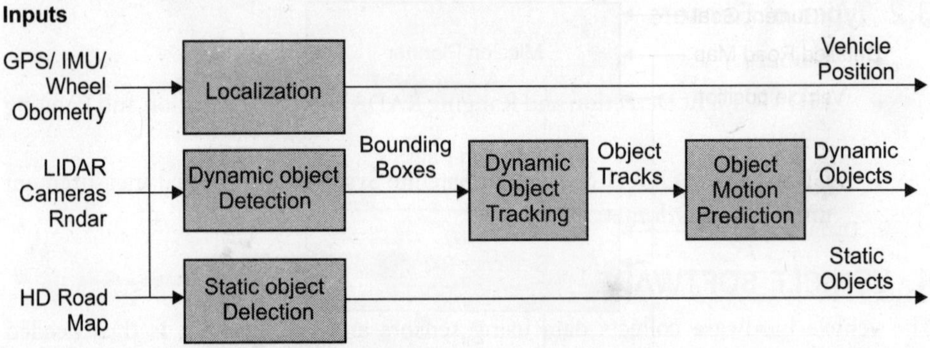


**Appendix.Fig.2:** Environment Perception

## 4.2 Environmental Maps

This is the step which gets the environmental maps of the area vehicle is currently driving in. There are 3 types of mas generated and all of these three maps have different purpose and function which helps the vehicle to drive safely.

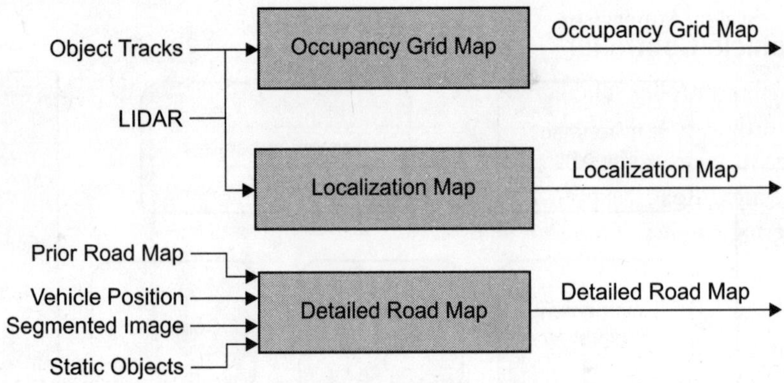


**Appendix.Fig.3:** Environmental Maps

## 4.3 Motion Planning

There has to be proper planning and decision to get the perfect trajectory and path of the vehicle which takes the velocity of other vehicles into account to reduce any possible chances of damage or accidents. [4] This is called Motion Planning and it consists of:

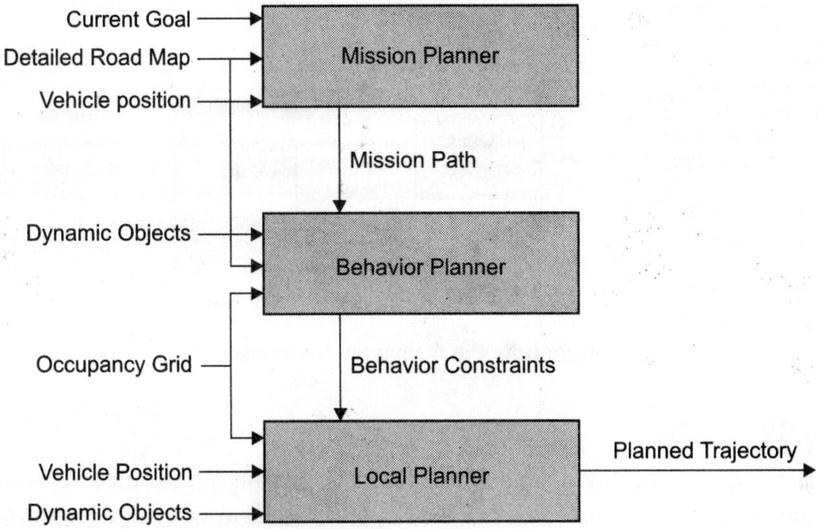


**Appendix.Fig.4:** Motion Planning

## 4.4 Vehicle Controller

The vehicle controller schemes and plans the velocity and direction of the autonomous vehicle driving on the road by calculating the data obtained by the sensors and hardware. It takes planned trajectory from the Motion Planner and Vehicle Position from Detailed Road Map and calculates the throttle percentage, braking percentage and Steering Angle required for smooth ride of the autonomous vehicle.

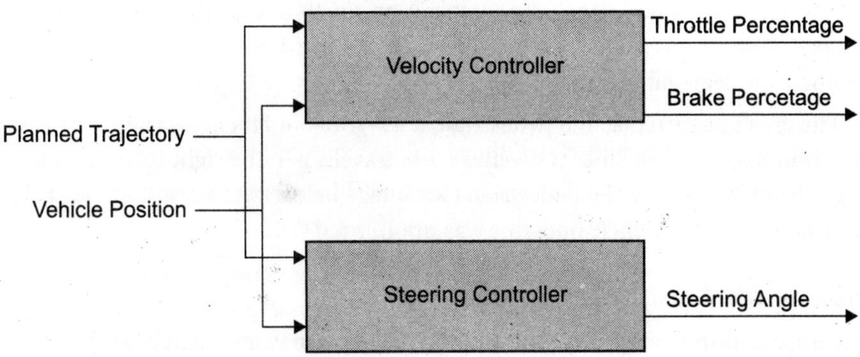


**Appendix.Fig.5:** Vehicle Controller

## 4.5 System Supervisor

The system supervisor consists of Software Supervisor and Hardware Supervisor which individually check and supervise the proper functioning of software and hardware of the vehicle respectively.

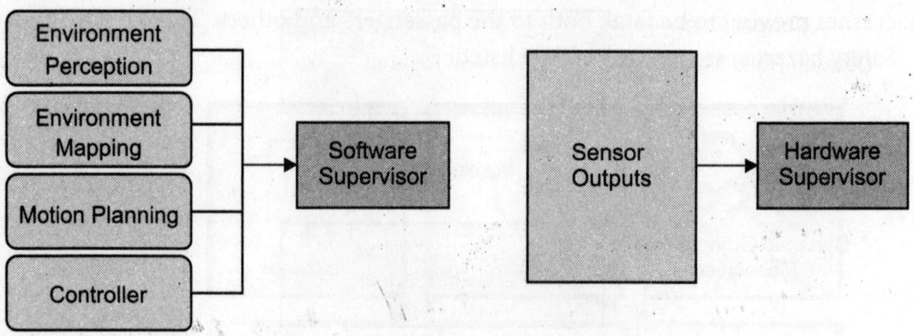


**Appendix.Fig.6:** System Supervisor

## 5. CASE STUDY

The safety and practicality of autonomous vehicles driving on the roads have always been questioned by the researchers and developers. The answer is crucial for developing sound policies to govern their deployment [7]. One proposal to assess safetyis to test-drive autonomous vehicles in real traffic, observe their performance and make statistical comparisons to human driver performance. [8] Thus to achieve safety and practicality of bringing autonomous vehicles to the real traffic and roads, we have to look at the autonomous vehicle crash reports of when they were out for real-time testing.

### 5.1 Uber Crash Report

About 9:58 p.m., on Sunday, March 18, 2018, an ***Uber Technologies, Inc.*** test vehicle, based on a *modified 2017 Volvo XC90* and operating with a self-driving system in computer control mode, struck a pedestrian on northbound Mill Avenue, in Tempe, Maricopa County, Arizona [9]. The Uber test vehicle was occupied by one vehicle operator, a 44-year-old female.

The crash occurred as the pedestrian, a 49-year-old female, walked a bicycle east across Mill Avenue. The Uber test vehicle was traveling in the right through lane when its right front side struck the pedestrian (see image below). As a result of the crash, the pedestrian died. The vehicle operator was not injured [10].

#### *Causes of the Crash*

There were multiple things that caused this crash and they are listed below: There were no real time checks on safety drivers.

After the woman was detected on the road (6 seconds before)[11], it was: first classified as unknown object then misclassified as a vehicle then a bicycle.1.3 seconds before, system tried to do emergency braking manoeuvre, but the vehicle had disabled it [12].

## 6. SAFETY HAZARDOUS AND ASSURANCE OF SAFETY

There are a lot of safety hazards to an autonomous vehicle which can lead to accidents or crashes proving to be fatal, both to the passengers and others. There are many types of Safety hazards, some of which are listed:

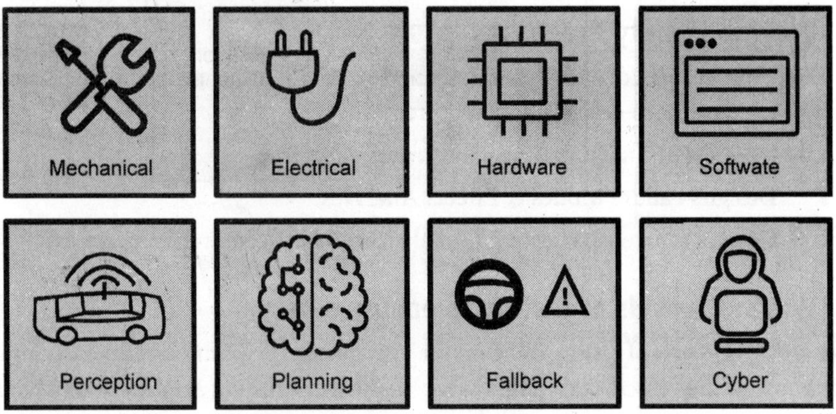


**Appendix.Fig.7:** Safety Hazardous

Thus, the autonomous vehicle developers and testers should make sure that these safety hazards are addressed and their issues resolved. Onlythen can the autonomous vehicles safely be allowed to drive on the road.

## 6.1 Waymo Safety Perspective

Waymo was founded years ago as the Google self-driving car project to design and build a safe self-driving car. In their first Safety Report on Waymo's fully self-driving technology, they detailed Waymo's work on and their commitment to safety. [11] This overview of Waymo's safety program underscores the important lessons learned through the 5 million miles Waymo's vehicles have self-driven on public roads and through our billions of miles of simulated driving.

## 6.2 Waymo: Safety Levels

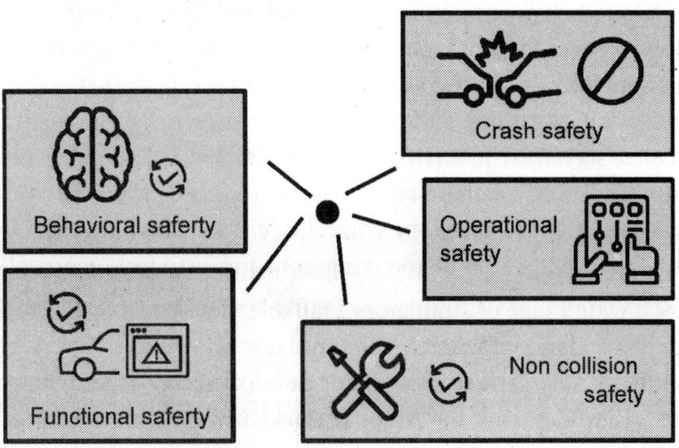


**Appendix.Fig.8:** Safety Levels introduced by Wamyo

The safety levels ensured by the self-driving car of the Google self-driving car giant are the various levels that ensure crash-less, smooth driving.

## 6.3 Waymo: Safety Processes

The safety processes Identify hazard scenarios & potential mitigations Use hazard assessment methods to define safety requirements

- Does Preliminary analysis Constructs Fault tree
- Designs Failure Modes & Effects Analyses
- Conducts extensive testing to make sure safety requirements are met

## 6.4 Waymo: Levels of testing to ensure safety

There are three levels of testing done on the Waymo's Self-driving cars, to ensure proper functioning of the vehicle (car in this case). These three testing are described as follows:

### *6.4.1 Simulation testing*

It is a type of testing in which the vehicle is tested rigorously with simulation, with thousands of variations, and fuzzing of neighboring vehicles.

### *6.4.2 Closed-course testing*

This testing follows 28 core and 19 additional scenario competencies on private test tracks. This testing focuses on four most common crashes Rear-end, intersection, road departure, and lane change

### *6.4.3 Real-world driving*

In this type of testing Starts with smaller fleet, expand steadily Already testing thousands of vehicles, with more on the way. [13]

## 7. CARLA SIMULATOR

A realistic simulation environment is an essential tool for developing a self-driving car, because it allows us to ensure that our vehicle will operate safely before we even step foot in it. Using a simulator, we can test all of the different modules that make up our system including perception, planning, and control, either together or independently. We can run sophisticated scenarios involving many AI controlled vehicles and pedestrians, and we can run variations on these scenarios, hundreds or even thousands of times to ensure our car consistently makes the correct decision. Most importantly, we can test our car in situations that would be too dangerous for us to test on actual roads. [14]

There are a wide range of simulators available, developed by teams from industry and academia alike. Here, we will use the simulator known as CARLA. CARLA stands for Car Learning to Act. Carla is a simulator developed by a team with members from the Computer Vision Center at the Autonomous University of Barcelona, Intel and the Toyota Research

Institute and built using the Unreal game engine. It features highly detailed virtual worlds with roadways, buildings, weather, and vehicle and pedestrian agents. Images of these environments can be captured in various formats including depth maps and segmented images.

The entire simulation can be controlled with an external client which can be used to send commands to the vehicle, record data and automatically execute scenarios for evaluating the performance of the car. [14]

## 8. TAXONOMY

Taxonomy or classification of autonomous driving is broadly explained in terms of requirements and levels. Requirements are explained in the 1st section. The levels however are divided as follows. The SAE recommended practice describes motor vehicle driving automation systems that perform part or all of the dynamic driving task (DDT) on a sustained basis [15]. It provides a taxonomy with detailed definitions for six levels of driving automation, ranging from no driving automation (level 0) to full driving automation (level 5), in context of motor vehicles and their operation on roadways.

### 8.1 Level 0

This is the first level of automation, also known as No Automation Level. In this level, all of the driving decisions, tasks and actions are performed by the driver. It is the full human perception, planning and control level.

### 8.2 Level 1

This level is also known as the Driving Assistance Automation Level. In this level, the vehicle assists the driver in driving actions but the driving decisions are entirely taken by the driver. In this level, either the Lateral control or the longitudinal control is present but not both at the same time.

#### *Example: Adaptive Cruise Control*

Adaptive cruise control systems can take control of the engine and brake in order to make the vehicle travel at a specific speed. Hence, the driver only has to steer.[16]

### 8.3 Level 2

The Level 2 is also known as Partial Driving Automation Level. In this level, the vehicle has both lateral and longitudinal control in specific driving scenarios, but the driver monitoring is always required.

#### *Example: General Motors (GM) Super Cruise*

General Motors Super Cruise is a true hands free system that uses high Definition maps, sensors watching the road, and an in-car monitoring System to make sure the driver is paying attention. [17]

## 8.4 Level 3

This level is also known as Conditional Driving Automation. In this level, the vehicle can perform Object Event Detection and Response (OEDR) to a certain degree in addition to the lateral control and longitudinal control. The driver may not need to monitor in certain scenarios as at the time of emergency and failure, the vehicle alerts the driver in time to intervene and the control must then be taken up by the driver. It is a controversial level of automation as it is not always possible for an autonomy system to know when it is experiencing the failure.

### *Example: Audi A Luxury Sedan*

The Audi A Luxury Sedan was an automated driving system that can navigate unmonitored in slow traffic.

## 8.5 Level 4

This level is also known as High Driving Automation Level. In this level, the vehicle is capable of reaching a minimum risk condition, in case if the driver doesn't intervene in emergency. Level 4 performs under limited ODD. The vehicle also performs lateral and longitudinal control as its basic performance. Hence, Level 4 systems can handle emergencies and are capable of keeping the passengers safe.

### *Example : Waymo*

The Waymo fleet can handle the driving task in a defined geographic area with a nominal set of operating conditions, without the need for a human driver.

## 8.6 Level 5

This level is also known as Full Driving Automation Level. In this level, the vehicle is fully autonomous with unlimited ODD. There are no examples of Level 5 automation level yet.

# 9. KINEMATIC MODELLING IN 2D

Creating a good vehicle model is essential for model based control development. Here, vehicle motion can be modelled by taking into account all the geometric constraints acting on the vehicle. Kinematic Modelling is more than sufficient to capture the motion of the vehicle at low speeds when the accelerations are not significant. Example of Kinematic Modelling is two wheeled robot, Kinematic Bicycle Model. Both the models will be modelled with respect to kinematic modelling in the following sub-sections.

## 9.1 Transformation of Coordinate Frames (Rotational matrices in 2D)

In many robotics applications, it is needed to attach several coordinates to a moving system and also represent elements from these frames in the inertial frame. Hence, transformation from one coordinate frame to another is required. A simple two wheeled robot with a single sensor has three frames to consider while s self-driving car can have dozens of coordinate frames.

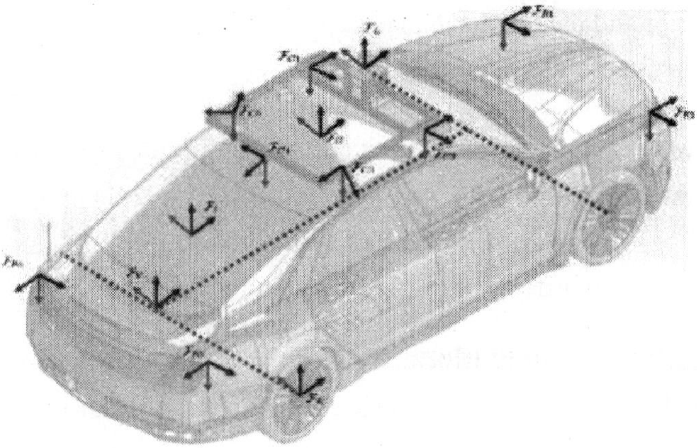

**Appendix.Fig.9:** Coordinate frames representation in a self-driving car

The rotational matrices can now be defined as:

- CEB: This rotational matrix transforms the vectors from frame b to frame e.

$$\text{CEB} = \begin{matrix} \cos(\theta) & \sin(\theta) \\ -\sin(\theta) & \cos(\theta) \end{matrix}$$

- CBE: This rotational matrix projects frame e onto frame b.

$$\text{CBE} = \begin{matrix} \cos(\theta) & -\sin(\theta) \\ \sin(\theta) & \cos(\theta) \end{matrix}$$

## 9.2 Coordinate Transformation with Translation of a Two Wheeled Robot

In this case, the position of a point P observed by the robot in the robot body frame b as shown in the figure below:

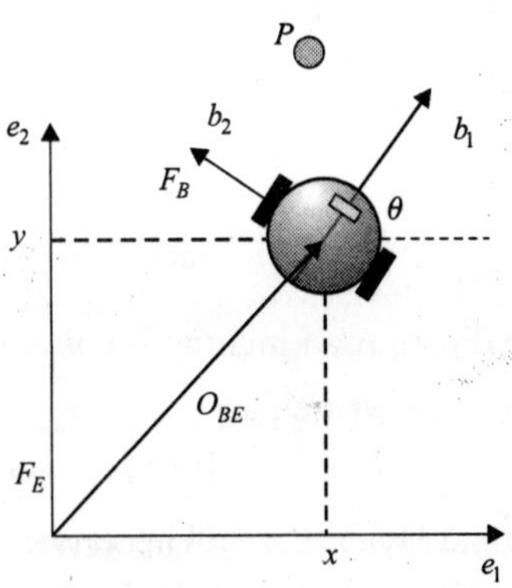


**Appendix.Fig.10:** Two wheeled Robot

The position of the robot with respect to the inertial frame is x and y and the orientation of the robot is theta.

The conversion between inertial frame and body coordinates is done with a translation vector and the rotational matrix. [18]

Location of point P in body frame B is:

$$\mathbf{PB = CEB\ (\theta)\ PE + OEB}$$

Where OEB is a translation term referenced in body frame B. Location of point P in inertial frame E is:

$$\mathbf{PE = CBE\ (\theta)\ PB + OBE}$$

Where OBE is a translation term referenced in inertial frame E.

## 9.3 Longitudinal Vehicle Model

Below is the full-fledged diagram of a vehicle on an inclined road with slope α.

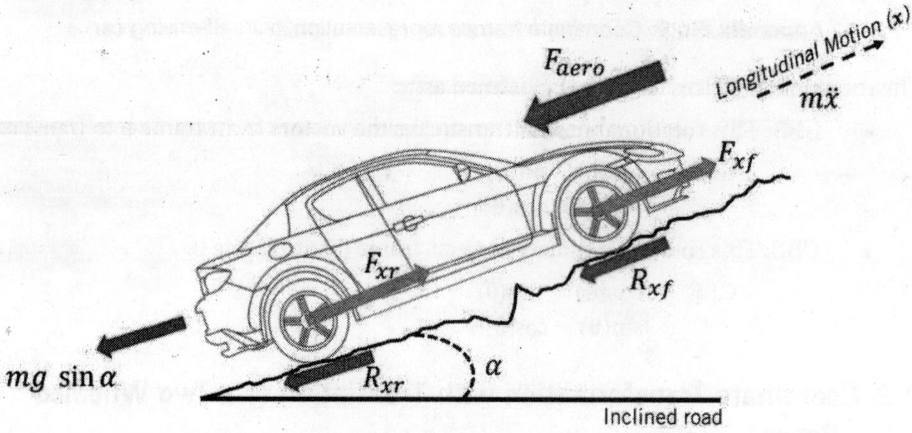


**Appendix.Fig.11:** Longitudinal Vehicle Model

The forces mentioned in the above diagram are:

- Front tire force, $F_{xf}$
- Rear tire force, $F_{xr}$
- Aerodynamic force, $F_{aero}$
- Front rolling resistance, $R_{xf}$
- Rear rolling resistance, $R_{xr}$
- Gravitational force due to road inclination, *mgsinα*

The dynamic equation can be written as:

$$mx = F_{xf} + F_{xr} - F_{aero} - R_{xf} - R_{xr} - mgsin\alpha$$

The simplified longitudinal Dynamics will become:

$$mx = F_x - \boxed{F_{aero} - R_x - mg\,\alpha}$$

Inertial Term    Traction Force    Total Resistant Forces ( Fload)

### *Assumptions*

Let $F_x$ be the total longitudinal force, then $F_x = F_{xf} + F_{xr}$ Let $R_x$ be the total rolling resistance, then $R_x = R_{xf} + R_{xr}$. Assume $\alpha$ is a small angle, $\sin \alpha = \alpha$

## 9.4 Lateral Vehicle Model

The following assumptions for the lateral dynamics of the bicycle model: Longitudinal velocity is constant

Left and right axle are lumped into a single wheel Suspension movement, road inclination and aerodynamic forces are neglected.

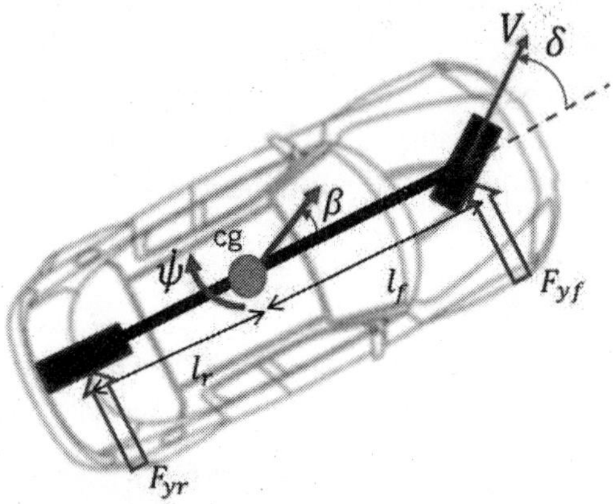


**Appendix.Fig.12:** Lateral Dynamics of the Vehicle

### *9.4.1 Lateral Acceleration*

$$a_y = \ddot{y} + \omega^2 R$$
$$= V\beta + V\psi$$

### *9.4.2 Lateral Dynamics Model Equation*

Vehicle mass    Side slip rate    yaw rate    front and rear tire forces

$$mV\left(\dot{\beta} + \dot{\psi}\right) = F_{yf} + F_{yr}$$

Vehicle velocity

### 9.4.3 *Angular Acceleration*

$$I_z \ddot{\psi} = l_f F_{yf} - l_r F_{yr}$$

Vehicle inertia

Center of gravity distance form front and rear tires

## 9.5 Other Factors to be considered for developing a real time model

There are many more factors that we have not considered for modelling our data since considering them will make the complete process tedious and hard to follow the back tracking approach.

### 9.5.1 *Engine Dynamics*

Tire force in terms of inertia and load force

### 9.5.2 *Tyre Slip Angle*

Tire forces are generally hard to predict exactly, and tire models tend to be linear and empirically identified. For normal driving conditions, the lateral tire forces are approximated as a linear function of the tire slip angle. This assumption is only valid for small tire slip angles

### 9.5.3 *Front and Rear Tire Forces*

The tire forces and slip angles are represented in terms of the cornering stiffness. The cornering stiffness of a tire is defined by its ability to resist deformation while the vehicle corners. [18]

# 10. VEHICLE ACTUATION

The vehicle actuation system consists of braking, throttling and steering and their functioning.

## 10.1 Coupled Lateral and Longitudinal System

The main input to the lateral system is the steering angle and the main input to the longitudinal system are throttle pedal position and brake pedal position. These inputs define some of the forces and moments that act on the vehicle and feed into the ordinary differential angle that govern the dynamics of the vehicle. The lateral and longitudinal dynamics can affect each other. The lateral forces and moments' drive the vehicle lateral dynamics, which produce a vehicle lateral velocity in the rate. The longitudinal forces drive the longitudinal dynamics which defines the forward velocity and displacement. The main task of vehicle control is to provide the suitable steering throttle and brake commands to keep the vehicle on the desired path and following a desired speed profile[19].

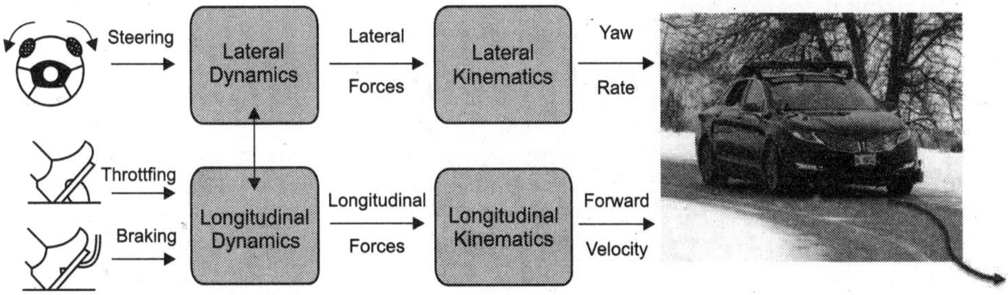


**Appendix.Fig.13:** Coupled Lateral and Longitudinal system

### *10.1.1 Steering*

The steering system model is simply the driver's command or the autonomy system's command to turn the vehicle to right or left. The steering angle is translated into a wheel angle through a special mechanism and gear ratios that provide the lateral forces to keep the vehicle in a curved path.

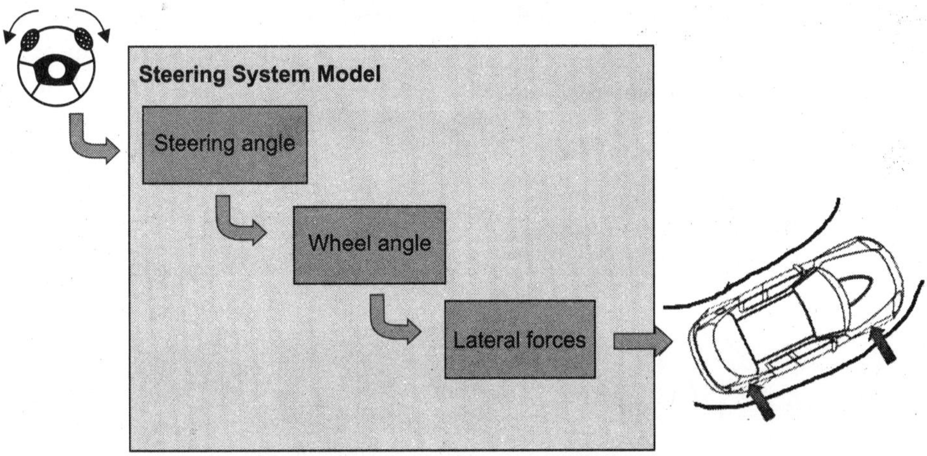


**Appendix.Fig.14:** Steering System Model

### *10.1.2 Throttling*

The driver put their foot on the gas pedal to define the level of torque demand needed to accelerate the vehicle. The actual response is a bit more complex and depends on the type of power generation unit involved.

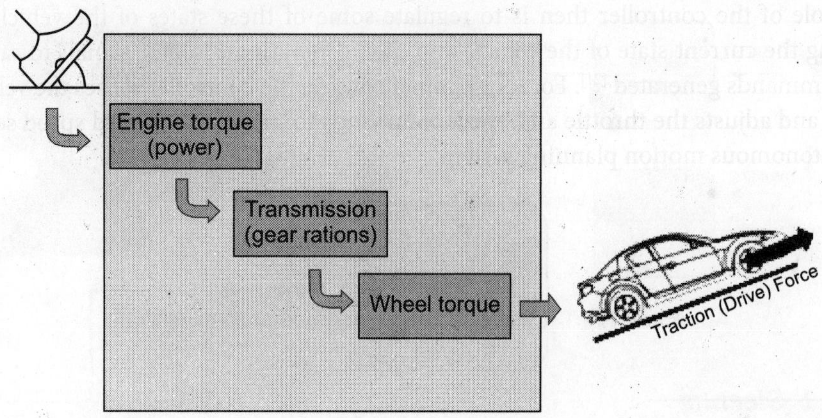


**Appendix.Fig.15:** Throttling

### *10.1.3 Braking*

The braking process starts from the driver commanded brake pedal position, which is translated into brake pressure by the electronic control unit.

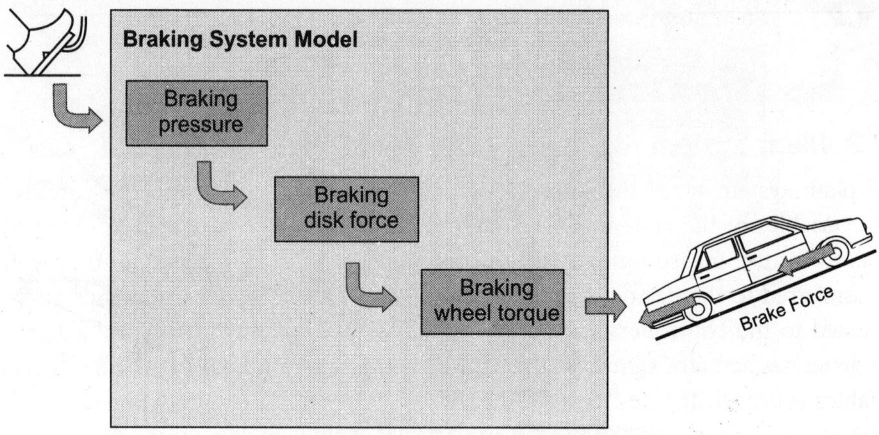


**Appendix.Fig.16:** Braking system

## 11. LONGITUDINAL VEHICLE CONTROL

The concept of Longitudinal Vehicle Control describes the regulation of speed in a self-driving car. Design of the longitudinal speed control underpins all vehicle performance on the road and is one of the fundamental components needed for autonomous driving[20].

### 11.1 Control Development

The kinematic and dynamic models developed before aim to capture how the dynamic system reacts to inputs command from the driver such as steering, gas and break and how it reacts to disturbances such as wind, road surface and different vehicle loads.

The role of the controller then is to regulate some of these states of the vehicle by sensing the current state of the vehicle and then generating actuator signals to satisfy the commands generated [21]. For longitudinal control, the controller senses the vehicle speed and adjusts the throttle and break commands to match the desired speed set by the autonomous motion planning system.

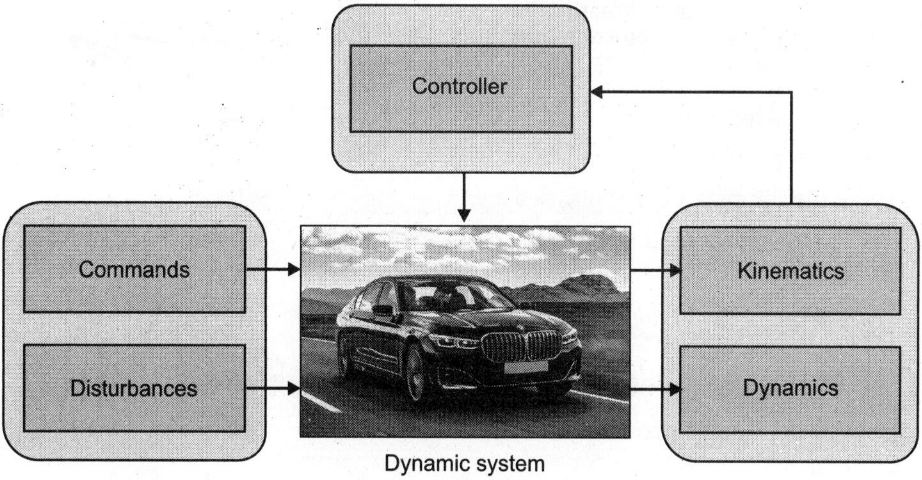


**Appendix.Fig.17:** Control Development

## 11.2 Plant System

The plant system takes the input as actuator signals and generates the outputs or state variables of the system. These outputs are measured by sensors and estimators are used to fuse measurements into accurate output estimates. The output estimates are compared to the desired or reference output variables and the difference or error is passed to the controller. The controller can be seen as a mathematical algorithm that generates actuator signals so that the error signal is minimized and the plant state variables approach the desired state variables. [21]The plant model be it linear or non-linear can be represented in several ways. Thetwo most common ways are:

- State space form which tracks the evolution of an internal state to connect the input to the output and transfer the function form which models the input to output relation directly.
- The next way is Transfer functions which are explained below:

A transfer function G is the relation between the input U and output Y.

$$Y(s) = G(s)U(s)$$

where, $s = \sigma + j\omega$

When s, a complex variable is expressed in Laplace domain, G(s) can be written as the function of numerator and denominator.

$$Y(s) = G(s)U(s) = N(s)/D(s)\, U(s)$$

The roots of the numerator are termed as zeroes and the roots of denominator are termed as poles

## 11.3 Controller

Control algorithm design can vary from simple such as constant gain multiplication, lookup tables and linear equations to more detailed methods based on non-linear functions and optimization over finite prediction horizons.[19] Some of the basic and classic controllers which are widely used in the industry are:

- Lead lag controllers.
- Proportional-Integral-Derivative Controllers.

Some of the complex algorithms used are:

- Non-linear methods: Feedback linearization, Back stepping mode and Sliding mode.
- Optimization methods: Model Predictive Control.

## 11.4 Proportional-Integral-Derivative (PID) Controller

PID control is mathematically formulated by adding three terms dependent on the error function.

- A proportional term directly proportional to error term E.
- An integral term proportional to the integral of error.
- A derivative term proportional to the derivative of error.

In time domain, the PID controller is written as:

$$(t) = K_P e(t) + K_I \int_0^t e(t)dt + K_D e(t)$$

where, $K_P$, $K_I$ and $K_D$ are proportional, integral and derivative gains.

In Laplace domain, the PID controller is written as:

$$U(s) = GC(s)E(s) = (KP + KI/s + KDs)\ E(s) = ((KD\ s^2 + KP\ s + KI)/s)\ E(s)$$

Hence, the PID controller can be finally written as:

$$G_C(s) = (K_D\ s^2 + K_P\ s + K_I)/s$$

Two zeroes added one pole added

From the above equation, following points can be concluded:

- The pole is at origin
- The zeros can be arbitrary places on the complex plane
- PID controller design selects zero locations, by selecting P, I, D gains
- There are several algorithms to select PID gains ( eg: Zeigler- Nicols Algorithm)

### *Characteristics of P, I and D gains*

When $K_P$ increases,

- Rise time decreases
- Overshoot increases
- Small change in Settling time occurs
- Steady state error decreases

When $K_I$ increases,

- Rise time decreases
- Overshoot increases
- Settling time increases
- Steady state error is eliminated

When $K_D$ increases,

- Small change in Rise time occurs
- Overshoot decreases
- Settling time decreases
- Small change in Steady state error occurs

## 11.5 Architecture of Vehicle Control Strategy

The vehicle control architecture is divided into four sections and are connected to each other.

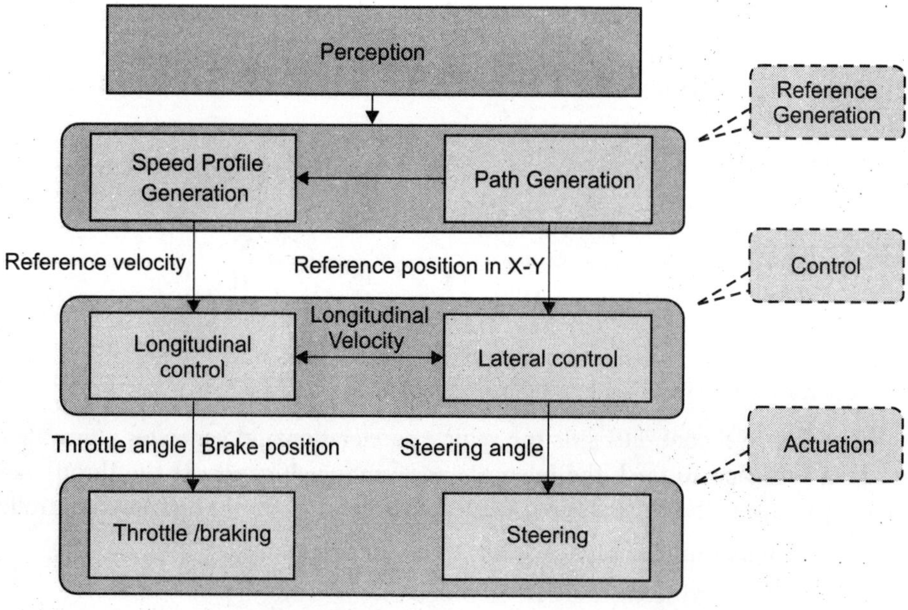


**Appendix.Fig.18:** Architecture of vehicle control

- The first section is the perception of the road and environment.
- The second section is the path generation and speed profile generation, which is known as drive cycle.
- The third section is the Longitudinal and lateral control.
- The fourth section is throttle, braking and steering.

One of the most well-known and commonly available control applications in automotive industry is cruise control vehicles operating on highways.

### *11.5.1 Cruise control systems*

In cruise control system, the speed of the vehicle is controlled by throttling and braking as requested by the driver and the system is kept at reference speeds [22].

The block diagram below shows the cruise controller and the plant model as a closed loop system designed to keep the vehicle velocity close to the reference velocity. The controller can be split into two parts high level controller and low level controller, both of them will be explained in later sections.

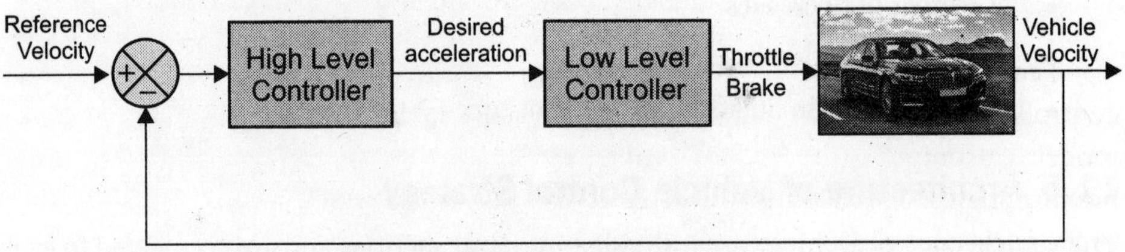


**Appendix.Fig.19:** Block Diagram

The high level controller takes the difference between the set point velocity and the vehicle actual velocity that generates the desired vehicle acceleration to close the gap. It also determines how much acceleration is needed at each time step based on the velocity error[22].

Mathematically, the desired acceleration for high level controller is:

Desired Acceleration  Reference velocity  Vehicle velocity

$$\ddot{x}_{des} = K_P(\dot{x}_{ref} - \dot{x}) + K_I\int_0^t(\dot{x}_{ref} - \dot{x})dt + K_D\frac{d(\dot{x}_{ref} - \dot{x}}{dt}$$

PID Gains

The low level controller gets the vehicle acceleration and generates a throttle or breaking actuation to track the reference acceleration. It generates the throttle and breaking signals to follow the desired acceleration calculated by the high level controller.

The assumptions in defining the low level controller are:

- Only throttle actuations are considered.
- The torque converter is locked.

- The tire slip is small.

In autonomous vehicle its best to apply a feedback as well as a feed forward model since it enables checking the errors from the previous state and giving the values to the next state will generate a much less error free model as compared with a normal machine learning model.

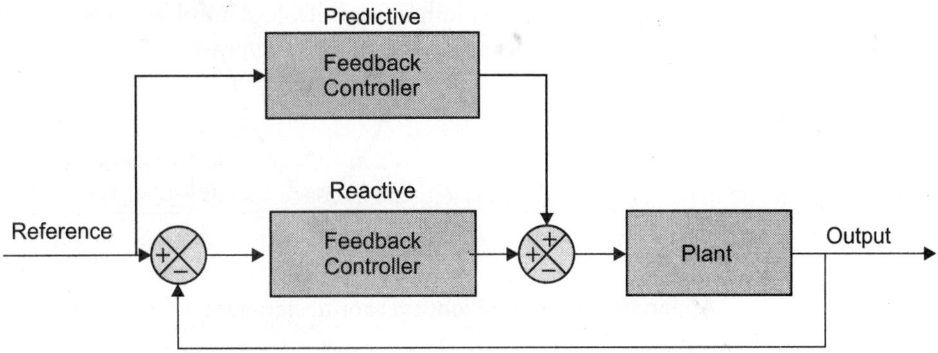


**Appendix.Fig.20:** Combined Feed forward and Feedback Control

Feed forward controller provides predictive response and non-zero offset. Feedback controller corrects the response and compensates for disturbances and errors in the model. The output of the feed forward and feedback control blocks are the throttling or braking angles to accelerate or decelerate the vehicle and keep the vehicle velocity close to the reference velocity. The feed forward controller generates the actuator signals ($u_{ff}$) based on the predefined table and the feedback controller generates the actuator signal ($u_{fb}$) based on the velocity error[22].

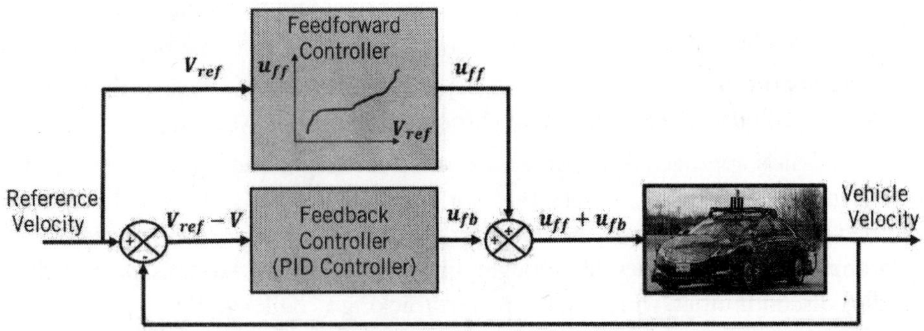


**Appendix.Fig.21:** Steering control

The below graph shows a comparative between PID, PID + feed forward and reference speed of the vehicle. It clearly shows that using feed forward model helps to get a desired result when it is added to the errors generate in PID.

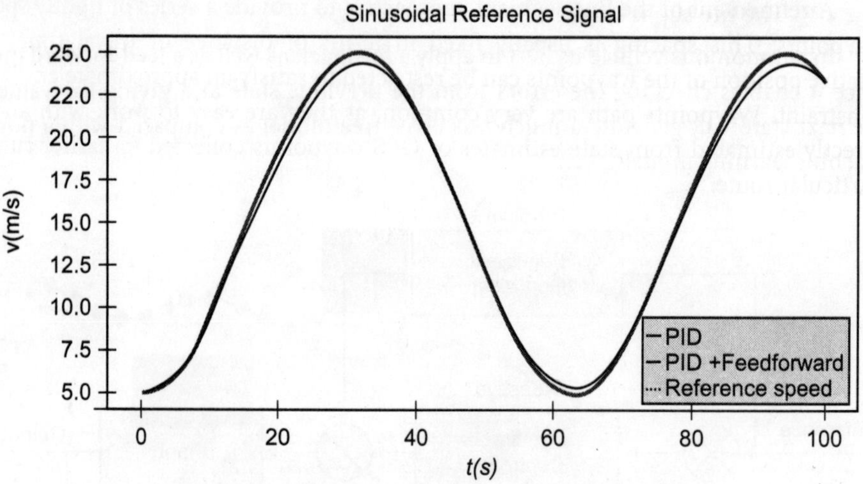


**Appendix.Fig.22:** Feedforward simulation results

## 12. LATERAL VEHICLE CONTROL

The main goal of lateral vehicle control which must select the steering angle required to correct any errors that accumulate and track changes in the path direction as they appear. To design the lateral vehicle controller, following things are taken into consideration:

- The error relative to desired path must be defined.
- A control law must be selected that drives errors to zero and satisfies the input constraints.
- The dynamic considerations to manage forces and moments added to vehicle must be added.

The approach to derive correct turns is classified as reference path for which following methods were formulated in chronological order:

The easiest approach is to define a sequence of straight line segments by requiring a sequence of end point vertices that are connected linearly. This path definition can be very compact and easy to construct, assuming points are well spaced and the environment mostly allows for straight line motion. However, this path includes heading discontinuities, which makes precise tracking a challenge. [23]

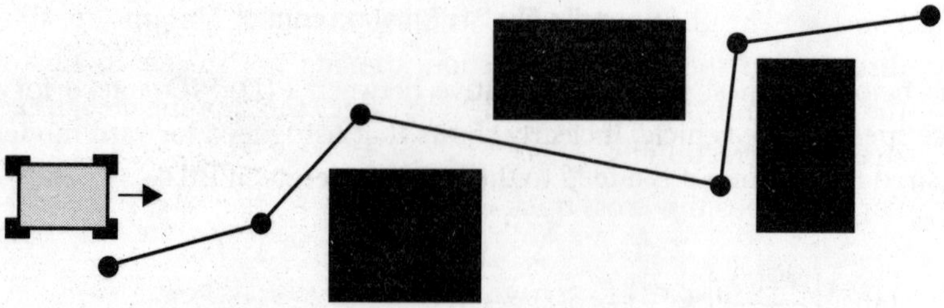

**Appendix.Fig.23:** Straight line segments

A refinement of the line segment approach is to provide a series of tightly spaced waypoints. This spacing is usually fixed in terms of distance or travel time. The relative position of the waypoints can be restricted to satisfy an approximate curvature constraint. Waypoints path are very common, as they are easy to work with and be directly estimated from state estimates or GPS waypoints collected in earlier runs of particular route.

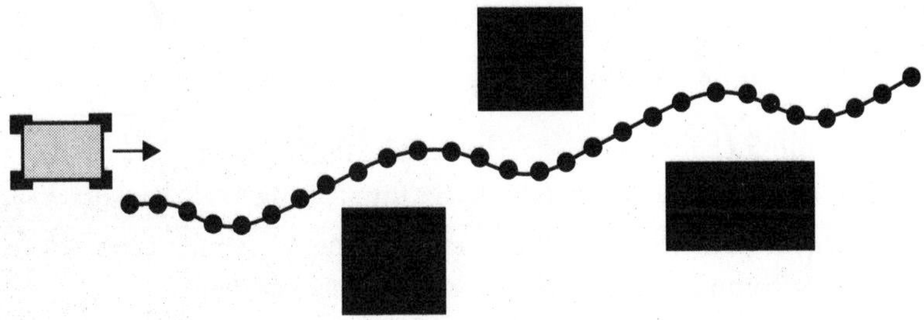

**Appendix.Fig.24:** Waypoints

It is also possible to define a path using a sequence of continuous parameterized curves, which can be either drawn from a set of fixed motion primitives or can be identified through motion planning through optimization. These curves provide the benefit of continuously varying motion and can be constructed to have smooth derivatives to aid in the consistency of error and error rate calculations.

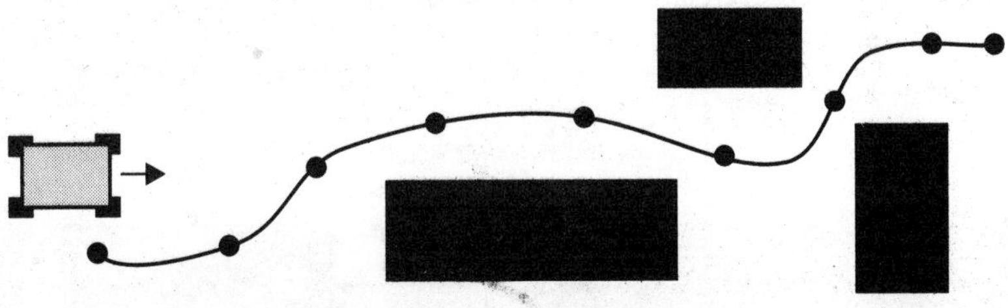

**Appendix.Fig.25:** Parametrized curves

In all cases of path following, the controller tries to eliminate the offset of the vehicle to the desired path and to align the vehicle heading to the path heading.

## 12.1 Control Law

The final control law can be considered in two categories:

- For large heading error, the steering command points in the opposite direction to the heading direction, causing the vehicle to turn to correct the misalignment with the path. The larger the heading error, the larger the steering correction[24].
- For larger positive cross track error,

$$\tan^{-1}\left(\frac{ke(t)}{v_f(t)}\right) \approx \frac{\pi}{2} \rightarrow \delta(t) \approx \psi(t) + \frac{\pi}{2}$$

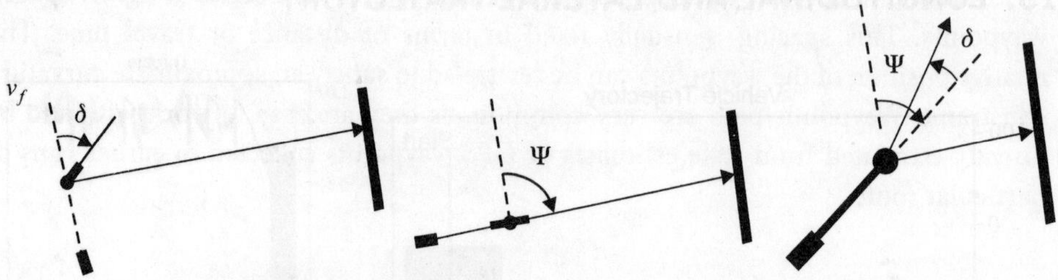


**Appendix.Fig.26:** Larger Positive crosstrack error

- As heading changes into steering angle, the heading correction counteracts the crosstrack correction, and drives the steering angle back to zero.
- When the vehicle approaches the path, the crosstrack error drops and the steering command starts to correct heading alignment[25].

## 12.2 Model Predictive Control (MPC)

The inputs to the MPC block which include the reference path and trajectory, as well as the vehicle states at each time step. The outputs of the MPC block are the lateral and longitudinal forces needed to follow the desired trajectory. These are however converted into throttle, braking and steering command as the output of the low level control. Finally, the actuation signals are applied to the vehicle at each time step and new vehicle state is achieved closing the feedback loop.

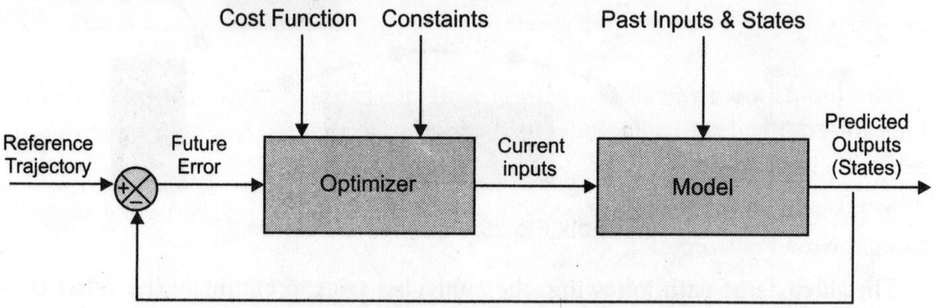


**Appendix.Fig.27:** MPC structure

There are two main blocks, namely, an optimizer block, which is the core MPC component and the dynamic model. The model takes in the past inputs and state from time t minus one and takes in the output of the optimizer which is the current sequence of input U at each time step in the horizon. The model then outputs predicted state at the next time step, which are compared to the reference trajectory and passed into the optimizer as the future or predicted error. The optimizer also receives updated constraints and the cost function to use, which can be fixed in advanced or varied based on changing operating modes. The optimizer then solves its optimization and the process repeats [27].

## 13. LONGITUDINAL AND LATERAL TRAJECTORY

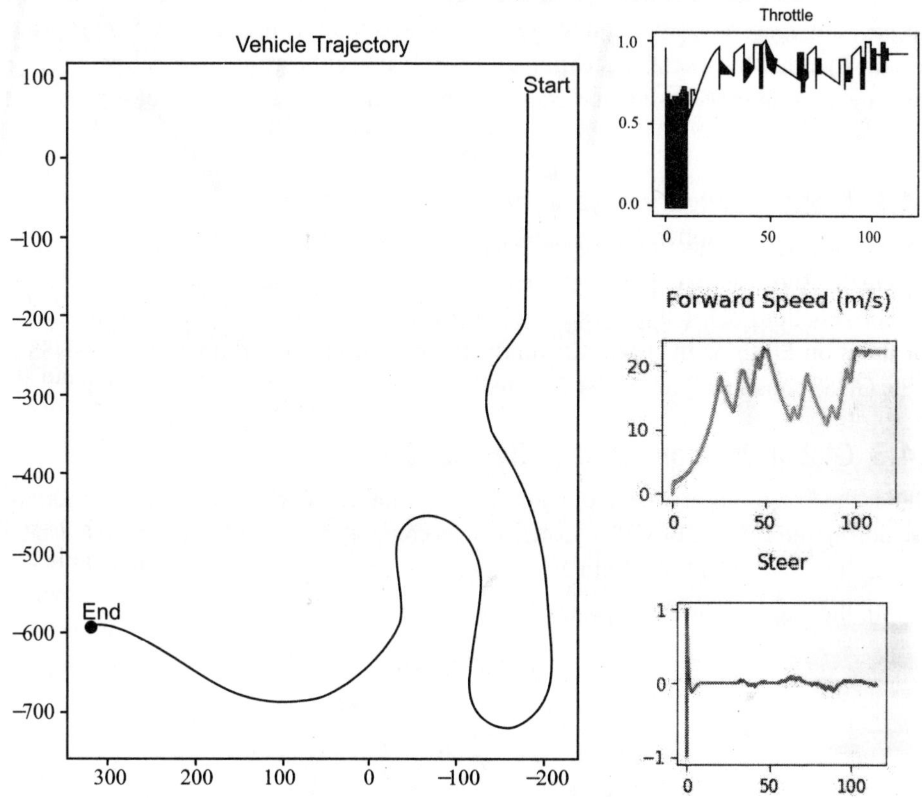


The inputs are given to the python program for generating a trajectory of the vehicle for a defined path. It includes its throttle brakes and steering. The vehicle model is self-sufficient

to take turns and reduce speed on the turns maintaining a particular angle by sensing the road in front of it.

The video demonstration of the car moving around in CARLA simulator based on the theory explained above can be viewed with the following link:

*https://drive.google.com/file/d/1LIncn_OmwHTCIOcmFJNmdhs3s7Mc5QdP/view?usp=sh ar ing*

## 14. SENSORS USED FOR VEHICLE ESTIMATION

There are many sensors that can be used to detect traffic and other obstacles present on the road. These obstacles can be an animal or another vehicle or even the road signs that can have a great impact on prediction of the path.

### 14.1 Inertial Measurement Unit

Inertial Measurement Units (IMU), sensors which comprise accelerometers and gyroscopes that use microcontrollers to process its collected measurements and

Bluetooth modules for system communication, are another technology growing in use for human motion tracking and analysis. [27]. IMUs, like accelerometers, are non-invasive and relatively easy to integrate into a wearable strap, making them appropriate sensors to utilize for wearable technologies aimed at healthcare and rehabilitation since they are capable of assessing and monitoring activities and symptoms of a particular movement disorder [28].

## 14.2 Global Navigation Satellite System (GNSS)

The term Global Navigation Satellite Systems or GNSS is a catch-all term for a satellite system that can be used to pinpoint a receiver's position anywhere in the world [29]. GNSS are constellations of satellites designed to provide positioning and timing information for users on Earth or in space. Currently, the most widely used operational GNSS is GPS. GNSS consists of nominally 24 satellites in approximately 12- hours' orbit [30].

## 14.3 Global Positioning Satellites (GPS)

GPS is the first modern system of Global Positioning Satellites. It was built for military use during the 1980s. The GPS constellation is composed of 24-32 satellites in 6 orbital planes. It has an altitude of about 20,200 kms and an orbital period of 12 hours [31].

In the diagram given below, the 7 satellites are visible:

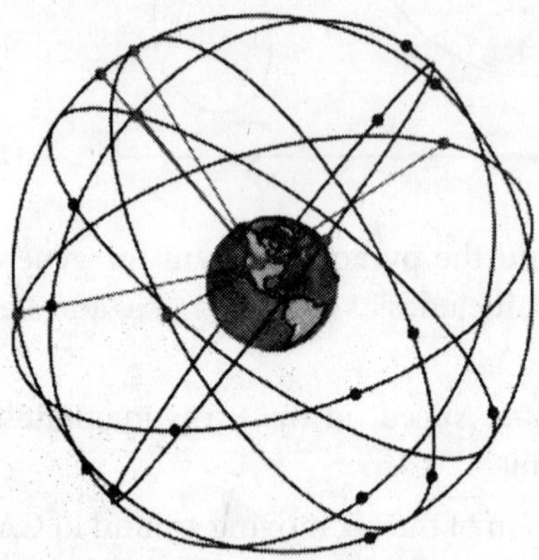

**Appendix.Fig.28:** Satellites broadcasting signals

Each satellite broadcasts on two different frequencies:

- L1 (1575.42 Hz, civilian + military)
- L2 (1227.6 Hz, military)

Each GPS satellite transmits a signal that encodes its position and time of signal transmission. To compute a GPS position fix in the Earth centered frame, the receiver uses the speed of light to compute distances to each satellite based on time of signal arrival. At least 4 satellites are required to solve for 3D position, and two for 2D if altitude is known [32].

## 14.4 LIDAR Sensing

LIDAR or Light Detection and Ranging has been an enabling technology for self-driving cars because it can see in all directions and is able to provide very accurate range information. LIDAR provides detailed 3D scans of the environment around the self-driving car. [33]

A LIDAR Sensor can be easily interpreted as a collection of 3 devices: -

### *Laser*

The laser emits a short pulse of light usually in the near infrared frequency band along some known ray direction. The laser pulse travels outwards from the sensor at the speed of light and hits a distant target. If the surface is too polished or shiny, then the laser pulse will scatter off in all directions and some of the reflected light will travel along the original ray direction.

### *Photodetector*

The main function of the photodetector is to catch a return pulse traveling along the original ray direction.

### *Stopwatch*

The stopwatch measures the time between when the light pulse first is emitted and when the photodetector catches the light pulse. This time is called **round- trip time.**

Hence, the distance using time-of-flight can be measured as:

$$r = 1/2\ c.t$$

Where r is distance, c is speed of light and t is round-trip time.

This technique is known as **time-of-flight ranging** and is applicable to radar and sonars.

## 15. INTERPRETING THE OBJECTS

The LIDAR sends signals in the form of point clouds, these are the signals generated by LIDAR sensors for state estimation. Let's say LIDAR scans a nearby tree off on the side of the road, and produces a point cloud that looks like this:

**Appendix.Fig.29:** LIDAR point clouds

A person can only see the points on the part of the tree that's facing the camera because the tree and leaves reflect infrared light. Using data structures, someone can store the LIDAR data. One common solution is to assign an index to each of the points, say1 through point n, and store the x, y, z co-ordinates of each point as a 3 by 1 column vector. These vectors can now be stored in lists or can be stacked side by side. [34]

The visual representation of storing LIDAR data is:

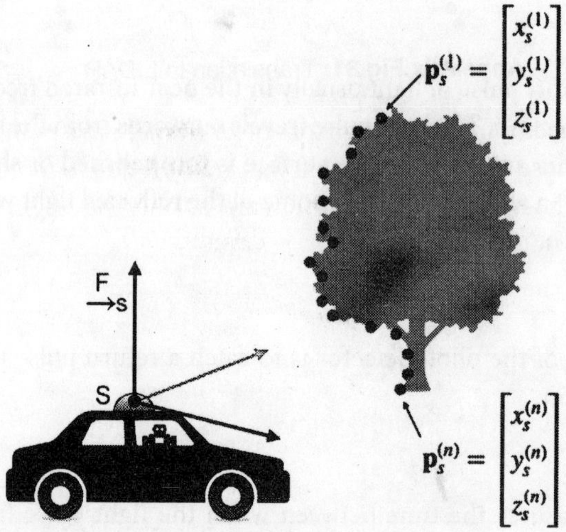


**Appendix.Fig.30:** Storing LIDAR Data

Mathematically, the 3 by 1 column matrix is written as:

$$P_s = \left[P_s^{(1)}\ P_s^{(2)}\ \dots\ P_s^{(n)}\right] = \begin{bmatrix} x_s^{(1)} & x_s^{(2)} & \dots & x_s^{(n)} \\ y_s^{(1)} & y_s^{(2)} & \dots & y_s^{(n)} \\ z_s^{(1)} & z_s^{(2)} & \dots & z_s^{(n)} \end{bmatrix}$$

## 15.1 Operations

There are three basic spatial operations that are important for carrying state estimation with LIDAR point clouds. The spatial operations on clouds mean physically manipulating the cloud while the reference frame stays fixed.

The three operations are dealt in detail below:

### *15.1.1 Translation*

Translating a point cloud means changing the origin of the point cloud while the basis vectors remain same in terms of both magnitude and direction.

The visual representation of translation in LIDAR point clouds is shown:

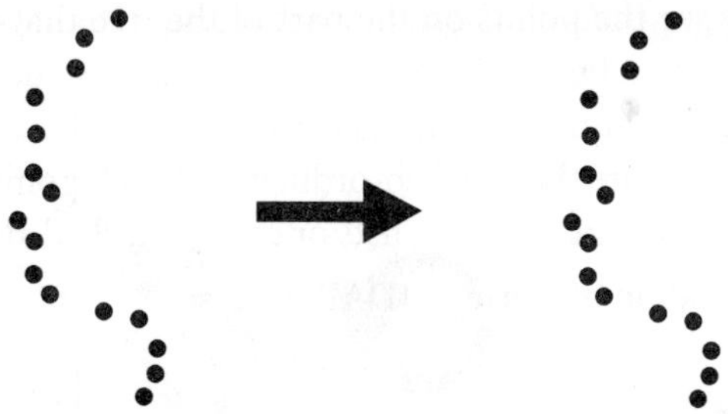

**Appendix.Fig.31:** Translation in LIDAR

For e.g., draw a vector from the origin of sensor frame, S to a point P. Now, consider a second frame, S' whose origin is translated w.r.t frame S due to motion of the vehicle. The basis vectors of the frame S and S' are the same as only the origin has moved. Now, draw another vector from the origin of S' to point P. [35]

Mathematically, the resulting vector is shown as:

$$\underrightarrow{r^{ps'}} = \underrightarrow{r^{ps}} - \underrightarrow{r^{s's}}$$

The resulting vector is represented in the diagram below:

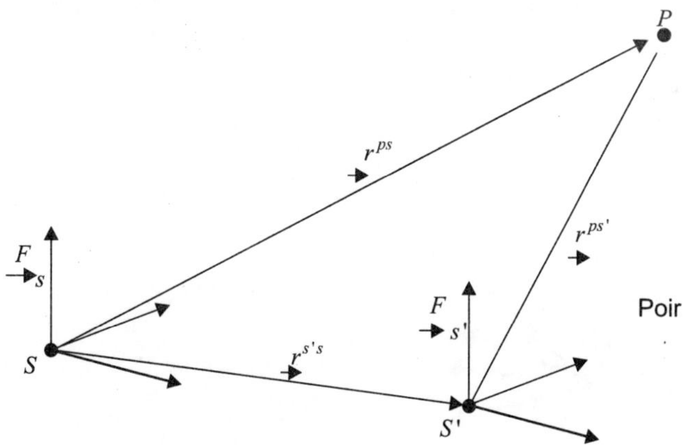


**Appendix.Fig.32:** Vector Translation

The point co-ordinates in the translated frame can be written as:

$$\begin{aligned} P_{s'}^{(j)} &= P_s^{(j)} - P_s^{s's} && \text{each point} \\ P_{s'} &= P_s - R_s^{s's} && \text{whole cloud} \\ R_s^{s's} &= \left[ r_s^{s's} \; r_s^{s's} \; \ldots \; r_s^{s's} \right] \end{aligned}$$

### *15.1.2 Rotation*

Rotating a point cloud means rotating the basis vector while the origin remains the same.

The visual representation of rotation in LIDAR point clouds is shown:

**Appendix.Fig.33:** Rotation in LIDAR

Consider the previous example, the only change will be that the basis vectors are rotated while the origin stays the same. [35] Mathematically, the rotation matrix which rotates co-ordinates from frame S to S' is shown as: $r_{s'} = C_{s's}\ r_s$

The resulting rotated vector is represented in the diagram below:

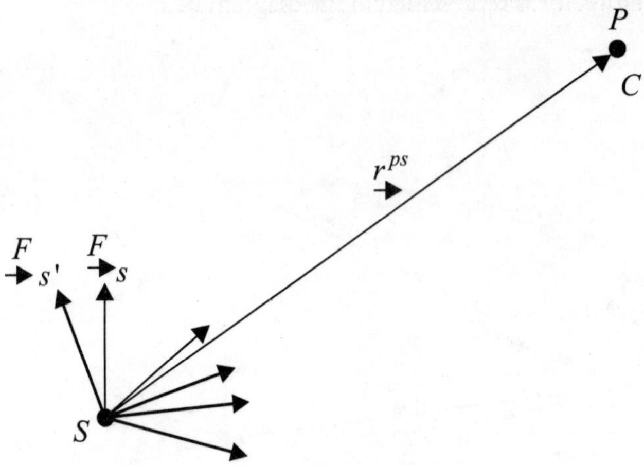


**Appendix.Fig.34:** Rotated vector

The point co-ordinates in the rotated frame are:

$$P_{s'}^{(j)} = C_{s's} - P_s^{(j)} \quad \text{each point}$$

$$P_{s'} = C_{s's} - P_s \quad \text{whole cloud}$$

### *15.1.3 Scaling*

Scaling a point cloud means altering the point cloud by magnifying each point cloud, where basis vectors and origin remain the same. The visual representation of scaling in LIDAR point clouds is shown:

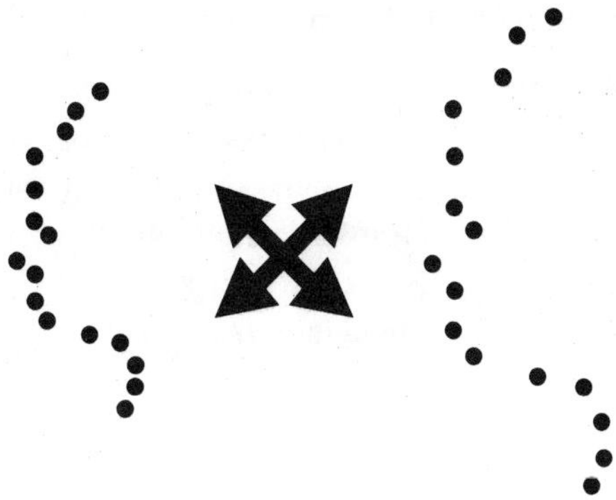

**Appendix.Fig.35:** Scaling in LIDAR

Consider the previous example, the only change will be that the length of the basis vectors will be changed. The scaling matrix is composed of scaling factors for each basis vectors of frames. mathematically, the scaling matrix is shown as:

$$r_{s'} = \underbrace{\begin{bmatrix} s_x & 0 & 0 \\ 0 & s_y & 0 \\ 0 & 0 & s_z \end{bmatrix}}_{S_{s's}} r_s$$

The resulting scaled vector is represented in the diagram below:

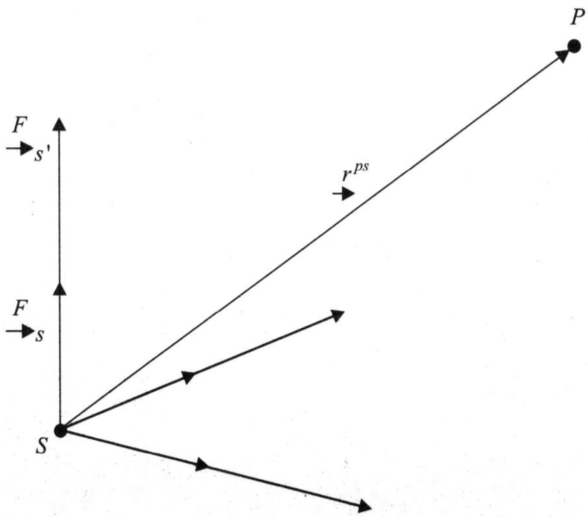


**Appendix.Fig.36:** Scaled vector

The point co-ordinates in the scaled frame are:

$$P_{s'}^{(j)} = S_{s's}\, P_s^{(j)} \quad \text{each point}$$

$$P_{s'} = S_{s's}\, P_s \quad \text{whole cloud}$$

## 15.2 State Estimation

The point set registration problem says that given 2 point clouds in different reference frames, and with the knowledge that they correspond to or contains the same object in the world, align them to determine how the sensor must have moved between the scans. [36] Hence, to find that optimal translation and optimal rotation between the two co-ordinate sensors frames that minimizes the distance between the 2 point clouds. The two reference frames and the point clouds generated by them are shown as:

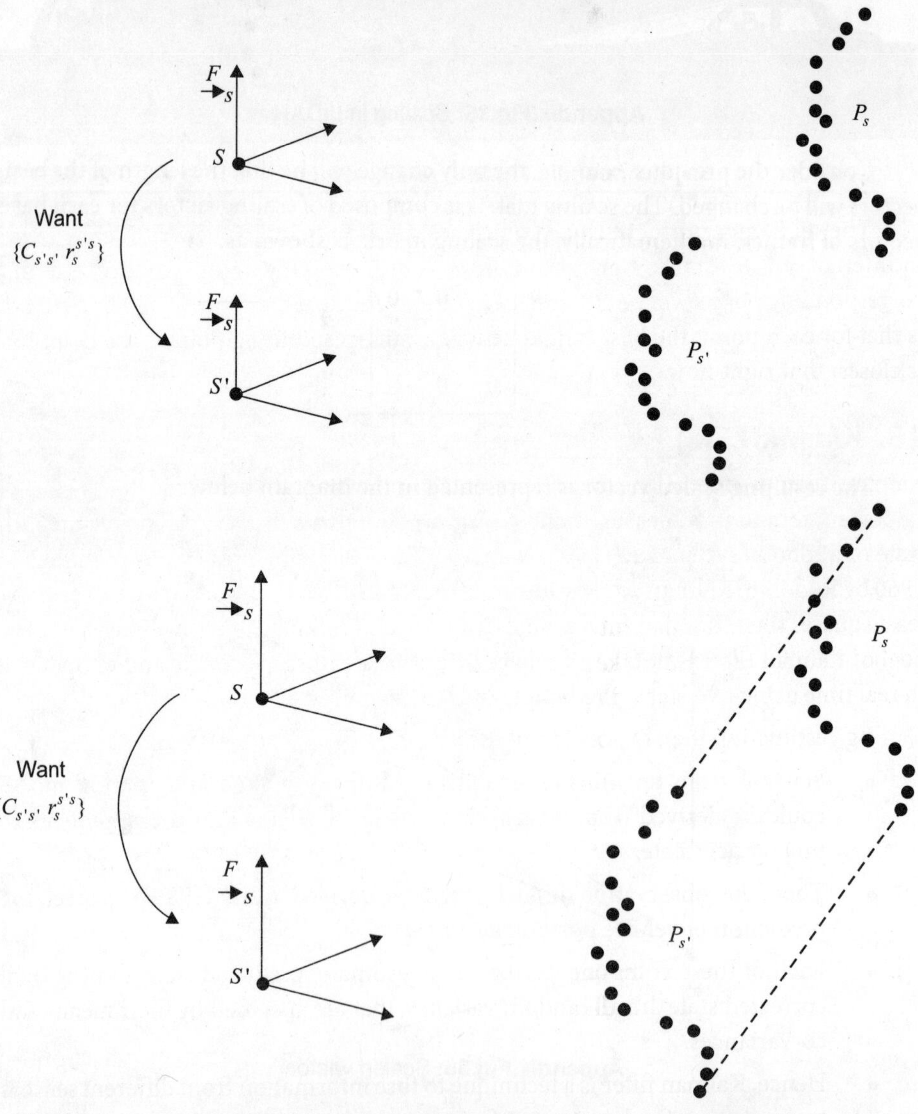


**Appendix.Fig.37:** LIDAR points clouds in S' frame and S frame and their convergence

Until now, it was assumed that the object from which the point cloud is generated by LIDAR was stationary but that is not the case in real world. In real world, the objects are rarely stationary. On the road, the vehicles are moving at particular speeds. In these cases, it might pose the problem for LIDAR to collect point clouds correctly. One way to do this is by fusing ICP motion estimates with the GNSS/INS measurements.

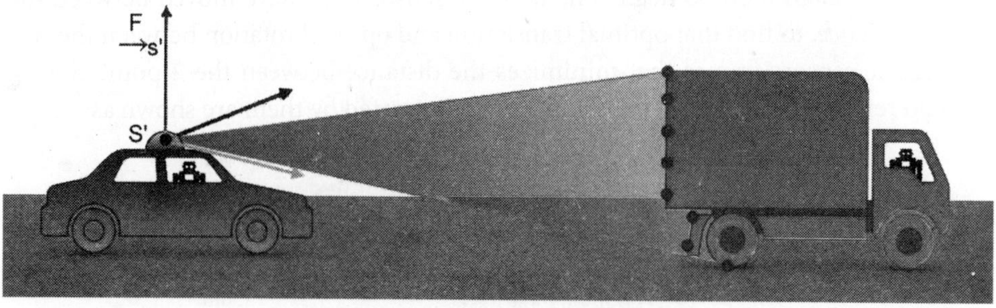


**Appendix.Fig.38:** Objects in motion

The ICP algorithm tells us which cloud points correspond to each other indifferent sensor frames. Here, the intuition is that when the optimal motion is found, corresponding points will be closer to each other than the other points. [36] The heuristic is that for each point, the best candidate for each corresponding point is the point that is closest to it right now.

## 16. KALMAN FILTER

Kalman filter is one of the most famous algorithms in engineering. It remains an important tool to fuse measurements from several sensors to estimate in real-time the state of a robotic system such as a self-driving car. The Kalman filter was published in 1960 by Rudolf E. Kalman. [37] The linear Kalman filter is very similar to linear recursive least squares filter. Kalman filter is able to update and estimate of an evolving state. The goal of Kalman filter is to take a probabilistic estimate of this estimate and to update it in real time using two steps: Prediction and Correction[38].

e.g., estimating the 1D position of the vehicle.

- Starting from an initial probabilistic estimate at time k-1, motion model could be derived from wheel odometry or inertial sensor measurements to predict new state.
- Then the observation model could be derived from GPS to correct the prediction of vehicle position at time k.[39]
- Each of these components, the initial estimate, predicted state and the final corrected state are all random variables that are specified by their means and co-variances.
- Hence, Kalman filter is a technique to fuse information from different sensors to produce a final estimate of some unknown state, taking uncertainty in motion and measurements.

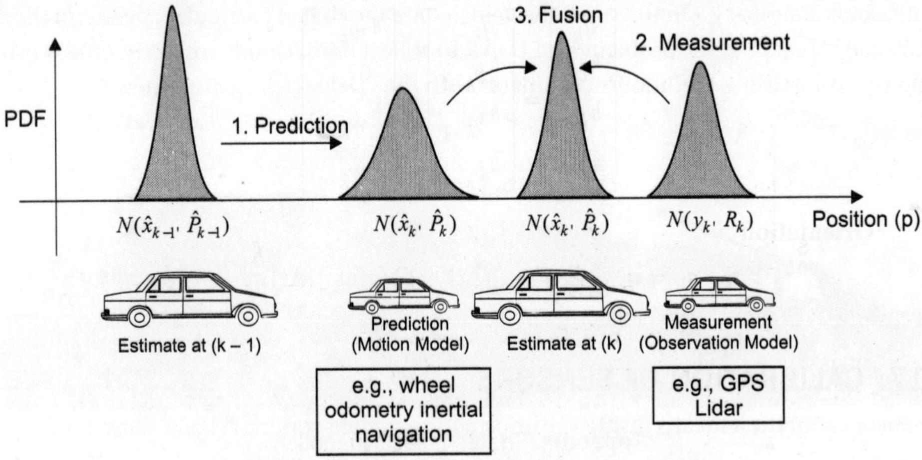


**Appendix.Fig.39:** Prediction and Correction

The IMU measurements are used as noisy inputs to the motion model. This will give a predicted state, which will update every time it has an IMU measurement. This can happen hundreds of times a second. At a much slower rate, it will incorporate GNSS and LIDAR measurements whenever they become available, say once a second or slower, and use them to correct the predicted state. For state, it uses a 10-dimensional state vector that includes a 3D position, a 3D velocity, and a 4D unit quaternion that will represent the orientation of the vehicle with respect to a navigation frame [40].

$$x_k = \begin{bmatrix} p_k \\ v_k \\ q_k \end{bmatrix} \in R^{10}$$

**Vehicle state** consists of position, velocity and parameterization of orientation using a unit quaternion:

**Position of the vehicle**

$$p_k = p_{k-1} + \Delta t v_{k-1} + \frac{\Delta t^2}{2}(C_{ns} f_{k-1} + g)$$

**Motion model** input will consist of specific force and rotational rates from our IMU:

$$u_k = \begin{bmatrix} f_k \\ \omega_k \end{bmatrix} \in R^6$$

**Velocity of the vehicle**

$$v_k = v_{k-1} + \Delta t\left(C_{ns} f_{k-1} + g\right)$$

**Quaternion Model** that will represent the orientation of the vehicle with respect to a navigation frame [41].

$$\begin{bmatrix} \bar{q}_k \\ {}^h b_k \\ {}^h \dot{b}_k \\ {}^g b_k \end{bmatrix} = \begin{bmatrix} \bar{q}_{k-1} \\ {}^h b_{k-1} \\ {}^h \dot{b}_{k-1} \\ {}^g b_{k-1} \end{bmatrix} + \begin{bmatrix} {}^q w_{k-1} \\ 0_{3\times1} \\ {}^h w_{k-1} \\ {}^g w_{k-1} \end{bmatrix}$$

**Orientation**

$$q_k = q_{k-1} \otimes q(\omega_{k-1}\Delta t) = \Omega\left(q(\omega_{k-1}\Delta t\right) q_{k-1}$$

## 17. CALIBRATION OF SENSORS

Sensor calibration means fusing the information or data coming from different sensors.

### 17.1 Intrinsic Calibration

This type of calibration deals with sensors specific parameters. In intrinsic calibration, we want to determine the fixed parameters of our sensor models, so that we can use them in an estimator like an extended Kalman filter. Every sensor has parameters associated with it that are unique to that specific sensor and are typically expected to be constant. For example, we might have an encoder attached to one axle of the car that measures the wheel rotation rate omega. If we want to use omega to estimate the forward velocity v of the wheel, we would need to know the radius R of the wheel, so that we can use this in the equation v equals omega times R. In this case, R is a parameter of the sensor model that is specific to the wheel the encoder is attached to and we might have a different R for a different wheel. [42]

**The strategies for determining intrinsic parameters are:**

- Manufacturer specifications: The easiest one is to let the manufacturer do the work. Sensors are often calibrated in factory, but this is not good enough to do state estimation.
- Measure by hand: This strategy involves more work as it suggests to measure the sensor parameters by hand which is not very easy.
- Estimate as part of the state: A more sophisticated approach involves estimating the intrinsic parameters as part of the vehicle state, either on the fly or more commonly as a special calibration step before putting the sensors into operation. This approach has the advantage of producing an accurate calibration that's specific to the particular sensor and can also be formulated in a way that can handle the parameters varying slowly over time. [43]

### 17.2 Extrinsic Calibration

Extrinsic calibration is equally important for fusing information from multiple sensors. In extrinsic calibration, the relative poses of all the sensors are determined w.r.t vehicle frame. For example, if we need to know the relative pose of IMU and LIDAR. So the rates reported by the IMU are expressed in the same coordinate system as the LIDAR point clouds. [44]

The strategies for determining intrinsic parameters are:

- CAD model: The CAD model of the vehicle is a powerful tool for determining extrinsic parameters where all the sensors are nicely laid.
- Measure by hand: This strategy involves more work as it suggests to measure the sensor parameters by hand which is not very easy.
- Estimate as part of the state: This can become a bit complicated for arbitrary sensor configurations, and there is still a lot of research being done into different techniques for doing this reliably. [45]

## 17.3 Temporal Calibration

An often overlooked but still important type of calibration is temporal calibration. We have assumed that in multisensory fusion, all of the measurements are captured exactly the same moment in time or at least close enough for a given level of accuracy. Here, it is important to check that two measurements are close enough to be synchronized. To do so, we would have to timestamp each measurement when the on-board computer receives it, and match up the measurements that are close to each other. [46]

The strategies for developing a better estimator are:

- Assume zero delays: The delay occurs when a sensor actually records the measurement and the time it receives the computer. By assuming this time delay to be zero, we can still get a better estimator though it won't be accurate enough [47].
- Hardware Synchronization: Another common strategy is to use hardware timing signals to synchronize the sensors but this strategy implementation is expensive.
- Estimate as part of the state: It is possible to solve the time delays as part of the state but it is a complicated strategy.

## 17.4 Range of Sensors

For sensors that observe the external world like LIDARs, SONAR, cameras or RADARs, their sensing range plays a very important role in safe operation. Most cars have long, medium, and short range sensing. If one of these malfunctions, it's often important to restrict movement so the malfunction doesn't affect safety. For example, in localization, we may use short range sensors for parking and to ensure we're not colliding with nearby vehicles. Medium range sensors may help in pedestrian and cyclist detection and in lane keeping. Longer one of thesefails, we have to take appropriate [48].

## 17.5 Case Study

As an example of a redundant system, consider the primary flight computer of the Boeing 777. The 777 operates on a triple redundancy principle. All major systems, including this flight computer, have two backups, each with independent power and separate programming and specifications. Here it can be seen that each of the flight computers has a different processor to ensure that a bug in the architecture itself doesn't affect all three computers. If one of the computers fails or malfunctions, the 777 uses a consensus algorithm to seamlessly switch to another one [49].

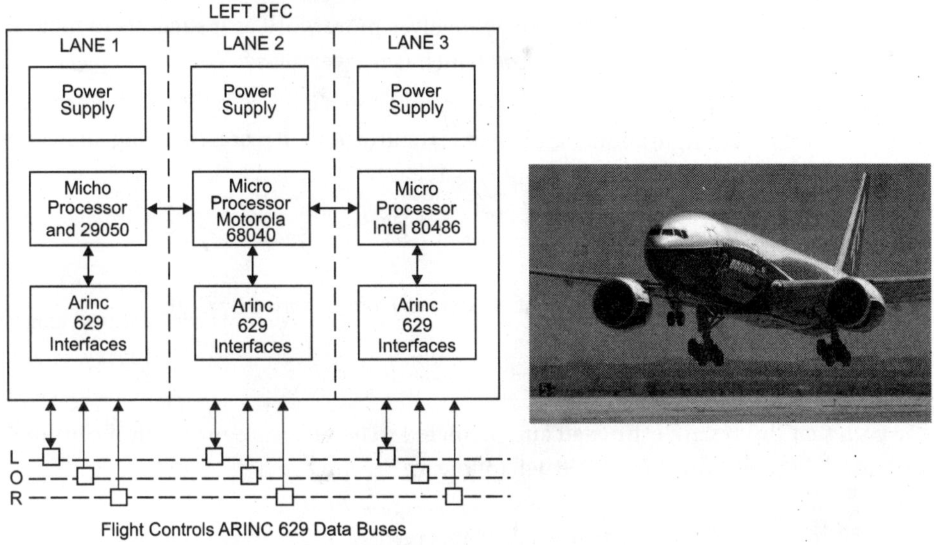


**Appendix.Fig.40:** Case Study of Boeing 777

## 18. VEHICLE'S VISUAL ODOMETRY

Visual odometry refers to the process of estimating a vehicle's 3D motion from visual imagery alone without considering the objects or motion hindrances. Visual odometry estimates local motion and generally has unbounded global drift. To bound estimation error, it can be integrated with simultaneous localization and mapping (SLAM) algorithms like Kalman Filter algorithm, which employ loop closing techniques to detect when a vehicle revisits a previous location. As loops are detected, a common approach is to construct a pose graph representing the spatial relationships and constraints linking previously observed viewpoints. Optimization of this pose graph results in a globally aligned set of frames. Following are the generated odometry of the vehicle model.

### 18.1 Ground Truth Trajectory

The path below shows the ground how the road looks to the vehicle and the trajectory that it has to follow. It is a 3 dimensional model representation of the 2 dimensional road model for better understanding since it enables to move the trajectory path over the ground plan or the X axis.

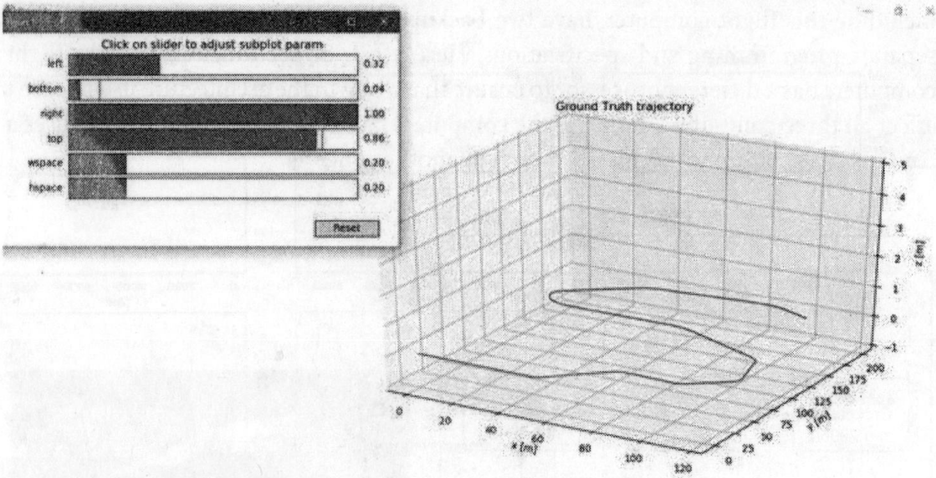


**Appendix.Fig.41:** Output of Ground Truth obtained by Carla

## 18.2 Estimated path

The path that the system estimated and predicted to be in accordance with the ground truth model shows how the vehicle will follow it.

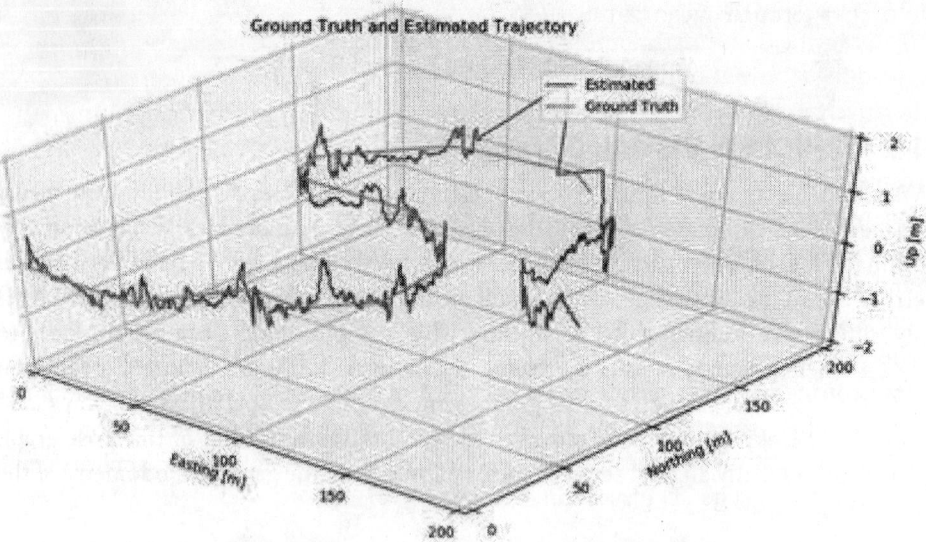


**Appendix.Fig.42:** The estimated path created for the vehicle model

Below are the error plots obtained after the creation of estimated trajectory of the vehicle model where the red lines represent the standard deviation of the model and blue the estimated motion about it.

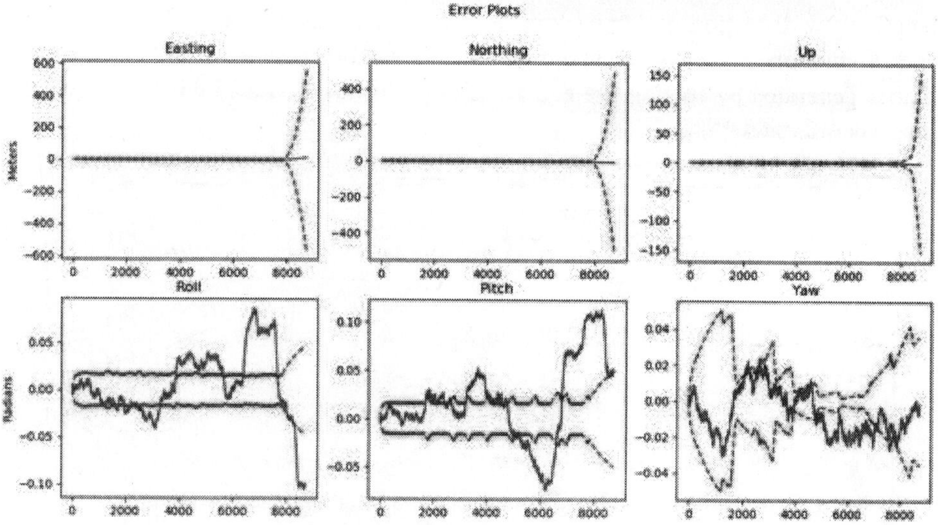


**Appendix.Fig.43:** Error Plots

## 19. CAMERA SENSOR

To help improve the error plots it's better to switch to a much safer and secure option by using cameras to detect the objects rather than focusing on other technologies. The camera is an important sensor that captures detailed appearance information of the things in front of the sensor. It has a very high rate of information capture and is relatively inexpensive. It is the most important sensor required for image formation. A modern day camera is a camera that captures photographs in digital memory [50]. Most cameras produced today are digital, and while there are still dedicated digital cameras, many more cameras are now incorporated into mobile devices like smartphones, which can, among many other purposes, use their cameras to initiate live video-telephony and directly edit and upload image to others [51]. Thus, modern cameras can serve the purpose of image capturing in relatively low cost and maintenance. The 3D points in the world coordinate frame can be projected to 2D points in the image coordinate frame using projective geometry equations. The autonomous vehicle needs to model the camera's projective geometry through coordinate system transformation [52]. The self-driving car models these transformations using matrix algebra and applies them to a 3D point to get its 2D projection on the image plane.

$$0_{image} = \begin{bmatrix} f & 0 & u_0 \\ 0 & f & v_0 \\ 0 & 0 & 1 \end{bmatrix} 0_{camera} = K0_{camera}$$

### 19.1 Camera Calibration

Camera calibration is the process of estimating intrinsic and/or extrinsic parameters. Intrinsic parameters deal with the camera's internal characteristics, such as, its focal length, skew, distortion, and image centre [53]. Extrinsic parameters describe its position and orientation in the world. These parameters can be extracted from the camera P matrix generated by solving the equations of projection of world coordinates to the image coordinates [54].

$$\begin{bmatrix} X_1 & Y_1 & Z_1 & 1 & 0 & 0 & 0 & 0 & -u_1X_1 & -u_1Y_1 & -u_1Z_1 & -u_1 \\ 0 & 0 & 0 & 0 & X_1 & Y_1 & Z_1 & 1 & -v_1X_1 & -v_1Y_1 & -v_1Z_1 & -v_1 \\ \vdots & \vdots & \vdots & \vdots & \vdots & \vdots & \vdots & \vdots & \vdots & \vdots & \vdots & \vdots \\ X_N & Y_N & Z_N & 1 & 0 & 0 & 0 & 0 & -u_NX_N & -u_NY_N & -u_NZ_N & -u_N \\ 0 & 0 & 0 & 0 & X_N & Y_N & Z_N & X_1 & -v_NX_N & -v_NY_N & -v_NZ_N & -v_N \end{bmatrix} \begin{bmatrix} p_{11} \\ p_{12} \\ p_{13} \\ p_{14} \\ p_{21} \\ p_{22} \\ p_{23} \\ p_{24} \\ p_{31} \\ p_{32} \\ p_{33} \\ p_{34} \end{bmatrix} = 0$$

## 20. STEREOPSIS

**Stereopsis is a term that is most often used to refer to the perception of depth and 3-dimensional structure obtained on the basis of visual information deriving from two cameras like by an individual with normally developed binocular vision.** A stereo camera sensor is constructed from two identical cameras aligned to produce a binocular vision. The two cameras have parallel optical axes and they project to Bird's eye view for easier geometry [55].

### *A Basic Stereo Algorithm*

**Given:** Rectified Images and Stereo Calibration.

For each epipolar line (the blue lines in above diagram),

1. Take each pixel on this line in the left image
2. Compare these left image pixels to every pixel in the right image on the same epipolar line
3. Pick the pixel that has minimum cost
4. Compute disparity, ***d***

## 21. IMAGE FILTERING

Image Filtering is a technique for modifying or enhancing an image. For example, we can filter an image to emphasize certain features or remove other features. Image processing operations implemented with filtering include smoothing, sharpening, and edge enhancement [56].

## 21.1 Feature Detection

Image Features are points of interest in an image. Points of interest should have the following characteristics:

- Saliency: distinctive, identifiable, and different from its immediate neighbourhood
- Repeatability: can be found in multiple images using same operations
- Locality: occupies a relatively small subset of image space
- Quantity: enough points represented in the image
- Efficiency: reasonable computation time

## 21.2 Feature Extraction

Repetitive texture less patches are challenging to detect consistently. Patches with large contrast changes (gradients) are easier to detect (edges). Gradients in at least two (significantly) different orientations are the easiest to detect (corners) [57].

## 21.3 Principle Component Analysis (PCA) for feature extraction

PCA is one of the most used linear dimensionality reduction technique. When using PCA, we take as input our original data and try to find a combination of the input features which can best summarize the original data distribution so that to reduce its original dimensions. PCA is able to do this by maximizing variances and minimizing the reconstruction error by looking at pair wised distances. In PCA, our original data is projected into a set of orthogonal axes and each of the axes gets ranked in order of importance [58].

## 21.4 Harris Interest Point Detection

Harris corner detector was proposed by Chris and Mike. Harris operator is an improvement of a basic technique of Principle Component Analysis. The PCA corner detector is one of the earliest corner detection algorithms and it defines interest points as points where there is a large intensity variation in every direction. The algorithm tests each pixel in the image to see if a corner is present. They proposed measuring the intensity variation by placing a small square window and then shifting this window by one pixel in each of the eight principle directions such as two horizontal, two vertical and four diagonal directions. The intensity variation for a given shift is calculated by taking the sum of squares of intensity differences of corresponding pixels in these two windows [59].

# 22. CONVOLUTION NEURAL NETWORKS

Convolutional Neural Networks (ConvNets or CNNs) are a category of Neural Networks that have proven very effective in areas such as image recognition and classification. ConvNets have been successful in identifying faces, objects and traffic signs apart from powering vision in robots and self-driving cars [60].

Deep Feedforward networks or also known multilayer perceptrons are the foundation of most deep learning models. Networks like CNNs and RNNs are just some special cases of Feedforward networks. These networks are mostly used for supervised machine learning tasks where we already know the target function i.e. the result we want our network to achieve and are extremely important for practicing machine learning and form the basis of many commercial applications, areas such as computer vision and NLP were greatly affected by the presence of these networks. [61]

The main goal of a feedforward network is to approximate some function f*. For example, a regression function y = f *(x) maps an input x to a value y. A feedforward network defines a mapping y = f (x; θ) and learns the value of the parameters θ that result in the best function approximation. [60]

The reason these networks are called feedforward is that the flow of information takes place in the forward direction, as x is used to calculate some intermediate function in the hidden layer which in turn is used to calculate y. In this, if we add feedback from the last hidden layer to the first hidden layer it would represent a recurrent neural network.

These networks are represented by a composition of many different functions. Each model is associated with an acyclic graph describing how the functions are composed together. For example, we might have three functions f(1), f(2), and f(3) connected in a chain, to form,

$$f(x) = f(3)(f(2)(f(1)(x)))$$

In this f(1) is the first layer, f(2) is the second layer and f(3) is the output layer.

The layers between the input layer and output layers are known as hidden layers, as the training data does not show the desired output for these layers. A network can contain any number of hidden layers with any number of hidden units. A unit basically resembles a neuron which takes input from units of previous layers and computes its own activation value. [62]

Now a question arises that why we need feed-forward networks when we have linear machine learning models, this is due to the fact that linear models are limited to only linear functions whereas neural networks aren't. When our data isn't linear separable linear models face problems in approximating whereas it is pretty easy for the neural networks. The hidden layers are used to increase the non-linearity and change the representation of the data for better generalization over the function [63].

A Feedforward Neural Network defines a mapping from input x to output y as:

$$Y = f(x; \theta)$$

- An N layer FNN is represented as the function composition:

$$f(x; \theta) = f^{(N)}\left(f^{(N-1)}\left(...f^{(2)}\left(f^{(1)}(x)\right)\right)\right)$$

- x is called the input layer

- The final function f(N) is called the output layer
- The functions f (1) to f(N-1) are called the hidden layers

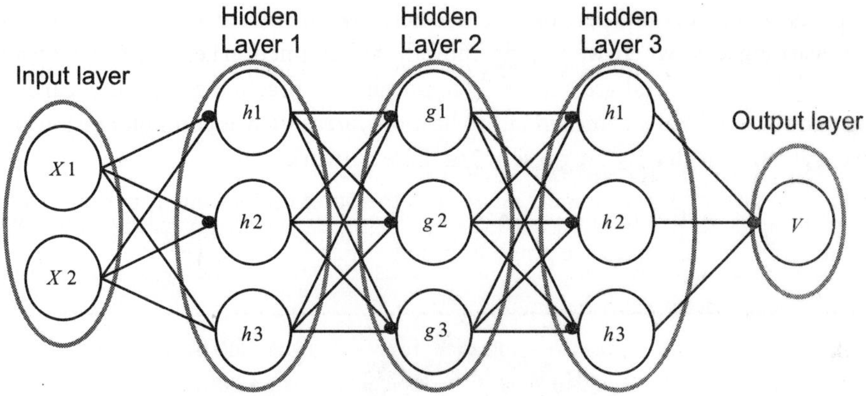


**Appendix.Fig.44:** Feedforward Neural Networks

## 22.1 Activation Function

It's just a function that we use to get the output of node. It is also known as Transfer Function. It is used to determine the output of neural network like yes or no. It maps the resulting values in between 0 to 1 or -1 to 1 etc. (depending upon the function). [64]

The Activation Functions can be basically divided into 2 types-

1. Linear Activation Function
2. Non-linear Activation Functions

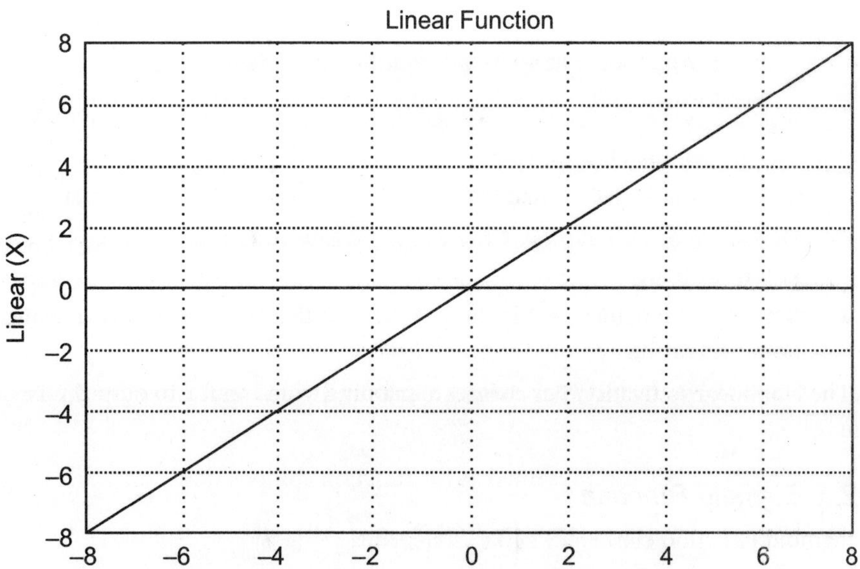


**Appendix.Fig.45:** Linear Activation Function

Linear or Identity Activation Function: As we can see the function is a line or linear. Therefore, the output of the functions will not be confined between any ranges.

Equation: f(x) = x

Range: (-infinity to infinity)

It doesn't help with the complexity or various parameters of usual data that is fed to the neural networks [65].

## 22.2 Non Linear Activation Function

The Nonlinear Activation Functions are the most used activation functions. Nonlinearity helps to makes the graph look something like this:

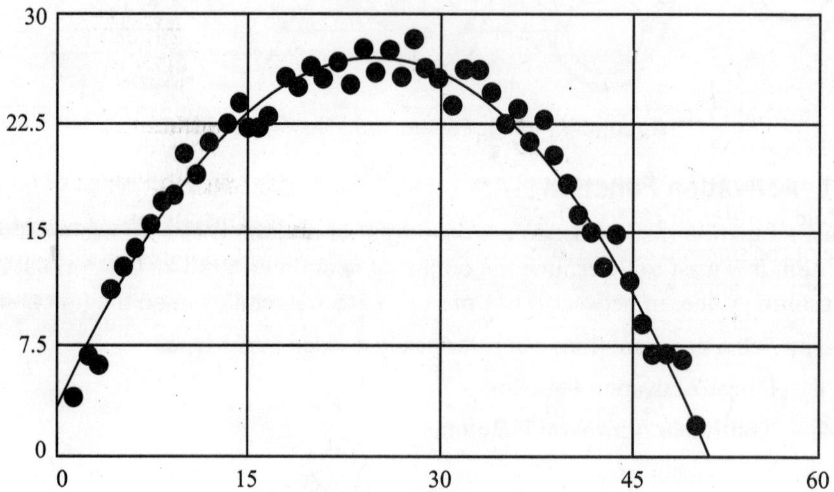


**Appendix.Fig.46:** Non-Linear Activation Function

It makes it easy for the model to generalize or adapt with variety of data and to differentiate between the outputs [66].

The main terminologies needed to understand for nonlinear functions are:

- Derivative or Differential: Change in y-axis w.r.t. change in x-axis. It is also known as slope.
- Monotonic function: A function which is either entirely non-increasing or non- decreasing.

The Nonlinear Activation Functions are mainly divided on the basis of their range or curves-

### *22.2.1 Sigmoid Function*

The Sigmoid Function curve looks like an S-shape.

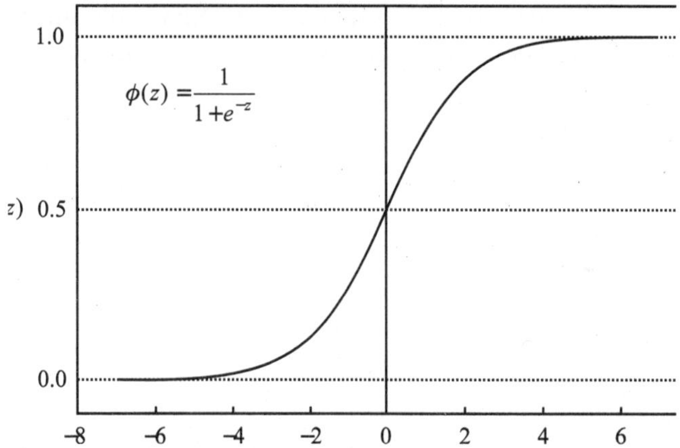


**Appendix.Fig.47:** Sigmoid Activation Function

The main reason why we use sigmoid function is because it exists between (0 to 1). Therefore, it is especially used for models where we have to predict the probability as an output. Since probability of anything exists only between the range of 0 and 1, sigmoid is the right choice. The function is differentiable. That means, we can find the slope of the sigmoid curve at any two points. The function is monotonic but function's derivative is not. The logistic sigmoid function can cause a neural network to get stuck at the training time. The softmax function is a more generalized logistic activation function which is used for multiclass classification. [67]

### 22.2.2 Tanh Activation Function

Tanh is also like logistic sigmoid but better. The range of the tanh function is from (-1 to 1). tanh is also sigmoidal (s–shaped).

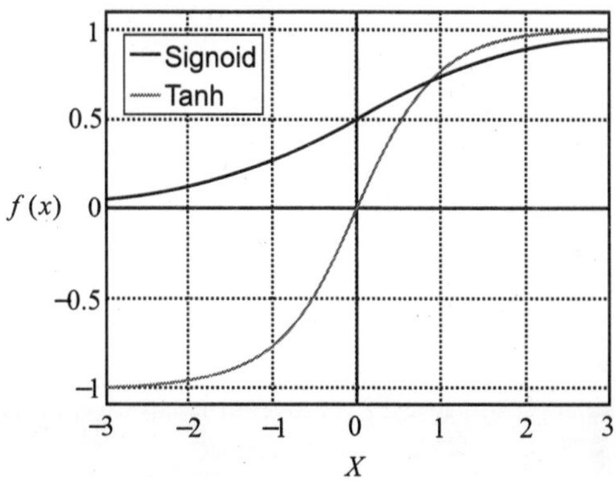


**Appendix.Fig.48:** Tanh Activation Function

The advantage is that the negative inputs will be mapped strongly negative and the zero inputs will be mapped near zero in the tanh graph. The function is differentiable. The function is monotonic while its derivative is not monotonic. The tanh function is mainly used classification between two classes. [68] Both tanh and logistic sigmoid activation functions are used in feed-forward nets.

### 22.2.3 ReLU Activation Function

The ReLU is the most used activation function in the world right now. Since, it is used in almost all the convolutional neural networks or deep learning.

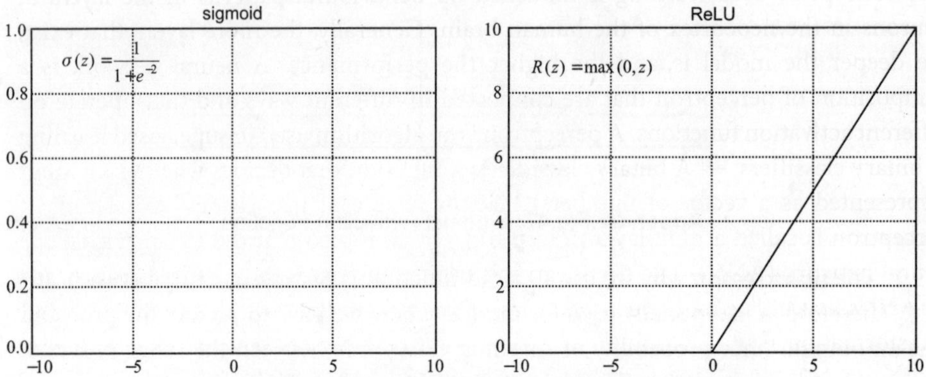


**Appendix.Fig.49:** Sigmoid v/s ReLU Activation Function

As we can see, the ReLU is half rectified (from bottom). f(z) is zero when z is less than zero and f(z) is equal to z when z is above or equal to zero. [69] Range: (0 to infinity)

The function and its derivative both are monotonic. But the issue is that all the negative values become zero immediately which decreases the ability of the model to fit or train from the data properly. That means any negative input given to the ReLU activation function turns the value into zero immediately in the graph, which in turns affects the resulting graph by not mapping the negative values appropriately. [70]

### 22.2.4 Leaky ReLU

It is an attempt to solve the dying ReLU problem.

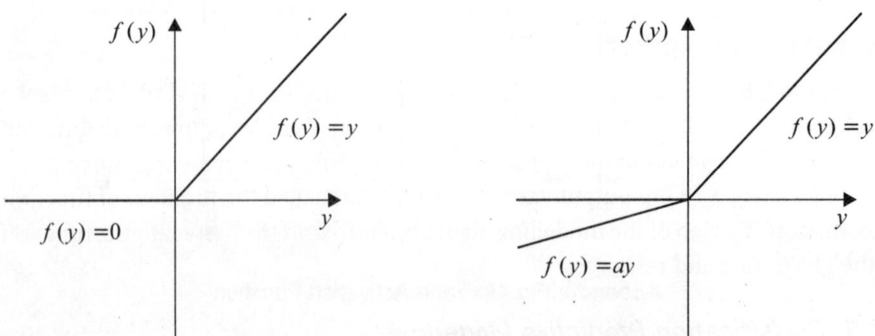


**Appendix.Fig.50:** ReLU v/s Leaky ReLU

The leak helps to increase the range of the ReLU function. Usually, the value of a is 0.01 or so. When a is not 0.01 then it is called Randomized ReLU. Therefore, the range of the Leaky ReLU is (-infinity to infinity). Both Leaky and Randomized ReLU functions are monotonic in nature. Also, their derivatives also monotonic in nature. [71]

## 23. OUTPUT LAYERS AND LOSS FUNCTIONS

The concept of deep learning is modelled on behavioural patterns in the layers of neurons in the neocortex of the human brain. Generally, the more layers that exist, the deeper the model is, and the higher the performance. A neural network is a composition of perceptron that are connected in different ways and that operate on different activation functions. A perceptron is an algorithm used in supervised learning of binary classifiers. [72] A binary classifier is a function that decides whether an input (represented as a vector of numbers) belongs in one of two classes. A network of perceptron is called a multilayer perceptron, which is also referred to as an artificial neural network (ANN). The deep learning architecture used today is primarily based on ANNs that utilize multiple layers of nonlinear processing for feature extraction and transformation. [73]

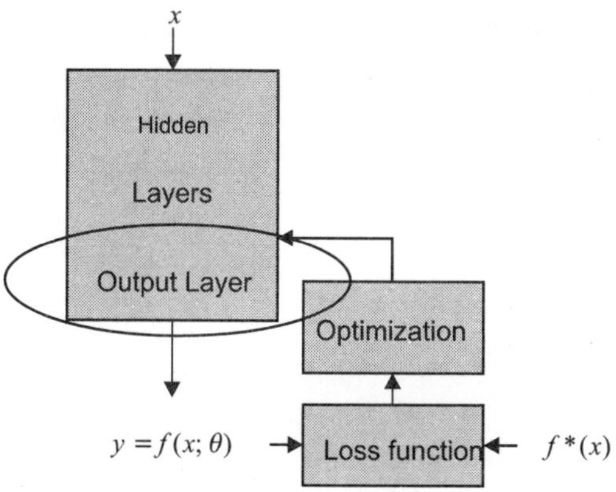


**Appendix.Fig.51:** Artificial Neural Network and Loss Function

### 23.1 Functional Approximation

Predictive modelling is the problem of developing a model using historical data to make a prediction on new data where we do not have the answer. Predictive modelling can be described as the mathematical problem of approximating a mapping function (f) from input variables (X) to output variables (y). This is called the problem of function approximation. The job of the modelling algorithm is to find the best mapping function with the given time and resources. [74]

#### *23.1.1 Classification Predictive Modelling*

Classification predictive modelling is the task of approximating a mapping function (f) from input variables (X) to discrete output variables (y).The output variables are often called labels or categories. The mapping function predicts the class or category for a given observation. [75]

### 23.1.2 Regression Predictive Modelling

Regression predictive modelling is the task of approximating a mapping function (f) from input variables (X) to a continuous output variable (y). A continuous output variable is a real-value, such as an integer or floating point value. These are often quantities, such as amounts and sizes. [75]

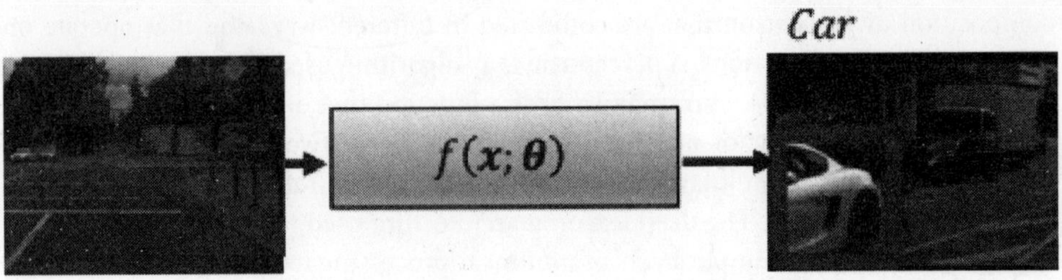


**Appendix.Fig.52:** Function Approximation

### 23.1.3 Softmax Function

Softmax function is often described as a combination of multiple sigmoids. We know that sigmoid returns values between 0 and 1, which can be treated as probabilities of a data point belonging to a particular class. Thus sigmoid is widely used for binary classification problems. [76]

The softmax function can be used for multiclass classification problems. This function returns the probability for a data point belonging to each individual class. Here is the mathematical expression of the same-

$$\sigma(z)_j = \frac{e^{z_j}}{\sum_{k=1}^{K} e^{z_k}} \quad \text{for } j = 1, \ldots, K.$$

While building a network for a multiclass problem, the output layer would have as many neurons as the number of classes in the target. For instance, if we have three classes, there would be three neurons in the output layer. Suppose we got the output from the neurons as [1.2, 0.9, 0.75].

Applying the softmax function over these values, we will get the following result – [0.42, 0.31, 0.27]. These represent the probability for the data point belonging to each class. Note that the sum of all the values is 1.

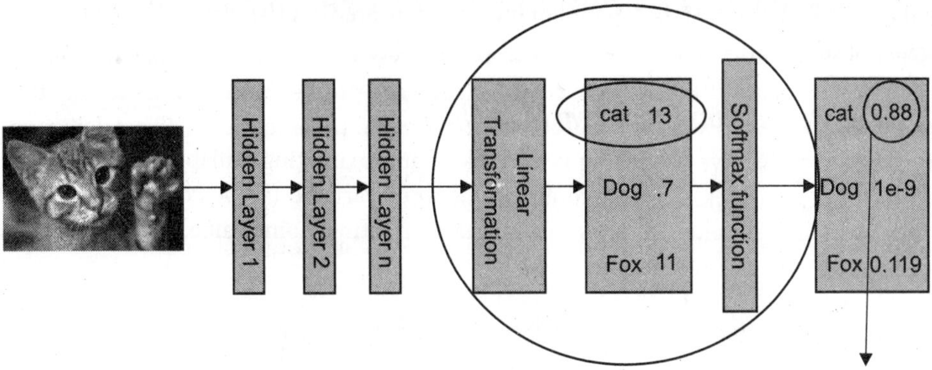


$$\text{softmax}\,(\text{h}_{\text{cat}}) = \frac{\exp(13)}{\exp(13) + \exp(-7) + \exp(11)} = 0.88$$

**Appendix.Fig.53:** Softmax Function

## 23.2 Cross Entropy Loss

Cross entropy indicates the distance between what the model believes the output distribution should be, and what the original distribution really is. Cross entropy measure is a widely used alternative of squared error. It is used when node activations can be understood as representing the probability that each hypothesis might be true, i.e. when the output is a probability distribution. Thus it is used as a loss function in neural networks which have softmax activations in the output layer. [77]

By considering the output of the softmax output layer as a probability distribution, the Cross Entropy Loss function is derived using maximum likelihood as:

$$L(\theta) = -\log(\text{softmax}(z_i)) = -\,z_i + \log\sum_j \exp(z_j)$$

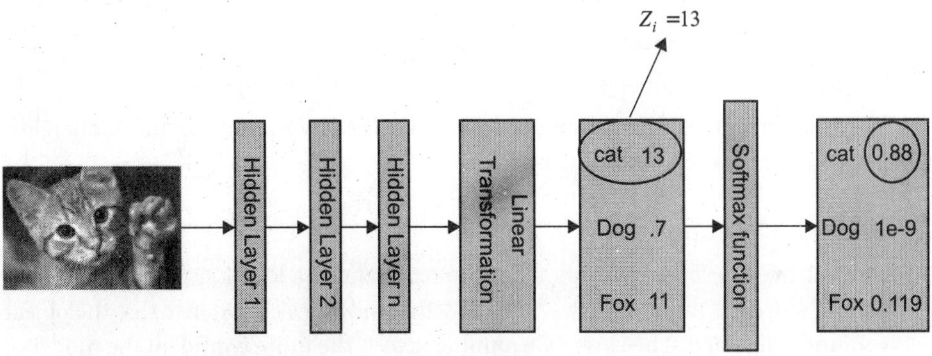


$$L(\theta) = -z_i + \log\sum_j \exp(z_j) = -13 + \log(\exp(13) + \exp(-7) + \exp(11)) = 0.12$$

**Appendix.Fig.54:** Softmax Output Layers

## 24. APPLICATION OF CNN IN CURRENT SCENARIO

Object Detection is not a trivial part of the process needed for a self-driving vehicle to drive on a road. It is one of the most important process which needs to function properly. There are always some problems that arise in 2-Dimensional object detection, some of which are:

- Extent of objects is not fully observed!
- Occlusion: Background objects covered by foreground objects
- Truncation: Objects are out of image boundaries
- Scale: Object size gets smaller as the object moves farther away
- Illumination Changes:
- Too bright
- Too dark

The image shows the view in front of a Mercedes-Benz car driving on a road. The image has different objects which are all Dynamic Objects–Truck, Pedestrians, Car, etc. These objects need to be detected on time and properly for vehicle to respond to the detection on time.

Applying Convolutional Neural Networks (ConvNets) for Object Detection,

$$f(x;\theta) = [x_{min}, y_{min}, x_{max}, y_{max}, S_{class1}, \ldots S_{classk}]$$

**Appendix.Fig.55:** Using ConvNets on the Objects

### 24.1 Output of vehicles

Locate the presence of objects with a bounding box

**Input:** An image with one or more objects, such as a photograph.

**Output:** One or more bounding boxes (e.g. defined by a point, width, and height), and a class label for each bounding box.

### 24.2 Error Detection

To interpret these results, we can look at the score and the location for each detected object. The score is a number between 0 and 1 that indicates confidence that the object was genuinely detected. The closer the number is to 1, the more confident the model is.

Depending on our application, we can decide a cut-off threshold below which we will discard detection results. For the current example, a sensible cut-off is a score of 0.5 (meaning a 50% probability that the detection is valid). In that case, the last two objects in the array would be ignored because those confidence scores are below 0.5:

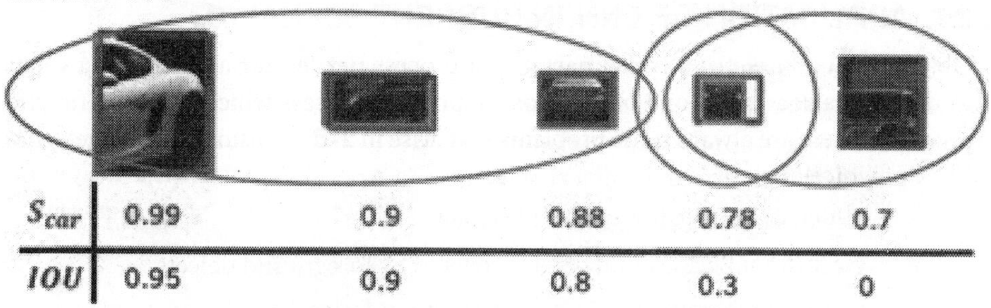


**Appendix.Fig.56:** Evaluation Matrices

**Table 1:** Confidence Score

| Score threshold | 0.9 | 0.8 | 0.7 | 0.6 | 0.5 | 0.4 | 0.3 | 0.2 | 0.1 |
|---|---|---|---|---|---|---|---|---|---|
| Precision | 1 | 0.75 | 0.6 | 0.6 | 0.6 | 0.6 | 0.6 | 0.6 | 0.6 |
| Recall | 0.5 | 0.75 | 0.75 | 0.75 | 0.75 | 0.75 | 0.75 | 0.75 | 0.75 |

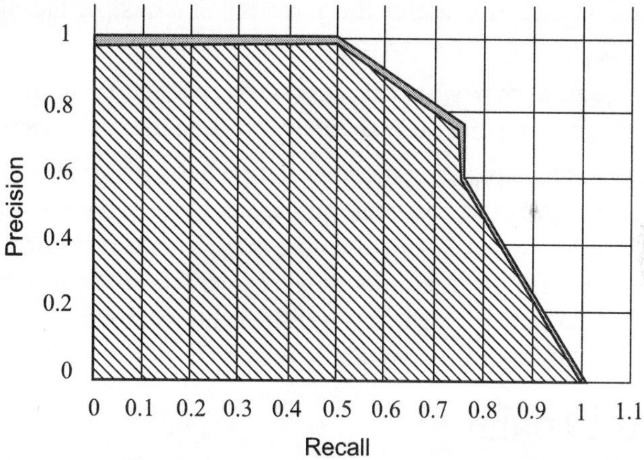


**Appendix.Fig.57:** Precision Recall Curve

Precision is a ratio of the number of true positives divided by the sum of the true positives and false positives. It describes how good a model is at predicting the positive class. Precision is referred to as the positive predictive value. Recall is calculated as the ratio of the number of true positives divided by the sum of the true positives and the false negatives. Recall is the same as sensitivity. Reviewing both precision and recall is useful in cases where there is an imbalance in the observations between the two classes. Specifically, there are many examples of no event (class 0) and only a few examples of an event (class 1). The reason for this is that typically the large number of class 0 examples means we are less interested in the skill of the model at predicting class 0 correctly, e.g. high true negatives. [78]

Key to the calculation of precision and recall is that the calculations do not make use of the true negatives. It is only concerned with the correct prediction of the minority class, class 1.

## 24.3 Traffic Signal and Signs Detection

Traffic signs and signals appear smaller in size compared to cars, two-wheelers, and pedestrians. Traffic signs are highly variable with many classes to be trained on. Traffic signals have different states that are required to be detected. In addition, traffic signals change state as the car drives. 2D object detectors can be used to perform traffic sign and traffic signal detection without any modifications. However, multi-stage hierarchical models have been shown to outperform the standard single stage object detectors.

# 25. SEGMENTATION

Deep learning and convolutional neural networks (CNN or ConvNets) have been extremely ubiquitous in the field of computer vision. ConvNets are popular for several computer vision tasks such as Image Classification, Object Detection, Image Generation, etc. Like for all other computer vision tasks, it has surpassed other approaches for image segmentation. Semantic image segmentation is the task of classifying each pixel in an image from a predefined set of classes.

Segmentation models are useful for a variety of tasks, including autonomous vehicles.

We need to equip cars with the necessary perception to understand their environment so that self-driving cars can safely integrate into our existing roads.

A naive approach towards constructing a neural network architecture for this task is to simply stack a number of convolutional layers (with same padding to preserve dimensions) and output a final segmentation map. This directly learns a mapping from the input image to its corresponding segmentation through the successive transformation of feature mappings; however, it's quite computationally expensive to preserve the full resolution throughout the network [80].

# 26. OCCUPANCY GRID

After all the filtering has been completed, there are still major map uncertainties due to the filtering methods used on the data, the complexity of the data at hand, and most of all, environmental and sensor noise. In order to handle this noise, the occupancy grid is modified to be probabilistic [81]. In probabilistic occupancy grid, the probability of occupancy is stored. For this, a belief map denoted by bel is built which can be represented as:

$$bel_t(m^i) = p(m^i \mid (y, x))$$

Current map cell

Sensor measurement for given cell

Hence, the threshold of certainty is used to establish occupancy. The sample probabilistic grid can be shown as:

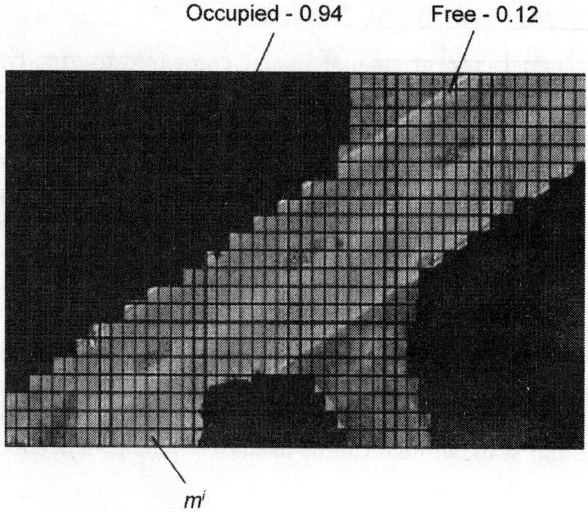


**Appendix.Fig.58:** Probabilistic Occupancy Grid

## 26.1 Bayes Update of Occupancy Grid

To produce the estimate of the vector of cellular posterior probabilities p, most of the existing methods factor the joint distribution of the cellular occupancies as pb(b)= ∏i pb(bi). Similarly, when conditioned on the collection of measurement vectors in JS, the joint distribution is assumed to be factored as pb|J (b|JS) = ∏i pb|J (bi|JS) which implies that the elements in the cellular occupancies are conditionally independent. As pointed out before, these simplifying assumptions limit the applicability of such methods in many practical situations. The general formulation (GF) presented in this section is intended to lift these restrictive assumptions. Throughout the development of this formulation, we assume that the sensor position at each time is reasonably accurate, i.e., the odometry errors are small enough to ignore. This is a valid assumption for sensory system deployed on many autonomous platforms, where a low velocity and small measurement error from the odometry sensors satisfies the ego-motion estimation for the vehicle [82].

Normalizer constant

$$bel_t\left(m^i\right) = np(y_t \mid m^i)bel_{t-1}\left(m^i\right)$$

Current measurement Previous belief map

Now, the beliefs are converted into log odds probabilities using the logit function. The logit function leads to cell values ranging from negative infinity to positive infinity avoiding the issue with numbers close to zero. The logit function takes the natural logarithm of the ratio of the probability p and 1 minus p. This conversion is represented as:

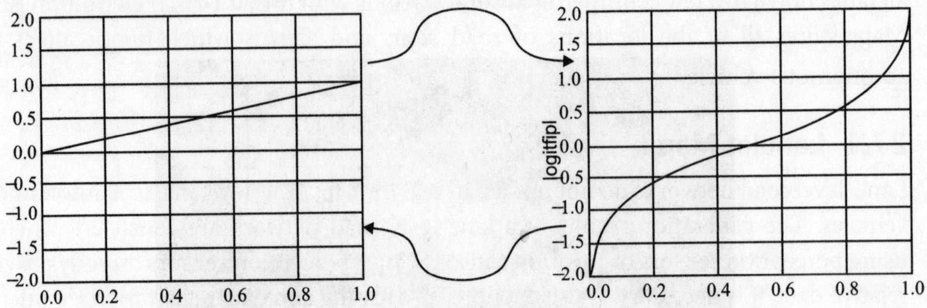


**Appendix.Fig.59:** Conversion of Beliefs to Log function

The occupancy grid updates account for filtering. The several filters that must be applied to the Lidar scan before it can be used to populate an occupancy grid are:

### *Downsampling*

Downsampling is the process of reducing the number of Lidar points to be considered by removing or ignoring redundant Lidar points. Common Lidar used in autonomous driving can produce up to 1.2 million points every second which provide very rich geometric descriptions of all the objects around the vehicle. It improves computation[83].

### *Removal of Overhanging Objects*

In removal of overhanging objects, all the LIDAR points are removed that are above a given threshold of the height limit of the car.

### *Removal of Ground Plane*

This filter involves removing points that are deemed to fall on the drivable surface. These are difficult to estimate due to several complications.

### *Removal of Dynamic Objects*

The dynamic objects are identified from the previous LIDAR frame. The history of dynamic object location can be used to identify parked vehicle as not all vehicles are dynamic, so they should be included.

### *Projection of LIDAR onto a 2D plane*

In this, all points are collapsed by zeroing the Z coordinate. Then the number of LIDAR points are summed up in each grid. More points indicate greater chance of occupation of that grid cell.

## 27. HIGH-DEFINITION ROAD MAPPING

A High-Definition Road Map is similar to traditional paper-based maps or online maps. However, the information contained within the High Definition map or HD map is significantly more detailed. While a traditional map stores the approximate locations of roads, the High Definition Road Maps stores the precise road locations including all lanes down to a few centimetres accuracy. Along with this, the High Definition Road Maps stores all of the locations of road signs and signals which might affect the autonomous vehicle[84].

## 27.1 Lanelet Map

Lane-level road networks do not update in real time for lane-level maps of autonomous vehicles. The generation results of a lane-level road network are consistent whether using perception sensors or position sensors. Since perception sensors directly provide relative data, it is necessary to use data pre- processing and data registration in order to obtain absolute data. More comprehensive and detailed reports on the lane-level road network generation process from perception sensors can be found in previous studies, although this is not the key concern in this study [85].

The High definition road is stored by a data type known as lanelet map.

The lanelet map has two elements:

### *Lanelet Element*

A lanelet element is an element which stores all information connected to a small longitudinal segment of a lane on a road which it represents.

### *Lanelet Boundaries*

It defines the edges of a driving lane. It is a list of pointers points(X,Y and Z co-ordinates) creating a polygonal line. The different operations that can be performed on boundaries are heading, curvature and centre line.

### *Lanelet Regulations*

The Lanelet regulations consists of two components, namely, elements and attributes. Elements are the list of points creating a line identifying stop location. E.g., traffic lights line, stop line. Attributes are a set of regulation attributes assigned to a lanelet. E.g., speed limit, crossing another lanelet. A new lanelet is created when a new regulatory element is encountered or ends.

### *Lanelet Connectivity*

Lanelet Connectivity is defined in terms of edges where 0 indicates next, 1 indicates left, 2 indicates right and 3 indicates previous.

### *Intersection Element*

It is a pointer to all lanelets which are part of an intersection. It helps with behaviour assignments.

## 27.2 Operations on Lanelets

The trajectory-based methods focus on lane centerline extraction. The single GPS trajectory-based method regards the GPS trajectory as the lane centerline, and this trajectory is recorded by a probe vehicle driving along the centerline of a lane. This method models lane geometry directly, so it is widely used. However, the accuracy of the lane geometry relies on the position accuracy of the probe vehicle. Research studies have focused on improving the accuracy and reliability of the probe vehicle position [86].

The various operations on lanelets can be:

- Path planning through complex road networks.
- Localizing dynamic objects.
- Interacting with other dynamic objects.

## 27.3 Creation of Lanelets

Perception-based methods usually extract lane markings to get the lane geometry (such as lane lines and arrows), since lane markings reflect the high intensity values on the road surface. Accordingly, the methods of previous studies have been mainly divided into two categories: point-cloud-based methods and geo-referenced feature (GRF) vision-based methods. A more detailed introduction to perception- based methods can be found in previous study.

There are three methods to create the lanelet map:

### *Offline Creation*

Offline creation is creating the map offline by driving the road network several times and collecting information, and then fusing both segmentation as well as localization information to improve the accuracy of the map. In this method, hand corrections are also possible if any mistakes are noted from the algorithms.

### *Online Creation*

Online creation is creating a lanelet map online while driving a road network for the first time. With the use of existing traditional maps and heavily relying on segmentation and object detection, it is possible to create the map as the autonomous vehicle drives through the road network for the first time. This method is highly computationally expensive both in terms of the motion planning task, as well as the perception tasks. It is highly error-prone and thus is rarely deployed.

### *Offline Creation with Online Updating*

The third approach for creating HD maps is to create the maps offline and then update them online if changes are detected.

# 28. MISSION PLANNING

The mission planning problem is to find the optimal path in the road network from the ego vehicles' current position, to the required final destination. The mission planning in driving environments is done with the help of Dijkstra's Shortest Path Algorithm and A* Algorithm.

## 28.1 Dijkstra's Shortest Path Algorithm

Dijkstra's algorithm is very similar to Prim's algorithm for minimum spanning tree. Like Prim's MST, we generate a SPT (shortest path tree) with given source as root. We maintain two sets, one set contains vertices included in shortest path tree, other set includes vertices not yet included in shortest path tree. At every step of the algorithm, we find a vertex which is in the other set (set of not yet included) and has a minimum distance from the source [87] .

The detailed steps used in Dijkstra's algorithm to find the shortest path from a single source vertex to all other vertices in the given graph.

### *Algorithm*

- Create a set sptSet (shortest path tree set) that keeps track of vertices included in shortest path tree, i.e., whose minimum distance from source is calculated and finalized. Initially, this set is empty.
- Assign a distance value to all vertices in the input graph. Initialize all distance values as INFINITE. Assign distance value as 0 for the source vertex so that it is picked first.
- While sptSet doesn't include all vertices
  a. Pick a vertex u which is not there in sptSet and has minimum distance value.
  b. Include u to sptSet.
  c. Update distance value of all adjacent vertices of u. To update the distance values, iterate through all adjacent vertices. For every adjacent vertex v, if sum of distance value of u (from source) and weight of edge u- v, is less than the distance value of v, then update the distance value of v.

## 28.2 A* Shortest Path Algorithm

A* is the most popular choice for path finding, because it's fairly flexible and can be used in a wide range of contexts.

A* is like Dijkstra's Algorithm in that it can be used to find a shortest path. A* is like Greedy Best-First-Search in that it can use a heuristic to guide itself. In the simple case, it is as fast as Greedy Best-First-Search:

The secret to its success is that it combines the pieces of information that Dijkstra's Algorithm uses (favoring vertices that are close to the starting point) *and* information that Greedy Best-First-Search uses (favoring vertices that are close to the goal). In the standard terminology used when talking about A*, g(n) represents the *exact cost* of the path from the starting point to any vertex n, and h(n) represents the heuristic *estimated cost* from vertex n to thegoal. In the above diagrams, the yellow (h) represents vertices far from the goal and teal(g) represents vertices far from the starting point. A* balances the two as it moves from the starting point to the goal. Each time through the main loop, it examines the vertex n that has the lowest $f(n) = g(n) + h(n)$ [88].

# 29. DYNAMIC OBJECT INTERACTION

The dynamic object interactions deal with handling interactions between dynamic objects and the ego vehicle. Dynamic modelling provides a view of a system in which control and sequencing are considered, either within an object (by means of a finite state machine) or between objects (by analysis of object interactions). This chapter addresses dynamic interaction between objects. Dynamic interaction modelling is based on the realization of the use cases developed during use case modelling [89]. For each use case, it is necessary to determine how the objects that participate in the use case dynamically interact with each other.

## 29.1 Motion Prediction

Motion prediction of the dynamic object attempts to estimate the future position, heading and velocity. It is important as it allows planning a set of manoeuvres to correctly interact with dynamic objects. It also avoids collisions on a planned trajectory.

### *Requirements for Motion Prediction Models*

The requirements for motion prediction models can be mandatory and optional. The mandatory requirements can be class of dynamic object, current position, heading and velocity. The optional requirements can be current high definition roadmap, image of the current dynamic object and the history of position, heading and velocity.

### *Simplification of Motion Prediction*

The motion prediction for cars can be simplified by considering some assumptions. These are as follows:

### *Physics-based Assumptions*

This is the first class of assumptions. These assume that the vehicles must follow a set of physical constraints governing their movement.

### *Maneuver-based Assumptions*

This is the second class of assumptions. These assume that a vehicle on the road, are made up of a finite set of maneuvers in a restricted domain in the environment.

### *Interactions-aware Assumptions*

This is the third class of assumptions and make assumptions same as Maneuver-based assumptions. The only difference here is that the dynamic objects react and interact with each other, instead of only evaluating each vehicle.

## 29.2 Constant Velocity Prediction Model

This model can be used to apply to both pedestrians and vehicles. It is simple and computationally efficient. It considers the assumption that the dynamic object maintains its velocity both in terms of heading and magnitude [90].

### *Algorithm*

The inputs to the constant velocity prediction model are: T – Time horizon to predict over.

dt – time between predictions.

xobj – current object dynamic state. xobj.pos – current object position. xobj.vel – current object velocity.

The outputs of the constant velocity prediction model can be: x1:t – list of future vehicle states.

The constant velocity prediction model algorithm can be given as: t ← 0

x0 = xobj

while t ∗ dt < T do t = t + x

t. pos ← x t – 1. pos + dt ∗ x t – 1.vel xt. vel ← x t – 1.vel

end while return x1:t

## 29.3 Map Aware Motion Prediction

The map aware motion prediction includes the information from the HD road maps too and define the motion of dynamic objects. The above map aware assumptions can be incorporated with motion prediction methods. These can lead to the improvements as follows:

### *Improved Position Estimation*

On roadways with natural curvature, vehicles on drive lane usually follow the given drive lane. Hence, the predicted path is set to follow the center of driving lane on which the dynamic vehicle is on.

### *Improved Path Prediction*

In the previous model, it was difficult to predict lane change maneuvers without extra information. Also, the multiple possible lanelets were difficult to predict when in an intersection.

When, the above assumptions are applied to the motion prediction model, the lane change maneuvers are predicted easily using multi-hypothesis approach. Multi-hypothesis approach considers the range of all possible motions such as left, right, stay stopped. It provides more information to local planner and is safer due to human error.

### *Improved Velocity Prediction*

Road curvature can be used to improve the velocity prediction over the path. The velocity prediction is improved based on regulatory elements in the environment such as lanelet priors, deceleration profiles.

## 30. TIME OF COLLISION

Time to collision is comprised of collision point between the two dynamic objects and Prediction of the time to arrive to the collision point.

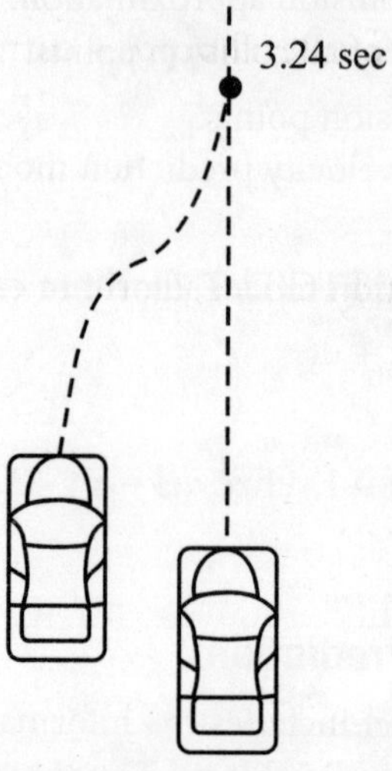


**Appendix.Fig.60:** Time to collision

The requirements of accuracy are:

- Accurate predicted trajectories for all dynamic objects.
- Accurate dynamic object trajectories.

The simulation approach simulates the movement of each vehicle as time passes and takes account of the vehicle model over time. It checks if any part of the two dynamic object has collided. It is computationally expensive and gives higher accuracy if simulated with high fidelity [91].

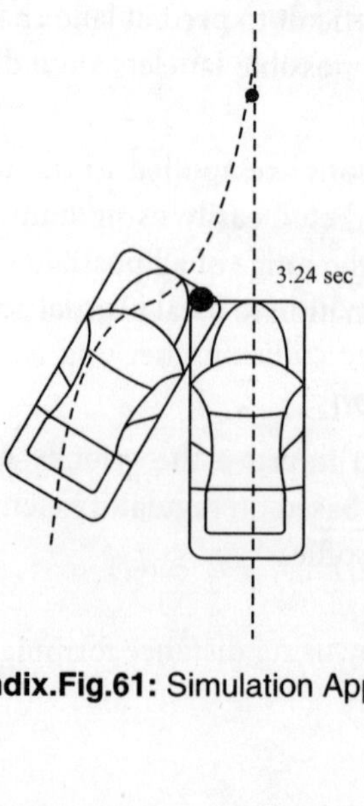


**Appendix.Fig.61:** Simulation Approach

The inputs to the simulation approach can be:

D – list of dynamic objects such as predicted paths. dt – time between simulation steps

Nc – number of circles for collision approximation. The outputs of the simulation approach are listed as: Pcoll – list of all collision points.

TTC – list of all time to collision points.

### ***The simulation algorithm is:***

Algorithm Constant Velocity TTC(D, T, dt, Nc ) t ← 0

x0 = xobj while t < T do t = t + dt

for i ∈ {1, ... D } do

di . xt ← PositionEstimation(di, t) for ∈ {i, ... D } do

dj . xt ← PositionEstimation(dj , t)

Pcoll,ij ← CollisionEstimation(di. xt, dj . xt, Nc ) if Pcoll,ij then

TTCij ← tend

end end

end while return Pc , TTC

In estimation approach, geometries of the vehicle are approximated over duration of the predicted path and the collision point is estimated based on the cars prediction. Many assumptions are usually made by this method usually to estimate time to collision. This approach is computationally inexpensive and gives less accuracy due to less approximations and estimations.

For this approach the vehicle is considered as a set of 3 concentric circles and the collision is checked with respect to the distance present between these circles.

In order to improve speed and robustness of both the methods, conservative approximations are used. Conservative approximations may report a collision even if there is not any collision, but never misses a collision if there is to happen any. The car can be encapsulated by three circles.

Swath along path is the union of each rotated and translated footprint. The swath computation is done by computing the area occupied by car along path generated by rotating the car's footprint by each x, y, θ along the path. The swath can now be checked for collisions. Swath based methods are useful for lattice planners, as the swath sets can be computed offline. Online collision checking is then simplified using lookup tables[92].

$$S = U_{peP}\ F\big(x(p), y(p), \theta(p)\big)$$

$$d_{ij} = \sqrt{(x_j - x_i)^2 + (y_j - y_i)^2},\ r_i + r_j \geq d_{ij}$$

The distance is computed by using distance formula applied on the closest points of the circle.

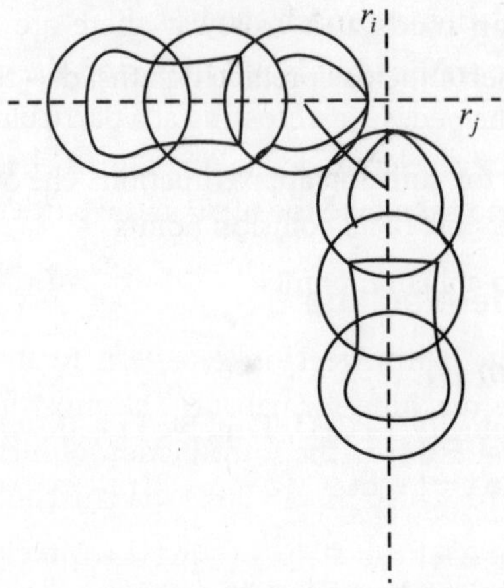


**Appendix.Fig.62:** Calculating Distance between two dynamic points

Here $r_i$ and $r_j$ represents the radii of the circles and their coordinates are used to obtain the value of *d(I,j)* is then compared with the sum of the radii to check if the vehicles will cause collision or not in real time frame.

Circle approximation is effective because it is fast to check if an occupancy grid point lies within a circle of radius *r* centred at (*xc* , *yc*). If obstacle in occupancy grid lies within circle, a collision is reported.

## 31. BEHAVIOUR PLANNER

A behaviour planning system plans the set of high level driving actions or manoeuvres to safely achieve the driving mission under various driving situations. A behaviour planner considers rules of the road, static and dynamic objects around the vehicle. The planned path must be safe and efficient. Hence a synchronous sequential circuit change is required that can change for every clock pulse based on the input therefore a Finite State Machine is considered. Where each state is a driving manoeuvre. Transitions define movement from one manoeuvre to another. They define the rule implementations that need to be met before a transition can occur. Here, entry action are modification to the constraints[93].

The input requirements of the behavioural system are:

- High definition road map.
- Mission path
- Localization information
- Perception information such as all observed static and dynamic requirements, occupancy grid)

The output of the behavioural system is the execution of the driving manoeuvre. The set of constraints which must be obeyed by the planning trajectory of the self-driving car include ideal path, speed limit, lane boundaries, stop locations, set of interest vehicles.

For the intersections on roads at a crossway there are multiple parameters to be considered that are if the traffic light is red then stop the vehicle within a suitable distance so it don't crosses the pedestrian crossing at a particular road. If the light turns green vehicle should start to accelerate, for taking a turn check for any other vehicle present at the intersection and then take the turn on the particular lane.

### 31.1 Hierarchical State Machine

Harel state charts bring the "Ultimate Hook" pattern to the logical conclusion by combining it with the state machine formalism. The most important innovation of state charts over the classical FSMs is the introduction of hierarchically nested states (that's why state charts are also called hierarchical state machines).

The fundamental character of state nesting in Hierarchical State Machines (HSMs) comes from combining hierarchy with programming-by-difference, which is otherwise known in software as inheritance. In Object-Oriented Programming (OOP), the concept of class inheritance lets us define a new kind of class rapidly in terms of an old one by specifying only how the new class differs from the old class. State nesting introduces another fundamental type of inheritance, called behavioural inheritance. Behavioural inheritance lets us define a new state as a specific kind of another state, by specifying only the differences from the existing state rather than defining the whole new state from scratch[93].

By using this concept the Scenario is handled easily by combining multiple Finite State Machines together as one. We can easily sum that intersection and drive lane both are interlinked scenario since a vehicle can change lanes at a particular intersection. So rather than putting all the same conditions of drive lane into an intersection it is better to make an intersection FSM diagram and a drive-lane independently and then connecting both together.

On a larger domain the multi-lane switching can be combined with the above set of Finite State Machines hence making it a larger and a complex structure hence it was better to use a hierarchical model rather than the normal FSM for better understanding of each individual structure.

## 32. TRAJECTORY ROLLOUT ALGORITHM

The trajectory rollout algorithm is divided into three steps – trajectory propagation, collision checking and path selection.

### 32.1 Trajectory Propagation

By holding velocity constant and varying the steering angle gives the candidate set of trajectories.

$$x_n = \sum_{i=0}^{n-1} v_i \cos(\theta_i)\Delta t = x_{n-1} + v_{n-1}\cos(\theta_{n-1})\Delta t$$

$$y_n = \sum_{i=0}^{n-1} v_i \sin(\theta_i)\Delta t = y_{n-1} + v_{n-1}\sin(\theta_{n-1})\Delta t$$

$$\theta_n = \sum_{i=0}^{n-1} \frac{v_i \tan(\delta_i)}{L}\Delta t = \theta_{n-1} + \frac{v_i \tan(\delta_i)}{L}\Delta t$$

### 32.1.1 Rollout Planner

It uses trajectory propagation to generate candidate set of trajectories. Among collision-free trajectories, it selects trajectory that makes the most progress to goal.

### 32.1.2 Trajectory Set Generation

Each trajectory corresponds to a fixed control input to our model. More sampled trajectories lead to more manoeuvrability. Fewer sampled trajectories improve computation time.

## 32.2 Collision Checking

Here, swath based collision checking is performed. Swath is generated for each candidate trajectory. Collision checking is performed for each point in the swath using occupancy grid. The ultimate goal of motion planning is rewarding progress to the goal point.

Distance to goal

$$J = \| x_n - x_{goal} \|$$

$$J = \alpha_1 \| x_n - x_{goal} \| + \alpha_2 \sum_{i=1}^{n} k_i^2 + \alpha_3 \sum_{i=1}^{n} \| x_i - P_{center}(x_i)$$

Curvature

Deviation from centerline

## 32.3 Path Selection

Path selection is done with the help of receding horizon control. In receding horizon control, only 1s and 2s of trajectory is executed at each planning iteration. Planning horizon end time recedes towards time point when goal is reached. This process is continued until goal is reached. This planner is greedy and sub-optimal, but is fast enough to allow for online planning [94].

# 33. PLANNING THE LATTICE USING PYTHON

## 33.1 Conformal Lattice

Conformal Lattice exploits road structure to speed up planning. The goal is to plan a feasible collision-free path to goal. Lattice paths are laterally offset from a goal point along road.

## 33.2 Goal Horizon

Goal point is dynamically calculated based on speed and other factors. The short look-ahead improves computation time, but reduces ability to avoid obstacles. The endpoints are sampled laterally offset from goal according to the heading along the road.

## 33.3 Spiral Generation

Now, spirals can be computed to each goal point. It focusses on kinematic feasibility. If a goal point cannot be reached with a spiral under the kinematic constraints, then that goal point is discarded [95].

$$\min f_{be}(a_0, a_1, a_2, a_3, s_f) + \alpha\left(x_s(p_4) - x_f\right) + \beta\left(y_s(p_4) - y_f\right) + \gamma\left(\theta_s(p_4) - \theta_f\right)$$

$$\text{s.t.}\begin{cases} |\, p_1 \,| \leq \kappa_{\max} \\ |\, p_2 \,| \leq \kappa_{\max} \end{cases}$$

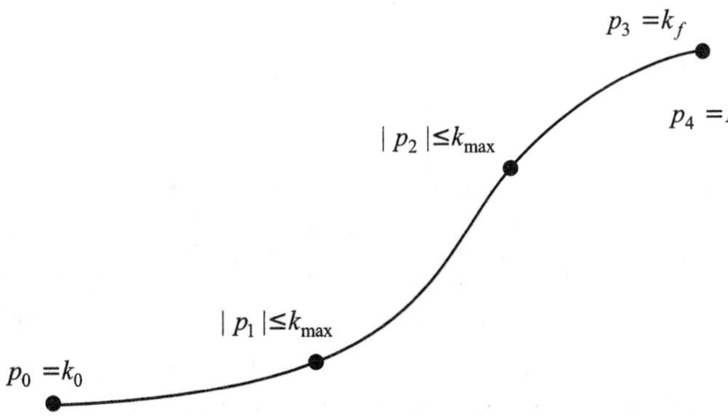


**Appendix.Fig.63:** Spiral Generation

## 33.4 Trapezoidal Rule

For each goal states, a spiral can be optimized to the goal point. A discrete path representation is obtained by using trapezoidal numerical integration.

$$x(s) = x_o + \int_o^s \cos\left(\theta(s')\right) ds' \qquad y(s) = y_o + \int_o^s \sin\left(\theta(s')\right) ds' \;\Rightarrow\; \int_o^s f(x)dx \approx \sum_{i=1}^{N-1} \frac{f(x_{i-1}) + f(x_i)}{2}(x_{i+1} - x_i)$$

## 33.5 Collision Checking

Collision checking can be performed through circle-based or swath- based collision checking for each point along each path. The parked vehicle in red represents obstacle, and the paths that would result in collision with it are marked red.

## 33.6 Path Selection

The best path among the collision-free paths need to be selected. The objective function of selection is a design choice. The paths can be rewarded that track centre of the road, and penalize paths that come too close obstacles. The best path is highlighted in blue. The path selection process is repeated for each planning step as car moves along road. The path converges to the centerline of the road, even when obstacles are present [96].

# 34. VELOCITY PROFILE GENERATION

The reference velocity needs to be computed. Behavior Planner Maneuver will also influence reference velocity. The curvature is recorded at intermediate points, ki. The velocity bounded by maximum lateral acceleration forms comfort rectangle. The final velocity selected as minimum of BP reference, lead vehicle speed and curvature speed limit.

It is an alternative profile. In this, the car decelerates to slower speed before stopping. It is useful for stop sign scenarios. The deceleration chosen should be well within comfort rectangle to maximize passenger comfort.

# 35. REFERENCES

1. Lateral Control of an Autonomous Vehicle https://ieeexplore.ieee.org/document/8286943
2. Longitudinal Vehicle Dynamics by Rajesh Rajamani https://link.springer.com/chapter/10.1007%2F978-1-4614-1433-9_4
3. R. Rajamani, "Introduction to Longitudinal Control " In: Vehicle Dynamics and Control https://link.springer.com/chapter/10.1007%2F0-387-28823-6_5
4. Vehicle Ego-localization by Matching In-vehicle Camera Images to an Aerial Image http://www.murase.m.is.nagoya-u.ac.jp/~ide/res/paper/E10-conference-mnoda-1.pdf
5. Sensing requirements for an automated vehicle for highway and rural environments by https://spectrum.ieee.org/transportation/advanced-cars/6-key-connectivity-requirements-of- autonomous-driving
6. WISE Drive: Requirements Analysis Framework for Automated Driving Systems https://uwaterloo.ca/waterloo-intelligent-systems-engineering-lab/projects/wise-drive- requirements-analysis-framework-automated-driving
7. *Driving to Safety*–How Many Miles of Driving Would It Take to Demonstrate Autonomous Vehicle Reliability? by Nidhi Kalra, Susan M. Paddock https://www.rand.org/pubs/research_reports/RR1478.html

8. AUTOMATED DRIVING SYSTEMS A Vision for Safety 2.0 by U.S. Department of Transportation https://www.nhtsa.gov/sites/nhtsa.dot.gov/files/documents/13069a- ads2.0_090617_v9a_tag.pdf
9. PRELIMINARY REPORT HIGHWAY HWY18MH010 by National Transportation Safety Board
10. https://www.ntsb.gov/investigations/AccidentReports/Reports/HWY18MH010-prelim.pdf
11. Uber's self-driving operator charged over fatal crash https://www.bbc.com/news/technology-54175359
12. Safety driver in fatal Arizona Uber self-driving car crash charged with homicide https://in.reuters.com/article/uber-selfdriving/safety-driver-in-fatal-arizona-uber-self-driving- car-crash-charged-with-homicide-idINKBN26708P
13. Safety driver charged in 2018 incident where self-driving Uber car killed a woman https://www.theguardian.com/us-news/2020/sep/16/uber-self-driving-car-death-safety-driver- charged
14. Safety Report by WAYMO https://waymo.com/safety/
15. CARLA- An open urban driving simulator https://d3c33hcgiwev3.cloudfront.net/2tyroyDyEem9HA6xGGaRfg_daf207a020f211e990ff7 3ab14e458cc_CARLA—An-Open-Urban-Driving- Simulator.pdf?Expires=1599004800&Signature=GbYTaLCpxIpBOBUqdetRkEf~ZhqCgh12 4u7D6d06Qo6LhRQxcn-4QiJMHxJre6TRylGaoLgS5WX3~Us7LB1ezhodFa0v8UCUUc~oz kVdSmdKLSluLbxZFk1CjuUDfUeWRkznNwozxaWYCf7EWa1OZF~HwYh-Gqgg1gHqcD olqD68Q_&Key-Pair-Id=APKAJLTNE6QMUY6HBC5A
16. Taxonomy and Definitions for terms related to Driving Automation Systems for On-road Motor Vehicles https://www.sae.org/standards/content/j3016_201806/preview/
17. Adaptive Cruise control https://www.ijser.org/researchpaper/Adaptive-Cruise-Control-
18. Towards-a-Safer-Driving-Experience.pdf
19. GM Super Cruise Self Driving Tech https://www.caranddriver.com/news/a30795396/gm- super-cruise-self-driving-2023/
20. Lateral Vehicle Dynamics https://www.springer.com/cda/content/document/cda_downloaddocument/9781461414322- c1.pdf?SGWID=0-0-45-1265143-p174267791.
21. Classical Control by Bruce A. Francis http://www.scg.utoronto.ca/~francis/main.pdf
22. Classical Dynamics By University Of Cambridge Part II Mathematical Tripos http://www.damtp.cam.ac.uk/user/tong/dynamics/clas.pdf
23. Tire Model by Moad Kissai, Bruno Monsuez, Adriana Tapus, Didier Martinez https://hal.archives-ouvertes.fr/hal-01690792/document

24. Feedforward Speed Control by Sailan, K., Kuhnert, K.D. by https://airccj.org/csecfp/library/Search.php?title=MODELING+AND+DESIGN+OF+CRUIS E+-CONTROL+SYSTEM
25. Lateral control of an Autonomous Vehicle by J. Jiang and A. Astolfi http://ieeexplore.ieee.org/stamp/stamp.jsp?tp=&arnumber=8286943&isnumber=8363076
26. Autonomous Automobile Trajectory Tracking for Off-Road Driving: Controller Design,
27. Experimental Validation and Racing by Hoffmann, G. et
28. al. http://ai.stanford.edu/~gabeh/papers/hoffmann_stanley_control07.pdf
29. Automatic Steering Methods for Autonomous Path Tracking Control by Snider, J.M.
30. https://www.ri.cmu.edu/pub_files/2009/2/Automatic_Steering_Methods_for_Autonomous_Au t omobile_Path_Tracking.pdf.
31. Predictive Active Steering Control for Autonomous Vehicle Systems by Falcone, P. et al. https://ieeexplore.ieee.org/document/4162483
32. Gordon Wetzstein's lecture on IMUs at Stanford University http://stanford.edu/class/ee267/lectures/lecture9.pdf
33. Wearable Technology in Medicine and Health Care https://doi.org/10.1016/B978-0-12- 811810-8.00009-9
34. The evolution of the various GNSS constellations https://www.geospatialworld.net/article/global-navigation-satellite-system-gnss/
35. GNSS applications and Methods by Scott Gleason , Demoz Gebre-Egziabher
36. Global Positioning System: Principles And Applications By Satheesh Gopi
37. Biotech's Dictionary of Global Positioning System by Pradeep Kumar
38. Lidar: Range-Resolved Optical Remote Sensing of the Atmosphere published by Springer,
39. New York, NY written by Ulla Wandinger Pages 1-18
40. LiDAR and Inertial Fusion for Pose Estimation by Non-linear Optimization by Haoyang Ye and Ming Liu https://arxiv.org/abs/1710.07104
41. State Estimation for Practice, Chapter 6, Section 1 and 2 about Point clouds http://asrl.utias.utoronto.ca/~tdb/bib/barfoot_ser17.pdf
42. State Estimation for Practice, Chapter 6, Section 4.3 about LIDAR sensing http://asrl.utias.utoronto.ca/~tdb/bib/barfoot_ser17.pdf
43. State Estimation for Practice, Chapter 3, Section 3 about Kalman filter http://asrl.utias.utoronto.ca/~tdb/bib/barfoot_ser17.pdf
44. Kalman's original article on the linear filter, courtesy of Welch and Bishop and hosted at UNC at Chapel Hill https://www.cs.unc.edu/~welch/kalman/kalmanPaper.html

45. Variable-State-Dimension Kalman-Based Filter for Orientation Determination Using Inertial and Magnetic Sensors by Angelo Maria Sabatini doi:10.3390/s120708491
46. By Stergios Roumeliotis et al. on the use of the error-state Kalman filter for mobile robot localization https://ieeexplore.ieee.org/document/772597
47. The Unscented Kalman Filters for Nonlinear Estimation by the Oregon Graduate Institute of Science & Technology https://www.seas.harvard.edu/courses/cs281/papers/unscented.pdf
48. Chapter 26–Technology and applications in interventional imaging: 2D X-ray radiography/fluoroscopy and 3D cone-beam CT by SebastianSchafer and Jeffrey H.Siewerdsen https://doi.org/10.1016/B978-0-12-816176-0.00031-4
49. Chapter 14–Vision-based sensing for assessing and monitoring civil infrastructures Sensor Technologies for Civil Infrastructures Sensing Hardware and Data Collection Methods for Performance Assessment Volume 1 in Woodhead Publishing Series in Electronic and Optical Materials 2014, Pages 383-409
50. Advances in Computers Volume 82, 2011, Pages 165-216 by GrahamThomas https://doi.org/10.1016/B978-0-12-385512-1.00005-0
51. Human Recognition in Unconstrained Environments Using Computer Vision, Pattern Recognition and Machine Learning Methods for Biometrics 2017, Pages 31-54 Ching-Hui Chen and Rama Chellappa
52. Temporal calibration in multisensor tracking setups by Manuel Huber; Michael Schlegel;
53. Gudrun Klinker doi: 10.1109/ISMAR.2009.5336465
54. A General Framework for Temporal Calibration of Multiple Proprioceptive and Exteroceptive Sensors by Jonathan Kelly Gaurav S. Sukhatme
55. D. Scaramuzza, A. Harati and R. Siegwart, "Extrinsic self calibration of a camera and a 3D laser range finder from natural scenes," 2007 IEEE/RSJ International Conference on Intelligent Robots and Systems, San Diego, CA, 2007, pp. 4164-4169, doi: 10.1109/IROS.2007.4399276.
56. Making of Boing https://www.icmrindia.org/casestudies/catalogue/Operations/Making%20of%20Boeing%2077 7-Operations%20Management%20Case%20Study.html
57. 3x4 Projection Matrix by Bob Fisher https://homepages.inf.ed.ac.uk/rbf/CVonline/LOCAL_COPIES/EPSRC_SSAZ/node3.html
58. Lecture 12: Camera Projection Reading: T&V Section 2.4 by Robert Collins CSE-486,
59. Penne State http://www.cse.psu.edu/~rtc12/CSE486/lecture12.pdf
60. Chapter 31–External tracking devices and tracked tool calibration of Handbook of Medical Image Computing and Computer Assisted Intervention 2020, Pages 777-794

61. Z. Zhang, "A flexible new technique for camera calibration," in *IEEE Transactions on Pattern Analysis and Machine Intelligence*, vol. 22, no. 11, pp. 1330-1334, Nov. 2000, doi: 10.1109/34.888718.
62. Y. M. Wang, Y. Li and J. B. Zheng, "A camera calibration technique based on OpenCV," *The 3rd International Conference on Information Sciences and Interaction Sciences*, Chengdu, 2010, pp. 403-406, doi: 10.1109/ICICIS.2010.5534797.
63. Y. Furukawa and J. Ponce, "Accurate, Dense, and Robust Multi-View Stereopsis," *2007 IEEE Conference on Computer Vision and Pattern Recognition*, Minneapolis, MN, 2007, pp. 1-8, doi: 10.1109/CVPR.2007.383246.
64. J. Singh and N. Rajpal, "Comparative analysis of image filtering techniques," *2015 2nd International Conference on Computing for Sustainable Global Development (INDIACom)*, New Delhi, 2015, pp. 139-152.
65. K. He, J. Sun and X. Tang, "Guided Image Filtering," in *IEEE Transactions on Pattern Analysis and Machine Intelligence*, vol. 35, no. 6, pp. 1397-1409, June 2013, doi: 10.1109/TPAMI.2012.213.
66. F. Song, Z. Guo and D. Mei, "Feature Selection Using Principal Component Analysis," *2010 International Conference on System Science, Engineering Design and Manufacturing Informatization*, Yichang, 2010, pp. 27-30, doi: 10.1109/ICSEM.2010.14.
67. Mrinal Kanti Bhowmika, Sandip Shilb and Priya Sahac, "Feature Points Extraction of Thermal Face using Harris Interest Point Detection" , International Conference on Computational Intelligence: Modeling Techniques and Applications (CIMTA) 2013 Procedia Technology 10 ( 2013 ) pp. 724 – 730, doi: https://doi.org/10.1016/j.protcy.2013.12.415
68. Goodfellow, Ian, et al. Deep Learning. United Kingdom, MIT Press, 2016.
69. Md. Rezaul Karim, Mohit Sewak, and Pradeep Pujari, Practical Convolutional Neural Networks: Implement Advanced Deep Learning Models Using Python ,Packt.com
70. S. Albawi, T. A. Mohammed and S. Al-Zawi, "Understanding of a convolutional neural network," *2017 International Conference on Engineering and Technology (ICET)*, Antalya, 2017, pp. 1-6, doi: 10.1109/ICEngTechnol.2017.8308186.
71. N. Jmour, S. Zayen and A. Abdelkrim, "Convolutional neural networks for image classification," *2018 International Conference on Advanced Systems and Electric Technologies (IC_ASET)*, Hammamet, 2018, pp. 397-402, doi: 10.1109/ASET.2018.8379889.
72. Chigozie Enyinna Nwankpa, Winifred Ijomah, Anthony Gachagan, and Stephen Marshall , "Activation Functions: Comparison of Trends in Practice and Research for Deep Learning" doi: https://arxiv.org/pdf/1811.03378.pdf
73. Xiaobin Hu , Peifeng Niu , Jianmei Wang, And Xinxin Zhang, "A Dynamic Rectified Linear Activation Units" doi: 10.1109/access.2019.2959036

74. Z. Dlugosz and R. Dlugosz, "Nonlinear Activation Functions for Artificial Neural Networks Realized in Hardware," *2018 25th International Conference "Mixed Design of Integrated Circuits and System" (MIXDES)*, Gdynia, 2018, pp. 381-384, doi: 10.23919/MIXDES.2018.8436869.

75. Alexander J. Smola; Peter Bartlett; Bernhard Schölkopf; Dale Schuurmans, "Probabilities for SV Machines," in *Advances in Large-Margin Classifiers* , MIT Press, 2000, pp.61-73.

76. A. M. Abdelsalam, J. M. P. Langlois and F. Cheriet, "A Configurable FPGA Implementation of the Tanh Function Using DCT Interpolation," *2017 IEEE 25th Annual International Symposium on Field-Programmable Custom Computing Machines (FCCM)*, Napa, CA, 2017, pp. 168-171, doi: 10.1109/FCCM.2017.12.

77. K. C. Kirana, S. Wibawanto, N. Hidayah, G. P. Cahyono and K. Asfani, "Improved Neural Network using Integral-RELU based Prevention Activation for Face Detection," *2019 International Conference on Electrical, Electronics and Information Engineering (ICEEIE)*,

78. Denpasar, Bali, Indonesia, 2019, pp. 260-263, doi: 10.1109/ICEEIE47180.2019.8981443.

79. J. Si, S. L. Harris and E. Yfantis, "A Dynamic ReLU on Neural Network," *2018 IEEE 13th Dallas Circuits and Systems Conference (DCAS)*, Dallas, TX, 2018, pp. 1-6, doi: 10.1109/DCAS.2018.8620116.

80. J. Xu, Z. Li, B. Du, M. Zhang and J. Liu, "Reluplex made more practical: Leaky

81. ReLU," *2020 IEEE Symposium on Computers and Communications (ISCC)*, Rennes, France, 2020, pp. 1-7, doi: 10.1109/ISCC50000.2020.9219587.

82. Charu C. Aggarwal, "Neural Networks and Deep Learning" *Springer International Publishing* 2018 *doi:* 10.1007/978-3-319-94463-0

83. Christopher M. Bishop. 1995. Neural Networks for Pattern Recognition. Oxford University Press, Inc., USA.

84. Snehashish Chakraverty; Nisha Mahato; Perumandla Karunakar; Tharasi Dilleswar Rao, "Differential Quadrature Method," in *Advanced Numerical and Semi-Analytical Methods for Differential Equations* , Wiley, 2019, pp.157-165, doi: 10.1002/9781119423461.ch15.

85. Venkata Yaramasu; Bin Wu, "Modeling of Power Converters for Model Predictive Control," in *Model Predictive Control of Wind Energy Conversion Systems* , IEEE, 2017, pp.149-176, doi: 10.1002/9781119082989.ch5.

86. Q. Rao, B. Yu, K. He and B. Feng, "Regularization and Iterative Initialization of Softmax for Fast Training of Convolutional Neural Networks," *2019 International Joint Conference on Neural Networks (IJCNN)*, Budapest, Hungary, 2019, pp. 1-8, doi: 10.1109/IJCNN.2019.8852459.

87. X. Meng, H. Kong, D. Tang and T. Lu, "Multimodal Image Captioning Through Combining Reinforced Cross Entropy Loss and Stochastic Deprecation," *2019*

*IEEE International Conference on Multimedia and Expo (ICME)*, Shanghai, China, 2019, pp. 1318- 1323, doi: 10.1109/ICME.2019.00229.

88. S. A. Khan and Z. Ali Rana, "Evaluating Performance of Software Defect Prediction Models Using Area Under Precision-Recall Curve (AUC-PR)," *2019 2nd International Conference on Advancements in Computational Sciences (ICACS)*, Lahore, Pakistan, 2019, pp. 1-6, doi: 10.23919/ICACS.2019.8689135.
89. N. Jmour, S. Zayen and A. Abdelkrim, "Convolutional neural networks for image classification," *2018 International Conference on Advanced Systems and Electric Technologies (IC_ASET)*, Hammamet, 2018, pp. 397-402, doi: 10.1109/ASET.2018.8379889.
90. C. Wang, L. Mauch, Z. Guo and B. Yang, "On semantic image segmentation using deep convolutional neural network with shortcuts and easy class extension," *2016 Sixth International Conference on Image Processing Theory, Tools and Applications (IPTA)*, Oulu, 2016, pp. 1-6, doi: 10.1109/IPTA.2016.7821005.
91. T. Collins, J. J. Collins and D. Ryan, "Occupancy grid mapping: An empirical evaluation," *2007 Mediterranean Conference on Control & Automation*, Athens, 2007, pp. 1- 6, doi: 10.1109/MED.2007.4433772.
92. T. Gindele, S. Brechtel, J. Schroder and R. Dillmann, "Bayesian Occupancy grid Filter for dynamic environments using prior map knowledge," *2009 IEEE Intelligent Vehicles Symposium*, Xi'an, 2009, pp. 669-676, doi: 10.1109/IVS.2009.5164357
93. H. Boche and U. J. Mönich, "Analytic Properties of Downsampling for Bandlimited Signals," *ICASSP 2019–2019 IEEE International Conference on Acoustics, Speech and Signal Processing (ICASSP)*, Brighton, United Kingdom, 2019, pp. 5008-5012, doi: 10.1109/ICASSP.2019.8683894.
94. W. Jang, J. An, S. Lee, M. Cho, M. Sun and E. Kim, "Road Lane Semantic Segmentation for High Definition Map," *2018 IEEE Intelligent Vehicles Symposium (IV)*, Changshu, 2018, pp. 1001-1006, doi: 10.1109/IVS.2018.8500661.
95. P. Bender, J. Ziegler and C. Stiller, "Lanelets: Efficient map representation for autonomous driving," *2014 IEEE Intelligent Vehicles Symposium Proceedings*, Dearborn, MI, 2014, pp. 420-425, doi: 10.1109/IVS.2014.6856487.
96. Fabian Poggenhans , Jan-Hendrik Pauls and Johannes Janosovits, "Lanelet2: A high- definition map framework for the future of automated driving" MRT KIT EDU, doi: https://www.mrt.kit.edu/z/publ/download/2018/Poggenhans2018Lanelet2.pdf
97. Ji-Xian Xiao and Fang-Ling Lu, "An improvement of the shortest path algorithm based on Dijkstra algorithm," *2010 The 2nd International Conference on Computer and Automation Engineering (ICCAE)*, Singapore, 2010, pp. 383-385, doi: 10.1109/ICCAE.2010.5451564.
98. X. Wang and D. Zhu, "A Fast Route Planning Algorithm," *2012 Spring Congress on Engineering and Technology*, Xian, 2012, pp. 1-4, doi: 10.1109/SCET.2012.6341969.

99. L. Yilmaz, "Automated object-flow testing of dynamic process interaction models," *Proceeding of the 2001 Winter Simulation Conference (Cat. No.01CH37304)*, Arlington, VA, USA, 2001, pp. 586-594 vol.1, doi: 10.1109/WSC.2001.977342.

100. C. Schöller, V. Aravantinos, F. Lay and A. Knoll, "What the Constant Velocity Model Can Teach Us About Pedestrian Motion Prediction," in *IEEE Robotics and Automation Letters*, vol. 5, no. 2, pp. 1696-1703, April 2020, doi: 10.1109/LRA.2020.2969925.

101. M. Bosnak and I. Skrjanc, "Efficient Time-To-Collision Estimation for a Braking Supervision System with LIDAR," *2017 3rd IEEE International Conference on Cybernetics (CYBCONF)*, Exeter, 2017, pp. 1-6, doi: 10.1109/CYBConf.2017.7985775.

102. R. L. Kovács, L. Nádai and Z. Hankovszki, "Modeling of commercial vehicles for vehicle dynamics control development," *2014 IEEE 9th IEEE International Symposium on Applied Computational Intelligence and Informatics (SACI)*, Timisoara, 2014, pp. 305-310, doi: 10.1109/SACI.2014.6840082.

103. V. Sklyarov, I. Skliarova, D. Mihhailov and A. Sudnitson, "Synthesis and Implementation of Hierarchical Finite State Machines with Implicit Modules," *2010 International Conference on Reconfigurable Computing and FPGAs*, Quintana Roo, 2010, pp. 436-441, doi: 10.1109/ReConFig.2010.29.

104. Lin Na and Bao Qihui, "Path selection algorithm based on Grey Incidence Decision," *Proceedings 2013 International Conference on Mechatronic Sciences, Electric Engineering and Computer (MEC)*, Shengyang, 2013, pp. 2372-2377, doi: 10.1109/MEC.2013.6885434.

105. B. Park, Y. Lee and W. Y. Han, "Trajectory generation method using Bézier spiral curves for high-speed on-road autonomous vehicles," *2014 IEEE International Conference on Automation Science and Engineering (CASE)*, Taipei, 2014, pp. 927-932, doi: 10.1109/CoASE.2014.6899437.

106. H. A. Najada and I. Mahgoub, "Autonomous vehicles safe-optimal trajectory selection based on big data analysis and predefined user preferences," *2016 IEEE 7th Annual Ubiquitous Computing, Electronics & Mobile Communication Conference (UEMCON)*, New York, NY, 2016, pp. 1-6, doi: 10.1109/UEMCON.2016.7777922.

# References


1. Dr. Rajiv Chopra, "Computer Graphics and Multimedia- A Practical Approach", S. Chand & Company Pvt. Ltd.; 4th Edition, Reprint 2019-20.
2. Adams, "Visualizations of Virtual Reality", Tata McGraw Hill, 2000.
3. Grigore C. Burdea, Philippe Coiffet, "Virtual Reality Technology", Wiley Inter Science, 2nd Edition, 2006.
4. William R. Sherman, Alan B. Craig, "Understanding Virtual Reality: Interface, Application and Design", Morgan Kaufmann, 2008.
5. Paul Mealy, "Virtual and Augmented Reality for dummies", Wiley 2018.
6. Tony Parisi, "Learning Virtual Reality", O'Reilly, 2016.
7. Grogorge C. Burdea et. al,"Virtual Reality Technology", John Wiley, 2003.
8. www.vresources.org
9. www.vrac.iastate.edu
10. www.w3.org/MarkUp/VRM

# Index

## R



## S



## T



## U



## V



## W



## X



## Y

# VIRTUAL AND AUGMENTED REALITY

## DR. RAJIV CHOPRA

## FEEDBACK FORM

1. Which topics from your examination point of view are inadequately or not covered in this book?

________________________________________

________________________________________

2. Is there any misprints/ mistakes/ factual inaccuracy in this book? If so, please specify.

________________________________________

________________________________________

3. What is your assessment of this book as regards the presentation of the subject-matter, expression, precision and price in relation to the other recommended books available on this subject?

________________________________________

________________________________________

4. Which competing books you regard as better than this? Please mention their author and publishers.

________________________________________

________________________________________

5. Any further suggestions/comments you would like to make for the improvement of the book?

________________________________________

________________________________________

***PS:*** *If needed, please attach a separate sheet.*

**Name** : ____________________

**College** : ____________________

**Address** : ____________________

**Email** : ____________________

**Mobile** : ____________________

*Please mail the feedback form at:*

**KHANNA BOOK PUBLISHING CO. (P) LTD.**

4C/4344, Ansari Road, Daryaganj, New Delhi-110002

*You can also email this feedback form at:*

contact@khannabooks.com or Whatsapp at +91 – 99109 09320

**BEST FEEDBACK WILL BE REWARDED SUITABLY**